The Story of Black

JOHN HARVEY

REAKTION BOOKS

For the fellowship,
senior and junior too,
of Emmanuel College,
Cambridge.

Published by
Reaktion Books Ltd
33 Great Sutton Street
London EC1V 0DX, UK
www.reaktionbooks.co.uk

First published 2013

Copyright © John Harvey 2013

All rights reserved
No part of this publication may be reproduced, stored in a retrieval system,
or transmitted, in any form or by any means, electronic, mechanical,
photocopying, recording or otherwise, without the prior permission
of the publishers.

Printed and bound in China

British Library Cataloguing in Publication Data
Harvey, J. R. (John Robert)
The story of black.
1. Black.
2. Symbolism of colors.
3. Black in art.
I. Title
155.9'1145-dc23

ISBN 978 1 78023 084 9

contents

1 Leonardo da Vinci, *Salvator Mundi, c.* 1500, oil on panel.

Introduction:
How Black Is Black?

LEONARDO DA VINCI was clear about black. 'Black is no colour', he said. Black, however, was still a pigment on his palette, and one he used often – for backgrounds. His *Lady with an Ermine* (1489–90) is painted with silvery, elusive colours – except for her clear red sleeve – but behind her there is only opaque, solid blackness. She also wears a black necklace. Again in Leonardo's *Salvator Mundi*, a ghostly Jesus floats before us – gazing, it seems, from the world of the dead, with brown, glazed, unseeing eyes – and behind him is the solid black of coal or soot (illus. 1). So if black, for Leonardo, was not a colour, still it made the perfect background against which colour showed.[1]

Other artists have been enthusiastic. Matisse said 'black is a force', while Renoir called black 'the queen of colours' and quoted Tintoretto's 'the most beautiful of all colours is black'. Historically there has always been the question: where does black stand in relation to colour? Black is not a colour in the spectrum: it cannot be, since the spectral colours are made of light. Aristotle, on the other hand, believed – and Goethe later came to believe – that bright colours could be made by mixing white and black. The ambiguity of black – is it thick stuff or nothingness, a colour or darkness? – has helped it to carry other opposite values: fertile soil or burned cinders; smart clothes or widow's weeds; the sexual mysteries of the night or death, depression and grief. Beethoven spoke of a 'black chord' in music. No other colour has been so identified with extremes that are opposite and absolute.[2]

Nor are these meanings constant. The history of this colour is like the record of an invasion. Black used to mark, mainly, the terrifying realms that lay outside human life, but over time we have brought black close to us: we have searched it out within our bodies and even within our souls. By stages this colour of death, terror and negation has come to occupy faith, art and the texture of social life. Seen in this perspective, the history of black is the history of the partial accommodation of the terrifying. Black has also loomed ever larger in the politics of race. But before addressing such themes, there are some basic issues with which I should perhaps begin: such as the relation in which black stands to light; and how we see it; and whether it is or is not a colour.

At the end of his own discussion of black, the colour historian Michel Pastoureau wonders whether black, at last, has become 'an average colour . . . a colour like all the others'. And black is a colour like others in the sense that we have black ink as well as blue and red ink, and black paint as well as terracotta. But black differs from other colours in that we cannot switch on a black light, while we can switch on a red or white one. Wittgenstein said that we could not, in a lamp, have a grey or brown light. But still grey or brown are made of light, while black is said to have no light. In this, black is like no other colour. Nor, in either lights or pigments, can we speak of a faint or pale black as we speak of faint red, light blue: there is only 'saturated' black.[3]

Black is, then, at once a colour and not a colour, and both these things are often said. Actually, if black is any colour, we would have to say that it is white. For no black item is utterly black: the blackest velvet, in deep shadow, still returns some photons to us. And as Thomas Young said in 1807, 'black bodies . . . reflect white light but in a very scanty proportion'.[4] Blackboard blacking still sends to our eye a near-zero level of light which is white. And 'near-zero' is an exaggeration: in reality a blackboard, or a piece of black cloth, may be sending us up to 10 per cent of the light that a sheet of white paper returns to our eye. If that light were not white, but tilted to red or blue, we would not call the blackboard black, but blue-black or black-brown. For black is not truly outside the spectrum, and neither does it have a narrow waveband like red or green: rather, it is white light's tiny brother. In laboratories there is a realm of 'meta-materials', of carbon nanotubes smaller than the wavelength of light, which may reflect less than 0.01 per cent of light; their applications range from solar panels to stealth jets, but even they are not totally black.

This white light shed by black things is, however, of so low a level that often we can scarcely say we see it. This raises the question: what do we see when we see black? And like the question of whether black is light or the absence of light, there is also the question: is seeing blackness a sensation, or the absence of sensation? The problem has been that sight, as we know, depends on light, and where no photon strikes the retina we expect no signal to be sent. At the same time, we feel that we 'see' a black thing; it does not seem to be a hole in our sight. The great optical scientist Hermann von Helmholtz said emphatically in 1856: 'Black is a real sensation, even if it is produced by an entire absence of light. The sensation of black is distinctly dif - ferent from the lack of all sensation.'[5] He was not perhaps fully able to explain this, since he also said that a black object sends no stimulus to the retina.

Recent studies have given body to his intuition, and if anything have reversed the idea that what we see is light, not dark. Professor Sir Alan Hodgkin has noted, of the cells in the retina, that 'it is dark-ness rather than light which makes the inside of the photo-receptor electrically positive and which releases a chemical transmitter to excite the next layer of cells.' It is as if the eye's primary need of light was in order to see where the dark places were. A distinguished neural scientist has speculated that, in the far evolutionary past, microorgan-isms may have needed to swim from the light towards the dark: at later stages, too, it may have been important to notice a dark cavity, which might mean safety – or hide a biding predator.[6]

There are further stages in the neural transmission. Both the 'rod' cells, which see tone, and the 'cone' cells, which see colours, emit the chemical transmitter to which Hodgkin refers – glutamic acid – onto the bipolar cells that make up the retina's second layer. One kind of bipolar cell sends a signal when light or colour arrives; the other kind sends a positive signal when light, or colour, is removed. The sum total of signals sent by the retina remains fairly constant (travelling up the ganglion cells to the brain). The signals say 'light here' or 'colour here', or 'darkness' or 'no colour here', giving black and dark a com-parable weight to that of light and colour.

This is the hard explanation for the intuition we have that black is a positive visual fact, and it is even possible that, in optical terms, black has a stronger presence than white. An easy test for this is to cross a piece of paper with black and white stripes of equal width. Does one see bars of whiteness against black night? Or black lines strong against white space? Though the white bars are replete with light in all wavelengths, and may for this reason look wider than the black bars, it is possible still to argue that the black bars have the stronger presence. This may be why mankind has preferred to write in charcoal on light stone rather than in chalk on slate, to use black rather than white ink and – in the 1980s – to switch the world's computers from light letters on a dark screen to black letters on white.

THERE IS THE other basic question of what exactly the word 'black', and words which we translate as 'black', mean. It is not hard to be sure that *noir, schwarz, nero* and *mavro* have the same meaning, as to hue and tone, as 'black'. Figurative use may differ from language to language – *dans le noir* means 'in the dark' while 'in the black' means 'in credit', although the 'black' market is black both in England and in France (*au noir*). As to hue, some uses may seem loose: we call a bruised eye 'black'; in Greece red wine and brown bread are black (*mavro*). But these might be called directional usages, indicating a move from the usual colour towards a tone nearer to black. The core meaning is understood to be black, in the sense of coal-black, black as ink (literally), and figuratively in the sense of unlucky, bad or terrible.

Colour-words in general are ambiguous, and we should be less sure of them the further we travel from our own time and place. The cultures of the past did not have our Munsell colour array, or very many saturated colours. Also, the further back in time one travels, the less it seems that 'colour-words' were mainly concerned with hue. The British prime minister William Ewart Gladstone wondered if the ancient Greeks had been colour-blind because Homer used colour-words so seldom and so loosely. In Latin the adjective *flauus* seems often to have a yellow sense, since it is applied to honey, corn, fair hair and gold, but it may also be applied to blushes, sparkling water and the underside of olive leaves. Many words which for us name colours descend from words which referred to the broader look that things can have. The English word 'green' has this dimension. It derives from the Indo-European *ghre-* root, to grow and flourish, which gives us both words in the phrase to 'grow green' and also led to 'grass'. Green is now a paint colour, and an 'elemental' colour in optics, but the older, broader meaning survives in our (fading) sense of green as unripe, callow, naive. Other words used once to refer more to brightness and dimness than to a particular hue. The English 'black' comes from the Indo-European *bhleg-*, meaning 'to shine, flash or burn', and from the Germanic *blakaz*, 'burned'. The Old English *blaec* chiefly meant 'dark' but also 'scorched'. It was in the Middle English *blak* that the hue sense became dominant, as the colour of soot, coal, pitch and ravens.[7]

Nor is it the case that all words that have to do with colour have evolved in the direction of a single hue. The Old English *salu* referred to dusky darkness, shading towards the brown, whereas the modern word 'sallow', which describes the look of a person's skin, would be hard to match against a Munsell chip. The whole subject of colour-words and their history is problematic, and I have tried to write with a sense of the complexities. Even when colour-words sound as though they mean the same as they do today, they still might not. Dyeing clothing black used to be difficult, and could only be done by overdyeing with woad, madder, galls and indigoes to produce a bolt of cloth which was called black, *noir*, *schwarz* or *nero*, but which might to us look a dirty purple. Fortunately paints and inks have usually been made from soot, whose black has not changed.

We should not, moreover, simplify the way in which we ourselves use colour-words, which often involve much more than hue and may at times seem fragrant (as when flower names are turned into colour-words, such as rose, fuchsia, lilac or lavender, which are applied to women's clothes more often than to men's). Nor, as to hue, are we actually precise or even consistent: we know that 'red' means a London bus, but still we call carroty or auburn hair red. The word 'black', manifestly, is far more than being simply the name of a hue (the colour of pitch). If we refer to a 'black hole' in Calcutta or in outer space, we are not imagining a cavity coated with tar, but rather a darkness – which may itself be more figurative than optical, referring to death in suffocation, or the total collapse of a star. And still black is black. The ancient Egyptians made from burned wood the black paint with which they painted the hair, and outlined the eyes, of the carved wooden figures they placed in tombs; they called this colour *km*, the word they also used for the black fertile mud of the Nile, from which they named their country Km. The word *km* had a range of meanings which could include all Egypt, but it also meant 'black', and their black was our black, as we see in museums still.

BUT NOR DO colours themselves depend on the words that we attach to them. Many birds have better colour vision than we do, way into the ultraviolet range. And the fact that they use saturated colours in their mating displays – including clear white and jet-black – shows that one does not need words to recognize and appreciate colours. Birds may have brilliant ultraviolet feathers which look dull grey to us. Again, a number of societies now, and more perhaps in the past, seem to have had a limited colour-lexicon, but the appreciation of coloured gems is universal. Some languages have used the same word for green, green-blue and blue, but again, everyone sees the difference between an emerald and a sapphire. Taking pleasure in colours seems general to humans with or without words; it can show in the making of beads of different coloured glass, or in wearing the brightly coloured feathers of birds, as the Incas and Aztecs used to do. It is not a simple pleasure. On the contrary, it can be finely aesthetic in places where formal aesthetics seem not to exist: for instance, in the subtle and beautiful way in which colours are combined in rugs made in villages. Berber rugs from Morocco may be subtle as well as bright in their colours, which often include black.

Nor does the study of colour vision, or of the changing use of colour-words, explain the value that we set on colour. In the first chapter of George Eliot's *Middlemarch*, two sisters share their mother's jewels, and the puritanical sister, Dorothea, exclaims,

> It is strange how deeply colours seem to penetrate one, like scent. I suppose that is the reason why gems are used as spiritual emblems in the Revelation of St John. They look like fragments of heaven. I think that emerald is more beautiful than any of them.

The casket does not include black stones – though jet, onyx, vulcanite and tourmaline were popular in the nineteenth century – but the sisters do discuss which jewels would suit best the black dress that Dorothea is wearing. Her black dress is not mourning, for her mother has been dead for many years: she wears black because she is a serious person, and because black was thought fine, even beautiful. In the event, she chooses an emerald ring with diamonds, and a bracelet to match.

As to Revelation (21:1–27), the precious stones St John saw in the walls of heaven were red (jasper, sardius, jacinth), green (emerald, chrysoprasus), blue (sapphire), violet (amethyst) and yellow to orange (topaz). I do not know if St John had a colour-vocabulary with which he could describe the exact hue of each stone. But he did not need one, since he knew the stones and we can see them. In any case colour-words give limited help, since a colour in a gemstone has a different character from colour on cloth or in a spotlight or on a butterfly's wing. And if we said that the heaven of St John was shining bright and also red, green, yellow and violet, this would give a poor idea of the transcendent wonder he sought to convey by enumerating the gems he saw in the walls, in whose beauty colour is important.

For colour-words do not describe colours: they simply give them a name. It is not easy – or perhaps even possible – to describe a colour sensation in words. Even describing black, which might seem easy, is difficult. Saying 'it is like seeing nothing', or 'like a dark night', or 'like being inside a cupboard without a light', does not describe the *blackness* of the black bag in which I carry my (black) mobile phone. I may say, 'it's like soot', or 'like Indian ink', but the bag does not look very like soot or like Indian ink. So I fall back on the word 'black', which points to blackness but does not describe it. All I can do otherwise is look for comparisons – or metaphors.

The delight in colour, combined with the uncertainty as to what exactly colour *is*, means that the nature of colour has always been discussed. Plato said that sight was a fire that came out from the eye, which made colours by interacting with the fire which shone from visible things. The discussion of colour in our own time – in recent decades especially – has been extensive and systematic. Most has been generated by the book *Basic Colour Terms* by Brent Berlin and Paul Kay, who argue that languages with few colour-words will almost always have words for the same few colours: first black and white (but including the sense of deep or dark tones versus light and also cool versus warm), then red, then yellow or green, then blue. Their thesis had been exhaustively tested, optically and linguistically, and in a qualified form it is held to be true. Their argument has done much to confirm what neurological studies also suggest: that colour vision is much the same in most fit human beings, though there is a slight variation between individuals, and in the same person at different ages; also that there is a predisposition, which is more biological than cultural, to identify certain principal colours, such as black, white, red, green, yellow and blue.[8]

The values attached to colours by different cultures may vary greatly, though here too the historical, aesthetic and anthropological literature suggests that similar roles have been assigned, in widely different cultures and over several millennia, to the 'primary' colours: white being predominantly benign, black predominantly negative and red predominantly vital. These particular identifications need not themselves be innate, since they relate to constants in human experience. In many cultures the word for 'white' may refer to mother's milk and also semen; the word for 'red' to blood; and the word for 'black' to soot, coal, charcoal, eyes and hair (and also faeces). There is also a wide cultural consensus as to the immaterial values of black as the colour of bad luck and of all the worst things: of sterility, hatred and death itself. Rudolf Steiner found black 'hostile to life . . . our soul deserts us when this awful blackness is within us'.[9]

It does not need to be said that a particular society, at a particular time, may have reasons to discriminate with extreme minuteness between the hues in a certain range: for instance, between the yellows, greens and browns that indicate the well-being of crops. Several noted studies have recorded the elaborate vocabulary the Dinka in South Sudan have developed to distinguish the fine shades between brown and reddish brown, and the different patterns of brown, black and white which determine the beauty of their cattle. On this subject, which they will discuss for hours, the Dinka sound – John Ryle has said – 'more like art-critics than stockbreeders'. A high value is set on animals that are entirely of a lustrous black, or of a particular reddish brown, and a higher value still on the piebald animals which they may breed, a paramount value being set on certain patterns of black and white.[10]

Without running to as many blacks as the Dinka have words for reddish brown, I do try to indicate the diversity of values that we attach to black, both as a colour which we see in different things, and as an idea, within our heads and words, deriving from that colour. I am aware that I sometimes slip quickly between different categories of black – in optics, pigments, words and conceptual domains – in a way that may seem promiscuous to the systematic analyst of a particular culture. But there is a point, I hope, in attempting a large but not overlong history of an idea, and the diversity of the data means that one must make quick leaps and comparisons. With my background in literary studies, I prefer to think of this as the poetic way of telling a history.

Through the centuries the colour black has been used to send messages to other people: by flying black flags, by wearing black clothes, by owning black things. And black is the principal colour we use when words (like these) are written down. Even a single colour has many meanings, changing again from culture to culture. I shall not try to tabulate further categories here, since it is more economical to introduce them in the order in which history brought them forward.

2 A specimen of obsidian, photograph by Hugh Tuffen, 2012.

ONE

The Oldest Colour

IN GENESIS DARKNESS rests on the deep before God proclaims light, or any colour can be. Other mythologies may begin with primal darkness, and in some versions of Greek myth there is at first empty darkness, and the only presence the black bird Nyx, or Night, who lays the golden egg from which the first god, Eros, will be born. Whether our own scientific cosmology begins with darkness is not clear, for it is not sure there was a 'before' before the Big Bang. It may be that we burst into being in flaring incandescence – which sank into a darkness of dissipated energy, until matter slowly began to collect.

Other myths imagine a beginning in light and heat. In Nordic myth, as related in the Eddas, 'first of all there was in the southern region the world called Muspel' – the land of eternal fire, whose border was patrolled by the fire-giant Surtur.[1] We may imagine a blazing landscape like the surface of the sun, and Surtur too we are able to see, because his name means 'black'. It is related to the northern linguistic root *svart*, 'black', which comes to us in 'swarthy'. Surtur stands gigantic in the furnace, black as coal or a burned-out forest.

When the flakes of fire from Muspel met the freezing mists of the north, drops of moisture condensed into the giant cow Audhumla, who licked from the frozen stones the beautiful figure of Bor, the first god. When our world ends, Surtur will lead his fire-giants north from Muspel, overwhelm the gods and dart fire about him to consume the universe; he will stay, in the heart of fire, an enigmatic, ultimate, implacable silhouette.

Not all creation myths are so dramatic. In Australian aboriginal myth, the Father of All Spirits gently wakes the Sun Mother in a peaceful, expectant cosmos. Where she walks, plants and creatures

wake. In this myth, and that of the African bushmen, fear and darkness come when the first night falls. The first men are terrified until
a new dawn brings salvation.

In various ways, night, the dark and blackness are a part of Creation.
The fearfulness that has accompanied black throughout its history
may in part date back to the terror night held, especially for nomadic
peoples who may not always have been able to kindle fires. Even now
a city blacked-out by a power cut can seem as dangerous as a jungle.

The myth of the First Night, which in several mythologies terri-
fies the first humans, is not peculiar to ancient tribespeople. Until the
nineteenth century, most people believed there had been a First
Night. Andrew Marvell described it in the seventeenth century when
Oliver Cromwell nearly died in a coaching accident. Marvell compared
the English nation, fearing it had lost its light, to the first man gazing in horror where the sun had set, 'while dismal blacks hung
round the Universe'. Till morning came,

> When streight the Sun behind he descry'd
> Smiling serenely from the further side.[2]

Cromwell's coach was not his hearse, and England was safe. And as
often happens in descriptions of night, lightless emptiness is treated
not as a void but as a jet-black substance: Marvell's 'dismal blacks'
were funeral curtains, which were hung both outside and inside a
house following an important death.

'Night' is itself one of the great Indo-European words which
has spread – like night – round the world. It is *nakti* in Sanskrit, *nyx*
in Greek, *nox* in Latin, *nacht* in German, *nicht* in Scots, *night* in
English, *nuit* in French, *notte* in Italian (also *noche* in Spanish, *noite*
in Portuguese and *noc* in Slovak). The expression 'black night' is
ancient: the idea that night is not merely lightless, but has the solid
colour of black. The ancient Greeks called night 'black Nyx', 'black-
winged Nyx' or 'sable-vestured Nyx'. Night was not black, however,
when she brought longed-for repose: then she is 'quiet Nyx' or (for
the Romans) 'dewy Nox'.

So Shakespeare, more than a millennium later, would refer to
'sable Night', or speak of night's 'black mantle', or call night a 'matron,
all in black'. Even when black, however, night was not always frighten -
ing. 'Come, gentle night,' Juliet calls from her balcony, 'come, loving,

black-brow'd night, / Give me my Romeo' (III.ii.20–21). For night is also the nest of love, and may be the further, dark lover who brings her lover to her.

ONE MIGHT ASK what was black, in actual history, before mankind appeared. For when our world cooled into a blue planet, all water and minerals, few of its materials were black. Most rocks are light-coloured, in the yellow-red-brown range. There are black stones like mudstones, or haematite (an iron oxide), or spirel (a mix of iron, chrome, aluminium and manganese), and black veins of serpentinite can be traced in the cliffs of the Lizard peninsula in Cornwall. Most of the minerals we would call 'jet-black' are, like jet (or like the 'black gold', oil), relatives of coal – that is, hugely compressed forms of long-dead vegetation. One might then say it was with organic life – and death – that black first became the colour of death.

Of the natural black stones, the most beautiful is obsidian (illus. 2). It was plentiful in the primal world, though fresh-made obsidian may still be found today. It is formed when – in a country like Iceland – molten lava falls on snow and ice and solidifies at once before there is time for crystals to form; hence its polished, freely curving surface. It sits heavy in the hand like a thick twist of jet-black glass. And obsidian is 50 per cent silica – glass – but black from the presence in it of iron, chrome, magnesium and manganese. Black granite has the same make-up, but is rougher because it crystallized slowly; it is also less black.

We speak of carbon-black, but the naturally occurring forms of carbon, such as diamonds, are not black: graphite is dark grey. Our carbon-black comes from burned organic things, mostly burned wood. But though plants may go black after death, very few plants are black in life. Most stems and leaves are green, since chlorophyll drinks in red and blue light, and reflects the green away. The petals of flowers are all the colours of the rainbow, and may also be of the deepest red-black or purple, but they almost never deceive the eye into seeming jet-black, even if they are called black poppies, or black mourning brides, or the coal-black pansy. No flower is quite as Alexandre Dumas *père* describes his black tulip: 'the whole of the flower was as black and shining as jet'. The reason for this is that the dark pigment used by plants, anthocyanin, has a red to purple colour which in low saturation makes flower petals pink, and in high concentration can be a deep chocolate purple, but is never quite black.[3]

Animals, by contrast, have melanin, which allows a true black, and black in the animal kingdom is a colour of life. Many creatures are truly black, in whole or in part. We may see a black swan, own a black cat or a black dog, ride a black horse or pay to see a toreador provoke a black bull. The black of all-black creatures is intense and lustrous, and demonstrably important in mating choices. Charles Darwin concluded that in species of birds where the male is black while the female is brown or mottled (like the blackbird, blackcock and black Scoter-duck), blackness was 'a sexually selected character'. As to other species where both sexes were black (like crows, and some cockatoos, storks and swans), he concluded again that their blackness was 'the result of sexual selection'. More specifically, a recent study has suggested that in the Gouldian finch, 'black male preference for black females' is 'lateralized' in the right eye, so that if that eye is covered, males are sexually disabled, while when black males sing to black females they gaze to them with their right eye especially. Other creatures anticipate the human taste for chequerboards and flaunt a strong contrast of black with white – lapwings, skunks, pandas, penguins – and in piebald creatures, too, such conspicuous colouring may be sexually selected while also sometimes serving as warning colour, as with the skunk. Other warning combinations include black with yellow, as in some snakes and in insects that sting: predatory great tits have, it appears, an inherited avoidance of black-and-yellow prey. Black with yellow may also serve as camouflage, as it does for a leopard stalking in long grass. But for whatever purpose an animal may be black or part-black, its colour is an asset to it. It has bred itself black slowly, from dull beginnings, because its blackness helped it to flourish. The older among us may speak of grey panthers, but we know that in the jungle few panthers are grey, while black panthers darkly burn with life.[4]

It is also clear that animals are not spooked by black in the way that humans are. To a cow, a black snake is no more frightening than a lime-green one, and you cannot spoil an animal's day by setting a black cat to cross its path. Animals are protected, it would seem, by the fact that since they do not have words, they also lack metaphors. It was a bad day for black animals when humans came on the scene, and began to speak, and to use metaphors too. Then the black of fearful night could be the black of misfortune, depression and death. A military or financial reverse could be black. The bad gods could be black gods, and black creatures their creatures; so black cats, goats and ravens became accursed, and even might *be* the Devil, or a devil, incognito.

Not all black creatures became simply bad once humans joined the world of creatures. For centuries the raven has had a black reputation because it likes lonely places and is glad to eat carrion. In the Bible the raven is held in abhorrence: 'And these are they which ye shall have in abomination among the fowls; they shall not be eaten, they are an abomination . . . every raven after its kind' (Leviticus 11:13–15). But reference to the raven may also be benign. Jesus Christ made a characteristic retort on ancient prejudice when he said, 'Consider the ravens: for they neither sow nor reap . . . and God feedeth them' (Luke 12:24). Perhaps because of the birds' intelligence, ravens were widely associated, in mythology, with prophecy. Ravens attended the Greek god Apollo, and also the Celtic god Lugus and the Norse god Odin. And in the Old Testament, when the prophet Elijah flees King Ahab, the ravens, at God's command, bring him flesh and bread at morning and evening. In a Bulgarian icon of around 1700 Elijah squats on the earth near the brook Kerith (which runs at the lower right of frame) while jet-black ravens bring food in their beaks (illus. 3).

The same icon shows another black creature of mixed credit in myth, the black horse. In the bottom right an inset panel shows Elijah ascending to Heaven in a chariot drawn by a black and a white horse. The Bible also says that Elijah went to Heaven in a whirlwind, but the whirlwind in turn bore a chariot and horses: 'behold, there appeared a chariot of fire, and horses of fire' (2 Kings 2:11). Those horses have no other colour than fire, which is represented in the icon by the rich red behind the chariot. Both the black and the white horse – together with the colour red – have presumably come from other books of the Bible. In Zechariah 6 the four spirits of the heavens have the form of horses drawing chariots: in colour they are red, black, white and grizzled. Zechariah says that 'the black horses . . . go forth into the north country' and in other mythologies, for instance Chinese, the colour black is associated with North. Because of its fierce cold, 'the north' could be a dark idea,

3 Bulgarian icon of Elijah, c. 1700.

but the black horses of Zechariah are not frightening; on the contrary, Zechariah's angel tells him that the black horses 'have quieted my spirit in the north country'.

Again, in Revelation 4, when the first four seals are opened, four horses emerge that are red, white, black and 'pale'. But though the colour black is often associated with death, the rider of the black horse is not Death – Death, famously, rides the 'pale' horse. The rider of the black horse carries a pair of scales, while a voice from their midst calls out the price of wheat and barley, and begs for the oil and wine not to be damaged. This rider is usually said to represent Famine, since his prices for grains are inflated, though the oil and wine may be those used by the Christian faithful in sacraments. Clearly an ominous prodigy of the Apocalypse, he is not more deadly than his fellows, who are identified with War and Conquest as well as with Death.

In art, in the oil paintings of later ages, black horses may have a magnificent beauty (see illus. 73), but in the symbolisms of myth and philosophy they are more likely to be alarming than exhilarating. In his *Phaedrus* Plato compares the soul to a charioteer with two horses in harness, one noble and white, the other unruly, ugly and dark or black: this horse represents the anarchic force of passion and lust. Other black creatures have still less ambiguity. Black cats have sometimes been thought lucky – supposedly King Charles I said his luck died when his black cat died – but most often black cats are evil embodied. The familiars of witches would take this form, as might the witches themselves, and in the Middle Ages black cats were sometimes tried, and burned alive or hanged. In a nineteenth-century drawing by Théodule Ribot, three witches crouch, absorbed in the ingredients of their cauldron, while the large black cat, on the shoulder of one of them, seems itself to have a hump. Its head, with pricked ears, could also be a horned head, presiding over the witches' work with glimmering eyes (illus. 4).

It was not only in the Middle Ages, or in remote villages, that black cats were thought devilish. The great art critic John Ruskin described the onset of his insanity in 1878:

A large black cat sprang forth from behind the mirror! Per -
suaded that the foul fiend was here at last in his own person
. . . I grappled with it with both my hands [and] flung it

4 Théodule Ribot (1823–1891), undated chalk drawing of three witches
seated around a cauldron.

with all my might and main against the floor . . . [Ruskin's
ellipsis] A dull thud – nothing more. No malignant spectre
arose which I pantingly looked for . . . I had triumphed!
. . . I threw myself upon the bed . . . and there I was found
later on in the morning in a state of prostration and bereft
of my senses.[5]

It is not known whether Ruskin attacked a real or an illusory cat. It
is interesting that, even as his sanity fails, he records that the cat was
merely a cat. His 'I had triumphed' then becomes ambiguous, since
he speaks as though he overcame the Devil, when it rather sounds as
though reality triumphed over delusion. Either way his victory felled
him with exhaustion – as might happen after a head-on struggle
with an age-old human error, such as the belief in evil powers who
could haunt us in the bodies of black beasts.

TO COME THEN to our own species, it is clear that since the human
race evolved in Africa, our ancestors were dark-skinned, to say the

least. It may be that when our line separated from the chimpanzees we had a light skin covered by hair. But as the hair disappeared we had to darken to survive the African sun. And from something over one million years BCE to less than 100,000 years ago we were as dark-skinned as any people now living in Africa. We began to lighten when we migrated northwards, but it is part of history that we were all black once, and were black for much longer than we have been any other colour.

The people of those early times have left no artefacts that we can touch, but they did, as they inched their way northwards, make marks on things that we can see. There were coloured clays one can use like chalk, and, once fire was controlled, charcoal and soot were plentiful. Soot, or manganese dioxide, found among the rocks, could be pounded with fat to make an ointment or a war-paint – or a crayon of hardened grease. What is clear is that when the first pictures were made – which we can still see in protected caves – the principal pigment was black. On the rock we see magnificent all-black bulls; black is used for the manes of horses, for the matchstick people who hunt the creatures, and for that momentous invention of visual art – the outline. The use of outlines can be seen in the background to the great, gracefully swaying, delicately footed, all-black cow in the 'nave' at Lascaux in southern France (illus. 5).

The outline was invented more than 30,000 years ago. It is completely artificial, for things and people do not have black lines round their edges. But we use it still, and probably will always use it. And throughout history, outlines have most often been black. Black is good because it is achromatic or neutral, without prejudice to the colour of the object drawn. Also, black is strong, and it is important to know where shapes and edges are. But from the beginning the black line has also been art. Deep in caves, the outlines of the heads of horses and lions can have a wonderful accuracy, economy, rhythm. There were clearly 'masters', from the start, who had the ability (which requires much practice) to carry an exact image in the head, since the lion would not have posed for them.

Doubtless, as in tribal cultures still, pigments were used for body art also, and black pigment perhaps for eye make-up (kohl is very old). The practice of tattooing goes back to at least 5000 BCE. Several colours were available, but it is a fair calculation that societies that left no other trace – beyond the pictures they made on rocks – gave

5 The Panel of the Great Black Cow, in the 'nave' at Lascaux; the painting is believed to be at least 17,000 years old.

a prominent place to black. From the start, black was strong for decoration. Also black has been and is, both for word and image, the principal colour of representation.

AT WHAT POINT and where men first began to think black materials luxurious, there is no knowing. We will never know who first gave to someone else, as a gift, a finely smoothed carving of ebony. Ebony has always had the advantage of being among the most densely solid woods (it sinks in water), as well as being of an intense, pleasing black when polished. In Egypt, in the tomb of Rekhmir, vizier to the fifteenth-century BCE pharaoh Tuthmosis III, there are well-preserved frescoes which show the people of Kush (Nubia) bringing tribute. They are black themselves, and their quality gifts include a hobbled giraffe, ostrich eggs, gold rings and logs of ebony.

Other black woods from Africa were quality items in the late Bronze Age. The shipwreck discovered off Uluburun in Turkey in 1998 – which was probably en route from Cyprus to Rhodes, and intended to carry gifts from one monarch to another – included in its cargo ivory, faience, gold and logs of African blackwood.[6] The use of black African wood was widespread through the ancient world. The carving of the goddess Diana at Ephesus was of ebony, according to Pliny. This is the Diana with many breasts (if they are breasts), which is well known from a Roman copy. We may think it white because the Romans copied it in marble, but originally it was wooden, and black.[7]

As to the people who exchanged these black luxuries, whether Nubian or Mediterranean, the part of them that was most often black was of course their hair. Hair that is raven-black may be viewed with suspicion, but there is little doubt that through history raven-black hair has also been thought vital, potent and beautiful. The beauty of Snow White, in the folk tale collected by the Brothers Grimm, consisted of her snow-white skin, her blood-red lips and her hair, as black as ebony. And in the hairstyles of the ancient world, black was beautiful. Both in Babylon and later in Assyria, black dye was regularly used, in addition to oils, curling devices and quantities of false hair, to ensure that the well-to-do of all ages had a gleaming, fragrant head of black hair, with trains of close-curled ringlets – and, for men, a large but tightly curling jet-black beard.

In these two empires and more widely, both men and women applied kohl to their eyes. There were various recipes – for instance, the soot of burned sandalwood mixed with clarified butter – and kohl was sometimes tinted with other colours, such as green. With their shining black hair and mostly black eyeliner, men and women, young and old, passed some of their leisure playing board games – the ancestors of our backgammon, draughts and chess – on boards that were often of ebony, or had an ebony veneer, while the pieces they moved were of ebony and ivory. If a portrait bust were made of a valued person, it might be cut in grey-black diorite or black granite. Gleaming black artefacts were treasured, and the apartments of the great might be faced with black marble. The Book of Esther (1:6) records that the bed-chambers of King Ahasuerus of Ethiopia had pavements of red, blue, white and black marble.

Black was also used externally. A courtyard or city square might have an obelisk of black limestone, recording the victories of an important monarch. The tiered walls of citadels could be black. Herodotus said that in the Medean city of Ecbatana the ranged battlements were, in ascending order, white, black, scarlet, blue and orange. It is not clear that Herodotus visited the eastern cities he described, but there is reason to think that the tiered walls of the ziggurats – the pyramidical temples built by Nebuchadnezzar and others – were faced with diverse colours, colours that had a celestial significance according to ancient Chaldean astronomy.[8]

It has been said that in Babylon and elsewhere the city walls were blackened with bitumen, and this is possible, since bitumen was the black glue which held many ancient buildings together. Herodotus claims that the city walls of Babylon were cemented with hot bitumen, and in the home bitumen attached mosaics of ivory, marble and pearl to the ebony chests of the rich.[9] Even so, the idea of coating a sun-seared city wall with bitumen sounds hazardous, and the traces of coloured stucco found at another ziggurat, at Khorsabad, allow one to suppose that where walls were coloured, they were plastered before being painted. In sum, the ancient ziggurats were probably not, in their prime, mounds of brown stone, but grand coloured wonders, perhaps stepping up through white, black, red and blue to orange at the summit. The thinking may have been more astrological than aesthetic, but the second, black tier would have been a strong component in their visual impact. Black was the colour of Saturn, known then as the furthest and coldest planet, and identified with the oldest of the gods.

There is no evidence that the pyramids in Egypt were coloured, but black had been an element in Egyptian visual style from a date at least as early as the rise of Babylon (around 2000 BCE). At the court of the pharaoh both men and women had their heads shaved and wore lush black wigs which again were fragrant, closely curled and gleaming with oil (which might descend from a small vessel at the summit of the hairpiece). One can still see in museums the exquisite small black vases in which both men and women kept the kohl for their eye make-up. Other cosmetics might be ground on palettes of near-black slate and kept in small pots of black steatite.

By the time of the Egyptians there were well-perfected ways of making black pigment for dyes, inks and paints. The best blacks came from the soot of burned oil – a dense, velvety black known as 'lamp-black' – or the soot of charred bones. Crushed ivory could be roasted until black, yielding the warm, slightly brownish 'ivory black'. The result is that on vases, on funeral plaques and in illuminated papyrus manuscripts we find hieroglyphs written in densely black ink, people and animals outlined in black, and some animals and the heads of some gods painted solid black.

If black had style and luxury, still it had its dark side. In ancient Egypt, as in many cultures, black was also the colour of death. Whether the death-god Anubis appears as a whole jackal, or as a man with a jackal's head, his jackal part is represented in saturated black, though jackals are not black. He may be seen weighing the soul of the scribe Ani in an illustration from the Book of the Dead of around 1250 BCE (illus. 6). We see his black muzzle in profile as he adjusts the plumb line of the balance. The crossbar and stem of his scales may be of ebony, and Ani himself and his wife Tutu, who enter respectfully from the left, have the glossy jet hair (or wigs) of Egyptian fashion. But if Anubis is black it is not for style, but because he is Death in person. The hieroglyphs beside him state that he is 'in the place of embalming', and during the embalming of high dignitaries the chief embalmer would wear a black jackal's-head mask. Both the embalmed body and its wrappings would become black from the chemicals used, while the mummy case would be black from a liberal coating of tar to protect it from damp. In the Book of the Dead, death is night and night is black. A voice from the underworld cries:

What manner of land is this into which I have come? It hath not water, it hath not air; it is deep, unfathomable, it is black as the blackest night, and men wander helplessly therein.[10]

But though Anubis was black and had a jackal's head – jackals were known to eat the dead – his role, as he stood at the gates of death, was to help the good when they were examined by the gods of the underworld. Like death he is frightening, but may not be our enemy. The god Osiris, who is normally shown with black or green skin and who might be called 'the dark one' or 'the black one', had himself passed through death, and become the king of the dead. He was dismembered by the jealous god of darkness, Set, but resurrected when the goddess Isis collected his scattered pieces. Death was a passage from which one wakened, and Osiris was associated also with rebirth and with the regeneration of nature each spring in the fertile black mud of the Nile.

The connection of Osiris with both death and fertility is often mentioned in modern accounts, but was also made in the ancient

6 Anubis weighing the soul of the scribe Ani, illustration from the
Book of the Dead, *c.* 1250 BCE.

world. Plutarch in his *Moralia* said 'Osiris . . . was dark because
water darkens everything', while 'the bull kept at Heliopolis . . .
which is sacred to Osiris . . . is black . . . Egypt, moreover, which
has the blackest of soils, they call by the same name as the black
portion of the eye, "Chemia" and compare it to the heart.'[11] It is
not surprising if blackness and the death-gods should be tied to
growing crops in a culture whose understanding of the universe was
profoundly cyclical.

    Not all black and fertility gods were necessarily gods of death.
The bull-god Apis governed the abundant herds; he had the form of
a black bull marked with white, like Egyptian cattle. The god Min,
of sexual reproduction, had black skin and an erect, prodigious penis.
The Greeks associated him with their priapic god Pan, who was half
a goat (a black goat, in Roman pictures) and went about with the god

Dionysus, called 'Dionysus of the black goat-skin'. Pan is remembered in Christian demonology when Satan takes the form of a monstrous black goat for the purpose of copulating not with maids, nymphs and goddesses – as Pan and Min used to do – but with hags and witches, and with beautiful but demonically possessed young women.

THE PANTHEONS OF many peoples have included a black god. Such deities may be gods of death and the underworld, as for the Hopi Indians. They may be known for their wrath, as among the Cherokee – in many mythologies gods turn black when enraged. They are seldom, however, malign and nothing else, as the black Devil of Christianity came to be. Black God, the fire god of the Navajo, is also the god of night, and of the stars and their creation. In the ritual dance the chanter who dances him wears a buckskin mask blacked with charcoal, with a white marking on it for the moon. He sprinkles the sky with the Milky Way, positions the constellations and lights them with his fire.

For black deities may be benign. The Aztecs had a god called Ixtlilton – the name means 'Little Black One'. He was the god of healing medicines, and also brought peaceful sleep to tired children. Such a figure, from old folklore, may survive in Italy's La Befana, a kind of female Father Christmas who arrives in January with a bag of children's presents, and is black because she has come down the chimney.

More frightening initially, though often also benign, is the 'great black god' Mahakala of Tibetan, Chinese and Japanese Buddhism (illus. 7). His name comes from the Sanskrit *maha* ('great') and *kala* ('black'), and in commentaries his blackness is said to represent totality, since all colours are absorbed in black. Though accompanied by skeletons and crowned with skulls and with a belt of severed heads, as in the nineteenth-century painting shown here, he is also in Tibet the protector of wisdom. In Japan he has become one of the Seven Lucky Gods who are still mass produced as small, brittle figurines. His blackness has shrunk to a flat black hat; he squats on bales of rice, smiling broadly, and is associated also with wealth and the kitchen.

Our best access now to the gods, and black gods, of ancient belief is through the major instance of a primordially ancient, polytheistic religion that thrives still in our contemporary world. It is celebrated by hundreds of millions of people all over the world – that is, Hinduism.[12]

In Hindu India a dark skin is not well regarded, since it suggests hours of toil exposed to the sun, and is found especially in the lower castes and in the aboriginal tribes. Nonetheless numerous gods have dark or black skin, either permanently or in many of their embodiments. Yama, the god of death, is black, and rides a black buffalo. When the demigod Virabhadra becomes enraged, he is terrible as death and his skin turns black. Agni the god of fire is often red, but may also be black; and Kama, the god of love and desire, is called 'the dark youth' and often shown with black skin. Of the greater gods, Vishnu is said to have as many colours as the ages of the world (which are white, then red, then yellow, then black), but he is normally depicted as black or dark blue (he is also said to have the colour of rain-filled clouds). His principal avatar is the beautiful, mischievous boy-god Krishna, whose name means 'black' and who again, in miniatures, is depicted as black, dark brown or dark blue. The name of Rama – the hero of the epic *Ramayana* – again means black.

In Hindu commentary different values are set on black – as the colour of death and disintegation, but also as the colour beyond all colours, and as the colour of the contradictions and the mystery of divinity. As the colour of divine energy, black can take harsh forms. The goddess Kali haunts cremation grounds, and is garlanded with skulls or severed heads (illus. 8). She is nearly naked and her skin is black (her name means 'black'). Her hair is wild from frenzied dancing, her eyes are red, her face and breasts are smeared with blood. But also she is full-breasted, and suckles babies tenderly. She is creator and destroyer: her two right hands offer blessings and gifts; her two left hands hold a bloodied sword and a severed head. When the skulls in her garland number 51, they allude to the letters of the Sanskrit alphabet, and if this seems a gruesome way to recommend literacy we may remember that worship of her flourishes especially among the disadvantaged castes in India's severely stacked society. She wears a skirt of severed hands, which may allude to souls freed from the pain of being. Like a nightmare wife she stands with both feet on her husband, the god Shiva – who is her partner when they dance, so wildly that they endanger the universe. And if she is tough, so too are her devotees. They have a freedom not available to Christians, Muslims or Buddhists. If their prayers are betrayed, they will visit Kali's temples not to give incense or flowery garlands, but to hurl at the goddess obscenities and excrement.[13]

Her husband Shiva is white, partly from the ashes of the cremation ground, though his whiteness may also be beautiful, as in the love hymns addressed to him by the great twelfth-century poet Akka Mahadevi:

Cut through, O lord,
my heart's greed,
and show me
your way out,
O lord white as jasmine.[14]

Like Kali, he is a god of death – he will destroy the universe – but he is also the most erotic of the Hindu deities. He wanders the world as a ravishingly attractive young man, so all women rush to adore him. In one legend the jealous men of the village seize him and cut off his penis, which then grows to a gigantic size, revealing his – and its – divinity. Though he can appear in many forms, for instance with ten arms and five faces, it is primarily in the form of his lingam, or penis, carved in black stone, that he is worshipped in the temples. For when embodied in his lingam, Shiva too is often black. In an eighteenth-century miniature the god himself, in the form of a garlanded jet-black member, rests happily erect in the white yoni, or female dish (illus. 9). The image is almost jaunty, with a fallen parasol resting at an angle. The emphatically phallic reading of the lingam is sometimes disputed, but the older carvings of his idol, in the form of a short black column, are often marked at the top to resemble a glans. Such carvings date back to at least the ninth century CE, and the phallic worship of Shiva is thought to be among the oldest of Hindu, or even pre-Hindu, practices.

The Shiva Purana records that at the beginning of time Brahma and Vishnu came upon the gigantic lingam of Shiva, and resolved to find its beginning and end. Brahma, as a swan, flew upwards, and Vishnu, as a boar, burrowed downwards. But though they continued for 4,000 years, they found no beginning and no end. Then Shiva appeared, in more personal form (with five faces and ten arms), and taught Brahma and Vishnu that the three of them were part of a single deity. It may be that this short, round-headed black stone column,

7 A 19th-century Tibetan painting of the *dharmapala* ('defender of the law')
Mahakala. Although benevolent, *dharmapala*s are represented as hideous and
ferocious in order to instill terror in evil spirits.

8 Popular print of Kali on the battlefield, striding over a recumbent Shiva, 1890s, coloured lithograph.

9 Lingam and yoni, 18th-century Indian miniature, gouache on paper.

which is adored and garlanded in many temples, and which normally stands in a basin or yoni of feminine shape, carries us back to the sense of fundamentals, and the reverence that they enjoyed, in the forgotten tens of millennia of the emergent human race.

10 Achilles and Ajax playing a board game, Attic black-figure amphora by Exekias, *c.* 530 BCE.

TWO

Classical Black

WE ASSOCIATE THE classical world of Greece and Rome with whiteness and light – with the high-grade limestone we call marble and with the radiance of Phoebus and of Apollo, gods of sunlight and civilization. And no ancient Greek would have sought to set a style by sauntering in the agora in a gleaming black tunic. But it was also in the classical world that black artefacts became common in daily use, that the colour black became a primary colour of art, and that blackness in the sense of death and the terrible found full recognition as a part of life. This is not to say that the classical world had the abstract, unitary sense of blackness that we do in the West, but the principal words for black (*melas* in Greek, *niger* and *ater* in Latin) had a wide and prominent currency.

However far we go back in the prehistory of Greece, we find some black goods. Around 7500 BCE, in the early Mesolithic period, the island of Melos was a source of obsidian. This black volcanic glass cannot be carved, but it can be chipped, like flint, into small blades for hunting. Other black stones, such as steatite and serpentinite, were hammered and split into tools, adzes and axeheads. During the Neolithic period, from 6000 to 4000 BCE, Greek expertise in pottery matured. In the 'Larisa style' the entire pot is stained black and is smoothed and burnished to a lustre. The Cycladic period, from 3000 to 1000 BCE, produced the curiously named 'frying pan' vessels – flat dishes with handles, again in the black-burnished style. It seems they were not used for frying but as mirrors, when a little water was poured into them and allowed to grow still over the blackened surface.[1]

In the Minoan civilization, which developed through the Cycladic period in Crete, black steatite and haematite were cut and polished into jewellery, small vases and seal-stones. Carbon black was used to decorate pots, and in the spacious pillared palaces – like that at Knossos – carbon-black was laid on the plaster of walls as an undercoat to set off the strong ochres, whites and blues of murals. These show banquets, galleys at sea, athletic youths bull-dancing. A swaying woman, seen in profile, will be strongly outlined in black, with black eyes and eyebrows, and curling, thick black hair.

When the Minoan civilization collapsed, quite probably influenced by the catastrophic volcanic explosion of nearby Santorini, elements of the Minoan style were continued by the Mycenaeans on the mainland. A recurring motif was the octopus, whose black, sinuous tentacles may be woven round a vase or dish in a beautiful winding dance.

The Mycenaeans thrived between 1600 and 1200 BCE. As we finally approach the period of the great city-states – Athens, Sparta, Thebes, Argos – the black patterns on pottery take on human shapes. In the seventh century BCE the black-figure style developed. Against the yellow-ochre background, bony people in black silhouette, with long noses and staring eyes, go to war or occupy their leisure. The designs can have a beautiful clarity, balancing perfectly the fine black figures against the negative bright space round them (illus. 10). Black heroes defeat black minotaurs, black ladies resist black satyrs, black athletes compete: much of their ancient world lives on in the strong black and ochre of the pots. Then, around 500 BCE, the darks and lights reverse, in the red-figure style (illus. 11). Now, against a lustrous, jet-black background, elegant, lightly red-brown people wrestle, dance or simply sit. They seem to think more, or may just relax gracefully. A fine tracery of lines suggests a supple musculature, or delineates with a lovely care the sensitive limbs of animals – as in the illustration shown, where the fawn of Apollo shrinks from the club of Herakles as he struggles with the god Apollo for possession of the sacred tripod of the Oracle of Delphi.

Behind these civilized individuals the black background is absolute. Vincent J. Bruno gives an apt description: 'in red-figured vases the uncompromising flatness of the black glaze around the figures, "its absolute insistence on a void", seems to magnify both the sense of the life and the formal strength of the figures'.[2] Perhaps the reference to 'a void' has an existential vibration that belongs more to our perspective than to that of ancient Greece. But it is true that black had a double role in Greek society, and away from the jewels and the murals and pots, black was the colour of despair, defeat, shame and death.

11 Red-figure calyx-krater vase attributed to Myson, *c.* 490–460 BCE, showing Herakles and Apollo fighting over the tripod of the Oracle at Delphi.

In the legend of the Minotaur, as retold by Plutarch, the ship which bore the tribute of young people to Crete – to be eaten by the Minotaur – had black sails, since they were heading to 'certain destruction'. Ancient ships were in any case largely black, because their seams were caulked with pitch and their timbers coated with tar: in the *Iliad* Homer refers regularly to 'the black ships' of the Greeks.[3] Sails were not usually black, however: they were the colour of the hemp or the flax from which they were made.

When Theseus boasted that he would kill the Minotaur, his father Aegeus gave the pilot white sails, to be hoisted if Theseus survived, and black ones to be used if he died. And Theseus did kill the Minotaur, with the help of Ariadne, the daughter of King Minos. But, preoccupied perhaps with Ariadne, he forgot to change the sails when he returned to Athens. When Aegeus, on a vantage point, saw the black sails, he threw himself down to be killed on the rocks.[4]

Black goods need not be deathly. Most pottery in daily use was black-glazed, and the Spartans drank black broth (*melas zomos*). But clothes were not normally black: surviving records describe them as white, blue-grey, saffron, purple; quince-coloured or frog-coloured; or the colour of natural fibre. They can sound modern, since some carried gold lettering. But stark black was kept for death. We can still see a Greek funeral in a good theatre, for at the start of his *Libation Bearers* Aeschylus brings a funeral procession on stage. Orestes exclaims, 'What's this crowd of women coming here / All wearing black?' The text has *melanchimois prepousa*, from the ancient Greek root for black, *melas* (which also gives us 'melanin', the black pigment in our hair and skin). The black mourners are the chorus, and we presently learn from them that black is also the colour of wrong-doing. When a man violates a virgin's bed – they chant – no river can cleanse his hand of 'the black blood which defiles him'. The play has a black symmetry, for when the Furies enter at the end to hound Orestes for killing his mother, they too come in dusky or dark-to-black robes.[5]

The text does not have the *melas* root here; nor do we see the Furies, since only Orestes sees them. But in the next play, *The Eumenides*, the Furies in turn are the chorus, and at once we see them, sprawled asleep outside the temple of Apollo, dusky or dark-to-black in their looks and in their dress. There clearly was a tradition, even apart from Aeschylus, that the Furies who pursued Orestes wore – or were – black. Pausanias, writing four or five centuries later, records that 'when the Furies were about to put Orestes out of his mind, they appeared to him black, but when he had bitten off his finger they seemed to him again to be white and he recovered his senses'. Virgil, in the *Aeneid*, refers to other stagings of the story, where Orestes' mother, Clytemnestra, 'pursues with torches and black snakes'.[6]

Aeschylus clearly had an eye for the effect black could have on stage. In *The Suppliant Women* the chorus consists of the many daughters of Danaus, fleeing the many sons of King Aegyptos of Egypt. The daughters' robes are called both luxurious and barbaric, and they themselves are compared to Libyans, Egyptians, Indians and Ethiopians – that is, they are black, or near-black. The pursuing Egyptians are also said to be black, in contrast to their snow-white clothes.

The sumptuous dark spectacle of Danaus and his daughters closes with the granting of sanctuary, not death. But death-black contributed to the spectacle of Greek theatre. In Euripides' *Alcestis* Death enters in person and bickers with Apollo: as to his appearance, Death is described by Herakles, later in the play, as the black-robed Lord of the Dead. Queen Alcestis, who gives her own life to spare her husband, King Admetus, is described as wearing black in preparing for death, and during the play Admetus changes his own royal robes for the black drapes of mourning, which are also adopted by his court. It should be said that the play, however black, has elements of comedy, and at the end Herakles lies in wait for Death, to wrestle with him. Being Herakles, he wins, and brings back Alcestis.

Within the poetry of the tragedies, references to black slide between the literal and the metaphorical. Black steeds must be black, but black shipwrecks may be black because of the death toll, rather than because the ships were tarred. To go to a central horrific incident, the gore that pours from Oedipus' eye sockets when he blinds himself with brooch-pins is described as black (*melas*). The new mask he wore when he came on stage blinded would presumably have been marked with black, though the blackness he speaks of must refer also to his extreme physical agony, to the horror and pollution of his father-killing and incest, and to the darkness of his blindness.

There is a strong sense in Greek tragedy that death, blackness and evil events are inescapable in human life. And behind the plays, and the Furies, and black Death in person, there was – in the Greek understanding of the universe – the actual dark place where the dead went. The 'Underworld' was literally that. It lay at no great distance beneath our feet, and we could climb down to it if we found the right cave. The gates to this realm were black, and black poplars grew there; the place itself was dark as night, though not completely lightless. The rivers that run there – the Styx, Lethe, Acheron – are dark and often described as black. The ruling god, Hades, is merciless but just. He may be called the dark one, or the black one, though at other times he is described as pale: he sometimes has black hair. His throne is sometimes of gold, at other times of the black wood ebony. He is attended by Death, and also by deaths – the individual deaths that

43

12 Jan Bruegel the Elder, *Orpheus in the Underworld*, 1594, oil on copper.

will visit each of us in turn. When he rides out his chariot is pulled by jet-black horses, and when mortals make offerings to him they sacrifice black animals, especially black sheep or black oxen. He has his own herd of jet-black cattle, managed by the demon herdsman Menoetes. He dispatches black-winged dreams to disturb the sleep of men. He has a daughter, Melinoe, whose limbs are partly black – from her father – and partly white, from her mother, Persephone. For in the grim-wonderful hell of the Greeks, though he is dark, his queen is bright. She is Spring, and each year she rises from the winter of death to clothe the earth with flowers and fruit. She is bright again in the painting by Jan 'Velvet' Bruegel, the son of the great Pieter Bruegel, which shows Orpheus playing his harp to her and to a not very dark King Hades (illus. 12). Hades the domain, however, is made of blacks, and clearly shows the continuity between the Greek, the Roman and the Christian underworlds.[7]

Both the primary importance of black as a colour, and the negative character it often had, are reflected in Greek theories of sight. When Plato explained how we see things, he described sight as a ray projected from the eye. We see things because our sight springs to meet them, and, subjectively, sight feels like that. We see white, he argued, when the ray of vision is at its widest, and black when it is at its narrowest contraction. His junior, Aristotle, thought this could not be right, since if sight was a ray that came out of the eye, we would be able to see in the dark. Actually this argument did not confute Plato, because he also spoke of a fire of visibility springing from objects, and in addition described the general ambient luminosity as a further subtle fire without which vision would fail.[8]

This theory involved many fires, and Aristotle gave a plainer account that also makes better sense to us: he argued that sunlight is reflected by objects into the eye. He did however agree with Plato that the primary colours were white and black, and that other colours could be made by mixing these in different ratios. Since it is thought that Plato had painted when young, and since Aristotle was a committed experimentalist, we may wonder whether there were impurities in their black and white pigments, which meant that the grey they mixed tilted now towards the red, now the green, now the blue.

Not that we should think of ancient colours and tones as being purely optical qualities. Democritus had called white smooth and black rough, and Plato compared blackness to an astringent or bitter taste in the mouth. For Aristotle white was an extreme of sweetness, and black an extreme of acrid bitterness. This is not to say that colour was literally identified with flavour, for bitterness, like blackness, is an idea unwilling to rest in its literal sense. Failure, betrayal, humiliation and ingratitude all have a bitter taste, just as misery is black, or the heart is black, or death is black, however bright the light. Aristotle gave his comparison force when he compared the sight of blackness to ashes and burned food in the mouth; but probably he did not find figs or peaches bitter when he ate them from gleaming, black-glazed dishes.[9]

The philosophers' remarks about the bitterness of black may be helpful when one thinks of the double role black had in Greek culture. For the beauty of black, and its sad bitterness, may not be wholly disconnected. Just as an appetizing dish may need to include a bitter herb, so the smart luxury of black may have a hidden tincture from the dark side of black. That element may be sunken, and yet give black artefacts, as it were, a *serious* value. The occluded, bitter side of black may give distinction to black designs. If then we return to the red-figure pots, in which dense black surrounds everyone, we might say that this decision for black contributes to our sense of a sophisticated culture. Even vases can grow serious. It is also possible that their blackness echoes the blackness that silver takes if it is not polished regularly.

Greek art had beauty, but severity too; and not only in its tragedies, but in its paintings. This may seem a strange thing to say, when almost no painting by ancient Greek hands survives. But the most famous Greek painter of all, Apelles, was praised for his *austeritas*. Pliny the Elder valued the grace of his figures, but especially he praised Apelles for the extreme, the absolute exactness, of his outlines, and for the minute verisimilitude of the portraits that he drew.[10]

Pliny also said that Apelles, and other Greek masters, used only four colours: white, black, red and yellow. It may be that Pliny exaggerates, for it is hard to see why Greek painters should not have used a blue pigment when the artists who painted the frescoes in Crete a thousand years earlier used a strong, beautiful blue both for the sea and for the plump, curving forms of dolphins. It is true, on the other hand, that the surviving Greek murals in the tomb complex at Vergina associated with Philip II of Macedon do seem to use only Pliny's four colours (which allow both vigour, and delicate tones of rose and grey). They are sophisticated works by an artist or artists who could paint a chariot and figures from a three-quarters angle, and the brushwork is – by modern standards – bold and expressive. It is perhaps only because they are not thought sufficiently brilliant that they are not attributed to Apelles, for he was alive at the time (he would have been 50) and was the court painter of Macedon. In any event, it does seem clear that Greek painters demonstrated their virtuosity partly through their handling of a deliberately restricted palette, and by giving their figures weight and substance with shading. In Petronius' *Satyricon*, when Encolpius enters the picture gallery, he tells us he was especially impressed 'when I stood before the work of Apelles, the kind which the Greeks call "Monochromatic"'. He praises the subtlety of touch in the outlines, but his words make clear that the works were painted, not drawn.[11]

Black certainly was important in the palette of Greek painters. An earlier artist was known as Apollodorus Skiagraphos (Apollodorus Shadow-Drawer) from his fame as the inventor of what we call chiaroscuro, the modelling of form by light-to-dark shading. Apelles himself was said by Pliny to have invented a new way of making *atra - mentum* (the Latin name for black pigment) by burning ivory where other artists had used calcined grape husks. Apelles was not in fact the first painter to use what we call 'ivory black', but burned ivory can yield an intense and also warm black which would have complemented the rose-to-crimson and the yellow-to-bronze registers of his other colours.

Pliny also praises Apelles for coating his paintings, when finished, with a thin (*tenuis*) layer of *atramentum*: it was this that gave his works their *austeritas*. In commentaries this final coat may be described as 'a dark varnish', but the Latin does not mention varnish, only black paint (*atramentum*). Presumably this coating had some protective ingredient, possibly gum arabic, but *austeritas* does not suggest the lustre, or the depth of hue, which varnish adds to paint. Many centuries later, the painter Turner temporarily toned down a dazzling canvas by adding a thin coating of lamp-black, and one may wonder whether – as a final touch – Apelles laid on a thin, dark wash which disciplined the stronger hues and left the surface matt.[12]

Not that Apelles' subjects were always sombre, at least as described by Pliny. Like gifted painters in other periods, he painted the great and the good of his day in a manner that pleased them. He painted Alexander the Great – from life – many times, sometimes with thunderbolts in his grasp. Also, Pliny says, he painted Alexander's concubine Pancaste so lovingly that Alexander gave her to him; he cannot have been too austere.

He did however produce elaborate didactic allegories, as we know from another composition, described by Lucian. Its subject was calumny, or slander, and we can, as it were, see a picture of this picture, since the Renaissance painter Sandro Botticelli (and others) attempted to reproduce it, working from Lucian's description. Botticelli's earlier painting of Venus hovering above the waves perhaps emulated the famous lost painting by Apelles of Aphrodite rising from the sea (not an easy subject to render in white, black, red and yellow). In *The Calumny of Apelles* a throned man with asses' ears reaches towards the figure of Slander, described by Lucian as 'a woman beautiful beyond measure'. Two other women, Ignorance and Suspicion, whisper into his ears, while Envy, represented by a wasted man, urges him to believe the lie (illus. 13).[13]

It is, however, the two figures to the far left who receive Lucian's climactic emphasis. They are

13 Sandro Botticelli, *The Calumny of Apelles*, 1494, tempera on panel, detail.

a woman dressed in deep mourning, with black clothes all in tatters – Repentance, I think her name was. At all events, she was turning back with tears in her eyes and casting a stealthy glance, full of shame, at Truth, who was approaching.

Lucian does not say that Truth was naked, and in making her so – beautifully so, in a slender, chaste style – Botticelli draws on the tradition of 'naked truth'. Here he may equal, or more than equal, Apelles. With the figure of Repentance, however, it may be that Botticelli falls short: she does clasp her hands ruefully, but also could be read as an ill-willed crone. Judging from Lucian, the Repentance painted by Apelles was a portrait of guilt that was at once eloquent and subtle. With tears in her eyes and stealth in her glance, filled with shame, she stands in the black mourning robes that she herself has torn.

Though we may only imagine her, still, by way of Lucian, Repentance shows us certain things: for instance, that mourning clothes in Greece were indeed black (Lucian's word is *melaneimon*, again from the *melas* root). She also shows that already in classical Greece, grief and repentance wore – and tore – the same robes. These things need to be said because in his book on black, Michel Pastoureau claims that black funeral processions began with the Romans, while penitential black was later and Christian.[14] The black tatters that Repentance wears, and which Botticelli paints, hark back to a world where simply to wear black had a visual violence. The mourners at the start of Aeschylus' *Libation Bearers* tear their skin and their hair as well as their clothes. If one wore black, one might, in the public eye, rip it to shreds – true grief, or consuming sorrow for the harm one has done, could demand no less.

Apelles was not an early Caravaggio, or an early Robert Motherwell. He was the great master of his age; also the first painter in history – and for many centuries the only painter – to be praised for the quality of his blacks.

TO JUDGE FROM Pliny, the Roman civilization to which he belonged had no painter to rival Apelles. There were notable artists, such as Iaia of Cyzicus – 'no one had a quicker hand than she in painting'. It seems she specialized in portraits – she was famous for a self-portrait

– and portraiture was a field in which Roman art excelled. The portraits that have survived, protected by the burial wrappings of their embalmed subjects, are lively and convincing. They are in the white-black-red-yellow register that Pliny mentions, and use black strongly for hair, eyebrows, eyes and (to a degree) for shading.

A more striking use of black, which still we can see, was in the frescoes painted on the walls of villas. Fortunately for us, some of these survive through a freak of history, preserved in the volcanic ash of Pompeii. In the time of the Emperor Augustus – in the tens of years BCE and CE – a style developed in which full-colour figures, rendered with some realism, were set before a flat field of saturated colour. This powerful background could be vermilion, but it also could be black. The solid blackness pushes space back, and against it the small figures take a poignancy: even more than on Greek vases, these figures seem set against a void. In the villa built at Boscotrecase near Vesuvius by a daughter of the Emperor Augustus and her husband, the walls of one room are solid black, except for a deep red panel at wainscot level (illus. 14). These walls, black as soot, are how - ever crossed by a few yellow-to-gold lines, thin as pins or pencils, which just sketch in the bare frame of a house or temple. There is an extreme of elegant slenderness, at once frivolous and precarious, against a dead blackness which seems not so much empty as thick, like impenetrable smoke.

The importance of black in Roman painting may be gauged from the fact that in his *Ten Books of Architecture* (written in the last decades BCE) Vitruvius devotes a chapter to the making of a good black for frescoes. The only colour to which he gives more space is vermilion, though he deplores the way his contemporaries splash it everywhere. For black, resin must be burned in a furnace, so its soot, passing through vents, sticks to the marble walls nearby. When the soot is scraped off, it is mixed with gum to make ink, or with size to make fresco-paint. Or, even better, if the lees of wine are roasted, then ground up with size,

> the result will be a colour even more delightful than ordinary black; and the better the wine of which it is made, the better imitation it will give, not only of the colour of ordinary black, but even of that of India ink.

14 The Black Room in the Roman villa at Boscotrecase near Vesuvius, *c.* 10 BCE.

For Vitruvius black was not bitter: his word, translated here as 'delight', is *suavitas* – the Roman word for sweetness in sound, taste and appearance.[15]

Frescoes were not suitable for rooms used in winter, where decorations could be spoiled by smoke from the fire, 'and the constant soot from the lamps'. Here Vitruvius recommends the use of black panels (with yellow ochre or vermilion accessories). In these rooms the floors might also be black, through the use of black marble, but he recommends especially the Greek form of flooring, which also provided for moisture absorption. I quote his details to give a fuller sense of Greek and Roman building practice, but it may be that his description would also have fitted the dining chamber in the villa of Alcibiades on the hill of Philopapou beside the Acropolis, where Socrates, Plato and their friends discussed politics, love and the nature of good.

> An excavation is made below the level of the dining room to a depth of about two feet, and, after the ground has been rammed down, the mass of broken stones or the pounded

burnt brick is spread on, at such an inclination that it can find vents in the drain. Next, having filled in with charcoal compactly trodden down, a mortar mixed of gravel, lime, and ashes is spread to a depth of half a foot. The surface having been made true to rule and level, and smoothed off with whetstone, gives the look of a black pavement. Hence, at their dinner parties, whatever is poured out of the cups, or spurted from the mouth, no sooner falls than it dries up, and the servants who wait there do not catch cold from that kind of floor, although they may go barefoot.[16]

The word for black in 'black pavement' is *niger*, the word most often used by the Romans for a satisfying or lustrous black; it was also the word they used to describe (without prejudice) the skin colour of Nubians and Ethiopians. For a more matt black they might use the word *ater* – the ancestor of our 'atrocious' – but *ater* too was not necessarily bitter, since it provided the name of the black paint which Vitruvius liked, *atramentum*.

There were diverse black items in the Roman world. The mosaics on the floors might be richly coloured, in the bronze-red to blue-green range, but often also the mosaics were black and white. They might show skeletons and veiled figures, but not all the monochrome mosaics are sombre. A mosaic from Ostia, the port of Rome, shows two ships passing each other, and the lighthouse of the harbour (illus. 15). The design has a free rhythm but is exact in its nautical detail, with both ships clearly using the same offshore wind. The

15 Mosaic of two ships passing the lighthouse of Rome's harbour at Ostia, *c.* 200 CE.

16 Romano-British Whitby jet pendant with a design of cupids as artisans, perhaps making a pot or cup.

ship to the left has the projecting prow of a warship and is using both mainsail and foresail, while the trading ship to the right is using only its mainsail, though the foremasts show clearly. Neither has stacked rows of sweating oarsmen (which are shown, compressed into centipedes, in Cretan-Minoan murals). In the foreground a dolphin sports sinuously, while light streaks in the water suggest the ships are making good speed.

In the Roman home, too, there were black *objets d'art*. Figures carved in black marble or ebony might stand in niches. The jewellery in a Roman matron's casket might include jet from Whitby in Yorkshire, carved into beads, bracelets or hairpins. Jewellery was functional, since Roman clothes were held together more by brooches than stitches. The brooches were often of the black stone onyx, or black glass, or niello (a black mix of copper, silver and iron sulphide). The matron's daughter might wear a jet pendant cut into a heart or, if betrothed, a pendant with cupids engaged on love's work, perhaps making a loving cup (illus. 16). The matron's father, her husband and her sons would each wear at least one ring, which might be set with onyx, niello or black glass, and cut so that it could stamp a seal. The less well-off men who worked in the household might also wear rings – perhaps of iron – which might be set with a cheaper black stone such as steatite.

Promenading out of doors, the Roman family would pass some buildings faced with black marble, and some with columns of black granite. Meeting an acquaintance in a black or blackish toga – the *toga pullus* – they would offer their condolences, for the Romans continued the Greek practice of wearing black mourning, and wore it for longer. At some point, parents would take a young family to the Lapis Niger, the Black Stone, an ancient shrine set to one side of the Forum. The origins of the shrine had been forgotten, but it was thought to mark the grave of Romulus, the founder of Rome. We may imagine the Roman father explaining these uncertainties to a family contemplating, with solemn faces, the beginnings of their city. Doubtless he traced with his finger the ancient inscription that laid a curse on whoever should disturb this sacred place, the words reading alternately from left to right, then back again from right to left, as they do in the oldest Latin inscriptions.

Whether, as they walked home, the Roman family would have seen other people wearing black not from grief, but for its smartness, we cannot be sure. Black wool was certainly valued for its softness and beauty. The colour which would have most impressed them, however, was not black, but purple. If the Roman father was in the Senate, his toga would have a purple stripe, as would the togas of his sons, and the toga of an acquaintance who had high standing as a priest.

As to the general use of purple – *purpura* – only the Emperor could wear a toga entirely of that colour; he would do so on cere-monial occasions. In the late Empire the use of purple began to be policed, while the privilege of wearing more of it than usual was sometimes granted to influential groups. Public benefactors could wear purple for life, and the officials at athletic contests could wear purple cloaks. In this regard Roman purple had something of the status which the finest black velvet had in, say, the sixteenth century, and actually its colour may not have been so different. The colour of this hugely expensive purple dye, which was made from the crushed remnants of the Mediterranean sea snail *Murex*, could vary between deep red and the deepest violet-black. Vitruvius said that the *purpura* that was harvested in Pontus and Gaul *was* black (*atrum*). Mark Bradley has noted that the redder purples were sometimes worn by those with liberal politics, while the dark-to-black purples were conservatively inclined. The Emperor Augustus would joke that the luxurious Tyrian purple sold to him was so deeply dark that he needed to stand in the sun, on his roof, for people to see that it was not in fact black. But he wore it.[17]

As to how close to black Roman clothes might sometimes be, there is the teasing evidence of those composite statues where the body is of white marble and the clothing of black. There is a more-than-life-size statue of Matidia, the sister-in-law of the Emperor Hadrian, where the revealing black marble gown she wears is clearly not a mourning robe. On display in the Hall of Statues at Antalya Museum in Turkey is a statue of a dancer sweeping forward, and her beautifully flowing and lifting dress is again, like her hair, of black marble – that is, of marble that once was black (illus. 17). How the originals of such dresses stood between the deepest black-purple and black is not certain, so it may be that we should not imagine that some Roman women appeared in black décolletée looking like Sargent's Madame X.

We can however note that when the poet Ovid advises Roman women on what they should wear, he says that a dress that is *pulla* suits a snow-white skin best. *Pullus* was the Roman colour of mourning and, though not necessarily black, it was perhaps of a deep grey like that we call 'charcoal'. Ovid notes also that Briseis of Troy was in mourning for her family, killed by Achilles, when she was carried off. Ovid implies that she was especially attractive in her grey/black robes, in a way that helped Achilles to fall in love with her, as he promptly did.[18]

Among the attractive colours worn by Roman women, Ovid includes Paphian myrtle. In her article on the colours of Roman textiles, Judith Lynn Sebesta suggests that this was dark green, since the leaves of the myrtle tree are a deeply dark green. However, she also notes that elsewhere Ovid calls the myrtle *nigra* – black – and that this tree can look black. The colour of Paphian myrtle would seem then to have been between a deep green-black and black. Sebesta notes too that the Romans could dye cloth black using iron salts with tannic acid from oak galls as the mordant. Some Roman fibres are described as *niger*, or even *coracinus*, raven-black.[19]

Roman black-dyeing was principally used to provide mourning wear, especially the *toga pullus*. The death-black of the Roman

17 A Hellenistic statue of a dancer in white and black marble, second half
of the 2nd century CE.

funeral might also be elaborated into a theatre of the grotesque – as in the black feast mounted by the emperor Domitian to caution hostile patricians. As Dio Cassius records, Domitian

> entertained the foremost men among the senators and knights in the following fashion. He prepared a room that was pitch black on every side, ceiling, walls and floor, and had made ready bare couches of the same colour resting on the uncovered floor; then he invited in his guests alone at night without their attendants. And first he set beside each of them a slab shaped like a gravestone, bearing the guest's name and also a small lamp, such as hang in tombs. Next comely naked boys, likewise painted black, entered like phantoms, and after encircling the guests in an awe-inspiring dance took up their stations at their feet. After this all the things that are commonly offered at the sacrifices to departed spirits were likewise set before the guests, all of them black and in dishes of a similar colour. Consequently, every single one of the guests feared and trembled and was kept in constant expectation of having his throat cut the next moment, the more so as on the part of everybody but Domitian there was dead silence, as if they were already in the realms of the dead, and the emperor himself conversed only upon topics relating to death and slaughter.

It was, however, a black comedy feast. Domitian's primary purpose was intimidation, and after his guests were conveyed to their mansions in solitary terror, further messengers arrived, bringing to each a copy of his place-slab, and of the black dishes, made now in silver and other costly materials. 'Last of all came that particular boy who had been each guest's familiar spirit, now washed and adorned.' By such means, it appears, Domitian restrained high-ranking opposition to the austerities of his regime. He gave the first black dinner party known to recorded history; others followed.[20]

The Roman realm of the dead is also, if anything, more black than that of the Greeks: its blackness is mentioned more often and with more zest. The river Phlegethon issues black flames, Statius says, and Black Death sits on an eminence. The fact that the Romans had several words for black enables them to not seem repetitive. A distinction is often made between the attractive, lustrous black of *niger* and the matt, repellent black of *ater*, but in describing the Underworld the two words seem interchangeable. In Statius the black river is *niger* and its black flames *ater*, while Death is *atra* (the feminine form of *ater*, since *mors*, 'death', is feminine). Ringing the black changes, Valerius Flaccus refers to a land of black night (Stygian, from the black Styx) and black dread (*niger*), where the Black One ('Celaeneus') sits dressed in black (*ater*). In Ovid the black Styx has black breath (*halitus niger*). The Roman queen of the dead, Proserpina (their Persephone), may be called 'the Stygian Juno'.[21]

Statius and Verius Flaccus are perhaps sensational in their blacks, for the underworld of Virgil is not so emphatically 'Stygian'. It is Virgil, however, who, twice in the *Aeneid*, plays with the oxymoron of black flames – in passages which presumably encouraged Milton to say that the flames of hell, in his *Paradise Lost*, shed 'darkness visible'. In a lightless cavern Hercules confronts the half-human Cacus, who belches out black fire (*atri ignes*). And when Dido accuses Aeneas of deceiving and deserting her, she promises to pursue him with black fires (*atris ignibus*), and in the next lines says that when icy death takes her, her ghost will surround him everwhere. The conjunction of black - ness, flames and frost – of fire with its two opposites, dark and cold – conjures a supernatural fire, blazing black and freezing too, to wither Aeneas in his guilt.[22]

In the poetry of Ovid the different blacks of Rome congregate and coordinate. Ovid, like Vitruvius, likes black. He tell us in his *Art of Love* that though he is easy prey for blondes he is glad to see a dusky Venus (*in fusco grata colore Venus*), while black hairs (*capilli pulli*) look good on a snowy neck (here *pullus* sounds more black than grey). Leda was famed for her black hair (*nigra coma*). His own hair, too, had once been black (*nigras*). He is alert too to black creatures, the black horses that draw the chariot of Pluto (the Roman Hades), who for Ovid is the Black God (*nigri dei*). In the *Metamorphoses* Aroe is trans - formed into a jackdaw with black feet and black wings (their blackness stressed in the Latin by alliteration and internal rhyming, *nigra pedes, nigris . . . pennis*). The hounds of Actaeon, who destroy him when he is transformed into a stag, include Black-foot (Melampus), black- haired Soot ('villis Asbolus atris'), Harpalos with the white mark on his black head, and Black (Melaneus). At the kill, Black-hair (Melan- chaetes) attacks his back while Killer and Climber bring him down.

It is not clear whether Black-hair is the same dog as black-haired Soot, and of course it hardly matters as the part-black pack rip his flesh into fibres and he issues a cry no deer could make, while his hunting companions urge the dogs on, at the same time wondering where Actaeon can have got to. It may be because Actaeon was Greek that, in naming the pack, Ovid uses Latin words based on the Greek *melas*.[23]

The black accents recur, adding a seriousness – even a fatality – to the extraordinary transformations that make up the *Metamorphoses*. Ovid's black can be epic in its impact and its quantity. In a primal conflict near the beginning of time, the sun-god Phoebus fights the monster snake Python whose coils cover mountains. When the snake dies, venom floods from its black wounds (*vulnera nigra*) – as if its bloodstream as well as its fangs run with venom, such that, when wounded, its own poison rots it black at once. Then again, Ovid will use his dark tones lightly. When Iris is tasked to rouse the god of sleep, Ovid multiplies darknesses humorously. Near the land of the Cimmerians, at the lightless end of the world, surrounded by fogs, in 'crepuscular' light, Iris enters a cave-mouth thick with poppies. As she works to wake the god, he keeps closing his eyes while his chin lolls again on his chest. He lies stretched out on an ebony bed with a cover that is black or near-black (*pullus*), stuffed with black feathers (*atricolor*).[24]

And in his most savage and cruel moments, the black emphasis reappears. When Philomela has just been raped and had her tongue cut out by Tereus, the brutal king of Thrace, Ovid imagines the cut-off tongue writhing like a wounded snake on the black earth (*terraeque ... atrae*). Since the earth of Thrace is not, and has never been said to be, black, its blackness here is poetic. The earth is black for the visual contrast, and black as blood-soaked earth may be, and black again with the darkness of the powers beneath the earth.[25]

Given the poetic use Ovid makes of blackness, there is an irony in the fact that this racy, daring, witty poet ended his days exiled among the Scythians by the Black Sea – a sea whose waters are far from black, but which even in antiquity may have derived its name 'Pontos Axeinos' ('Inhospitable Sea') from the Scythian *aksaina*, meaning lightless and dark.[26]

18 The Black Madonna of Altötting, Bavaria, 14th century, wood.

THREE

The Black of God

TO A ROMAN the colour black need not be harsh: it could be sweet, and luxurious, and erotic. But in temples it would be worn by mourners, not by priests; nor was the primary god – Jupiter – identified with darkness or with blackness. Priests and vestal virgins wore white or purple. A great change would need to come, in the universe of the spirit, before a god could be worshipped as lord of all – and as the light of the world – whose home would be in the deepest darkness that could be imagined by man.

AMONG THE PEOPLES absorbed into the Roman Empire, some had native black traditions. When the geographer Strabo describes the people of Lusitania (Portugal) he sounds as though he has found a race of ancient Victorians: 'All the men dress in black . . . but the women always go clad in long mantles and gay-coloured gowns.'[1] Clearly the tradition of Iberian black goes further back than Philip II of Spain, since a prime local product was black. Strabo has particular praise for Iberian wool 'of the raven-black sort. And it is surpassingly beautiful; at all events, the rams are bought for breeding purposes at a talent a piece.' Not all black wool was so expensively fine, and the 'rough black cloaks' which many men wore may have been of black goats' hair. Strabo is again referring to herdsmen when he says the people of the Cassiterides (possibly the Scilly Isles) wore long black garments that reached to their feet, and carried canes so that they looked like the goddesses of vengeance in tragedies – that is, the Furies. The canes were presumably an early form of shepherd's crook.

While Iberian women may have dressed gaily, further north there were other women, dressed in black, who resembled the Furies to more frightening effect. In 60 CE, when the Romans invaded Mona (Anglesey), a centre of druid opposition, they were met – Tacitus says – by armed warriors 'while between the ranks dashed women in black attire like the Furies, with hair dishevelled, waving brands'.[2] All around stood druids, lifting their hands to heaven, and 'pouring forth dreadful imprecations'. Though they were the veterans of many campaigns, the legionaries 'stood motionless . . . their limbs paralysed', until their general urged them 'not to quail before a troop of frenzied women'. Then they advanced, 'smote down all resistance' and laid waste the druid groves.

The women of Anglesey would again have worn black wool. Tacitus describes them as wearing funeral robes, and funeral wear was one destination for the black wool which so impressed Strabo. He found it at other extremities of the Empire. Of Laodicea in the Near East he says that the sheep there 'are excellent, not only for the softness of their wool . . . but also for its raven-black colour, so that the Laodiceans derive splendid revenue from it'.[3] Black wool was not worn only at funerals, for presumably it also provided some of those *pullus* garments which – Ovid said – suited women of light complexion. The *palla*, the Roman shawl, may also have been *pulla*.

Black in another sense were the nation of the Huns with whom the Romans cooperated (before falling victim to them). They were known as the Black Huns through the Near East because they were the northernmost Hun tribal grouping: black being widely associated with compass-points north. But for the Romans they were dark both in their skin colour and in their ferocity. The author Jordanes said 'they made their foes flee in horror because their swarthy aspect (*pavenda nigridinis*) was fearful, and they had, if I may call it so, a sort of shapeless lump, not a head, with pin-holes rather than eyes'.[4] It was said that they slashed their faces, and smeared black earth into the scars, so as to be more frightening. Attila himself was described as short, flat-nosed and swarthy, though Priscus, the Roman who negotiated with him, was impressed by his frugal eating, by the civility of his wife and by the excellent carpentry in his wooden compound.

Body art at this time might be black and might be blue. As shown on their coinage, many Celtic peoples had facial tattoos, for which a dark concentration of woad (wood indigo) was used. Julius Caesar said the Britons dyed their bodies blue before going into battle; probably their woad was mixed with beef dripping, which also gave protection from the cold. And Pliny said that British women and girls stained their bodies, not blue, but black all over. They used the herb 'glastum', which made them look 'like Ethiopians' as they performed sacred rites 'in a state of nature'.[5] The comparison would have been clear to his readers because, on the southern rim of the Empire, there *were* the Ethiopians, who had their own tradition of body art – of scarification and tattooing – using the black dye henna. Though never conquered by the Romans, the Ethiopians contributed archers to the multiracial force of the Roman legions; Ethiopia also provided the ebony that furnished many Roman villas.

Beyond the material culture was the religious. When British girls went naked, and black, it was to perform fertility rites. The pestles and mortars where the 'glastum' was pounded might be decorated with phallic shapes, and semen might be used as a binding agent.[6] For here too, as in ancient Egypt and elsewhere, blackness had a place in the cycle of Nature. The gods themselves might be black. The Celtic god Crom Dubh (his name means 'Crooked and Black') was black because he spent half the year underground, and bent from the weight of the sheaves that he carried. He sounds like Hades and Persephone in one, rising from the death of winter to preside over abundant harvests.

Other black gods were less abundant. It is not surprising that Nott, the northern goddess of night, wore black clothes and was drawn by black horses. Nor that Morrigu, the Celtic goddess of battles, hovered over the carnage as a black crow or raven. Nor that the Nordic goddess of the dead, Hel, was half white as a corpse and half black as decomposition and night. Since the northern peoples did not then produce written texts, some of these gods are now obscure to us, like the Celtic god Leug (from the Indo-European root *leug*, black), who was associated again with ravens, or like the Slavic Czernobog (literally 'Black God').

There is, on the other hand, nothing obscure in the description given of the Celtic god Ogmios as seen in a picture by the rhetorician Lucian of Samosata in the second century CE. The pantheisms of Greece and Rome were hospitable to other pantheisms, and classical writers were accustomed to finding their own gods worshipped under other names in other religions. Even so, Lucian is astonished by the form the Celts have given to Hercules:

The Celts call Heracles Ogmios in their native tongue, and they portray the god in a very peculiar way. To their notion, he is extremely old, bald-headed, except for a few lingering hairs which are quite grey, his skin is wrinkled, and he is burned as black as can be, like an old sea-dog. You would think him a Charon or a sub-Tartarean Iapetus – anything but Heracles! Yet, in spite of his looks, he has the equipment of Heracles: he is dressed in the lion's skin, has the club in his right hand, carries the quiver at his side, displays the bent bow in his left, and is Heracles from head to heel as far as that goes.[7]

Gazing at the picture, Lucian is still more astonished by the companions of Ogmios, for he draws behind him a crowd of men tethered by the ears, and the delicate chains that lead them – 'fashioned of gold and amber, resembling the prettiest of necklaces' – are fastened to Ogmios' tongue. Happily Lucian has an educated Celt for a companion, who explains to him that Ogmios is the god of eloquence and can be identified with Hercules because of the power that eloquence has. He is elderly because eloquence only finds its full vigour when combined with the wisdom of age.

Neither Lucian nor the Celt explain why the god of eloquence is black. We might wonder if he is dark from the ambiguity of eloquence, for to post-Christian eyes Ogmios could look like the Devil, by subtle words leading people astray. Lucian's Celt has no such thoughts, however, nor is there any suggestion that Ogmios is a dark fertility god of the underworld, nor that his club is phallic. Perhaps, then, the blackness of Ogmios is a purely visual emphasis: it shows he is a different order of being from those he leads. He is the god of eloquence, not an allegory of it, nor a particular orator. His blackness is not natural, it is supernatural: he is a god. For there are many black gods in the myths of the world, and in the myths of many peoples living far from Africa. The blackness of some is associated with death and wrath and pestilence; of others with black silt and rainclouds and soil; of others with fire, ash and embers and again with light and the constellations.

It may be that the dark gods should be viewed more broadly: that there is a connection between blackness and divinity. One could consider the mystery of any black surface. For a truly black surface

19 Herakles fighting Amazons, black-figure vase, *c.* 530 BCE.

differs from other coloured things because the eye reaches into it as into space, and finds only endlessness and no place to rest, as if sight could reach through black solidity. An all-black surface combines opacity with infinity. Such a character could suit the more-than-natural nature of the gods; their power is frightening though their purposes are opaque. If one thinks of the omniscience of the gods, and of their elusiveness and indifference to our needs, and of the way they outreach us though they reach deep within us, then it may not be surprising if in the pantheons of many cultures there are some gods who are black.

To return to Ogmios, and his teasing connection with Hercules – the Roman name for Herakles. Hercules/Herakles is a figure to consider when one contemplates the relation of human beings with the gods. He survives in popular narrative now as the mythological version of the circus strongman, good for cudgeling many-headed monsters. But worship of him was widespread in the ancient world. For Herodotus he had been an Egyptian god before he became a hero for the Greeks, and for the Greeks he was in different places a man, a demigod and a god. On the island of Thasos he was first worshipped

as a god, as the paramount god, before he was worshipped, in a separate temple, as a demigod. His story has mystery, and darkness
too. Before starting his labours he had slaughtered his family, having
been made mad by Hera. He was to die in horrific torment, his flesh
devoured by the venom in the black blood of the black-haired centaur
Charon. When Odysseus meets him in the Underworld in Homer,
he resembles black night, glancing fiercely round, bow and arrows at
the ready.[8] On vases of the sixth century BCE a black Herakles may
be seen fighting white Amazons (illus. 19).

For the ancient world Herakles was a giant, sacred, tragic figure,
the son of god and of man – of Zeus and Alcmene – the living union
of the human with the divine. If we compare him with the other
Son of Man – and of God – who was born into that world of gods
in a small nation on the fringe of the Empire, we may see both the
potency and the weakness of Graeco-Roman religion. For it is not
just that Hercules did not walk on water, nor heal the sick; more
importantly, for all his muscles, it seems that he had nothing to say.
Actually, none of the gods of Greece or Rome are remembered much
for what they said, and in their myths they often behave as though
they had half the brain that the Greek philosophers had. Whereas
Jesus – though he may have spoken from revelation – sounds as
though he spoke from a searching observation of human motive
(for instance, of the deep, bad work done in everyone by jealousy),
and of human need in relation to life, death, love, right and wrong.
And at all events, in spite of his humble origins and criminal death,
Jesus came to conquer that inclusive, faltering Graeco-Roman world.

On the island of Thasos the columns from the temples of
Hercules were reused – with Greek crosses cut in them – inside the
new Early Christian churches, where a relief of Hercules himself
was incorporated into the masonry. Both the columns and the relief
can be seen on site, with no fence round them, at Alikes on the
southern coast. Incidentally, in the succession from many gods to the
One, the value of the colour black changed fundamentally.

IN THE RELIGIONS with many gods, who may live in a big com -
munity somewhere between a family and polity, up on a high place
like a mountaintop, above but not too far above our world, often there
is among them a pre-eminent being who is more than their monarch

or governor: in some sense this being contains them, or may have made or borne them. In proportion as such figures are separated above the others, and recognized as primary godheads, they are likely to be identified with light, or the Light, engaged in a fundamental contest with darkness. The contrast of light and dark, and day and night, is so fundamental to us that things could perhaps not be otherwise. In the Bible, in the beginning, darkness lies upon the face of the deep, until God says let there be light, and there is light – which God sees, and approves, and then He divides the light from the dark, which He calls night.

The Jewish prophets were not alone in promoting the worship of an emergent single god. Their great enemy and captor, ancient Egypt, had an interlude – within the millennia of their worship of an animal-headed throng – when an eccentric pharaoh sought to im - pose the worship of a single god. During his reign of seventeen years, in around 1320 BCE, Akhenaten – the husband of Nefertiti – estab- lished temples to the great creating power, the Aten, which was also the disc and the god of the sun. In his hymn to Aten, Akhenaten sang:

How manifold are the things that thou has made . . .
O sole god, like whom there is no other.[9]

The Aten is praised for creating the primal river, the Nile, which flows both in the underworld and in the blessed land of Egypt: for if life depends on water, still it is quickened by the light of the sun.

Or in the Persian religion of Zoroastrianism the divinity Ohrmazd dwelt in endless light, and made of that light fire, then ether, then water, then earth, while the evil spirit Ahriman slept in endless dark- ness. When Ahriman woke, he turned the sky to dark night, inflicted the dark power Mihr on the world and set a 'dark moon' against the moon. In Zoroastrianism the Light that shone at the beginning of time gives the light of goodness in our world, and in each of us, while the evil of Ahriman is also the dark, bad part of us.[10] The forces of the cosmos are the giant counterpart of the motives inside us; as again they are in the pantheistic religions, where Aphrodite and Diana may be the magnified equal of the sexual passion, and the ascetic impulse, within the individual.

Zoroastrianism, and its offshoot Mithraism, appealed to the quest- ing spirit of the failing Roman world. Temples to Mithras were built in pockets of the Empire, including Londinium (London). It was however a men-only faith, and though it naturally appealed to legionaries, it was evidently insufficient to meet the larger need; this came to be supplied by the Christian faith, which brought Light inside the lives of all men and women.

A cosmic war between light and darkness is not, however, quite the same as a war between light and blackness. Christianity completed a change which was latent in all of the light–dark imagery when it equated the darkness with sin, and at the same time made sin black. This is an abstract way of putting things, I realize, and it may be helpful to look more closely at the actual colour of sin. Because sin, before the rise of Christianity, had not been primarily black. Sin had to have a colour, because in a recurring biblical metaphor, sin is conceived as a 'stain'. It is a stain upon the soul because it does not come from the centre of the soul, and may, through penitent prayer, be removed. In the Bible, as also in Greek poetry, there is a running imagery of washing, and of the great difficulty of washing off sin, or guilt, or evil. The sin that cleaves to one may be black – as when the chorus in *The Libation Bearers* speak of the black blood of guilt which a rapist cannot cleanse. But more often, in the Old Testament especially, sin is red. And it is red because, like the rapist's black crime, it is the colour of blood and bloodshed. The Lord speaks 'of Saul and his blood-stained house' (2 Samuel, 21:1) and Isaiah cries, 'For your hands are stained with blood, your fingers with guilt' (59:3). And as in Greek tragedy (and later in Shakespeare's *Macbeth*), the actual difficulty of washing real blood from your hands is equated with the difficulty of cancelling guilt. 'Although you wash yourself with soap and use an abundance of cleansing powder,' Isaiah says, 'the stain of your guilt is still before me' (63:3).[11]

The Bible recurs many times to the trope of being washed 'whiter than snow'. 'Purge me with hyssop, and I shall be clean', says Psalm 51; 'Wash me, and I shall be whiter than snow.' The colour to be washed off is again red, since the Psalmist also says 'Deliver me from bloodshed.' The red of sin is not however always that of blood: there are other sins than bloodshed, and they too may be scarlet or crimson. 'Though your sins are like scarlet,' says Isaiah, 'they shall be as white as snow; though they are red like crimson, they shall become like wool' (1:18). A sin that is scarlet or crimson sounds more in the domain of forbidden pleasure – the more lurid for the prohibition

– than that of forbidden violence, but the linkage with blood is not forgotten. On the contrary, it is reinforced by the further equation of blood with red wine, and red wine with both drunkenness and illicit sex. In Revelation 'the great harlot' sits on a scarlet beast and is arrayed in purple and scarlet; the inhabitants of the earth are 'drunk with the wine of her fornication', while she herself (she holds a golden cup) is 'drunk with the blood of the saints' (17:2–6). The image of red stains runs through the Bible, now of sin, now of wine, now of blood, in changing equations. 'I have trodden the winepress alone; from the nations no one was with me', Isaiah says again. 'I trod them down in my wrath; their blood spattered my garments, and I stained all my clothing' (63:2–4).

If sin lives in a red triad of bloodshed, drunkenness and crimson fornication, one might ask how sin came also to be black. This change came especially with Christianity, through Christianity's growing equation of sin with death. For if sin means death, or the death of the soul, and death itself is the result of sin – brought into the world by our first parents' sin – then sin will deserve to take death's colour. And this insistence on the identity of sin with death is of the New Testament. The Church later drew a distinction between venial and mortal sin, but that distinction is already made in the First Epistle of John, 'There is a sin unto death' (5:17). Again the doctrine of Original Sin, bringing death into the world, was later elaborated by the Church, but had been initiated in Paul's Epistle to the Romans, 'as by one man sin entered into the world, and death by sin, so death passed onto all men, for all have sinned' (5:12). Jesus Himself did not preach that sin was death – an idea that seems at odds with his emphasis on forgiveness, and on the importance of simply stopping, so that one 'sins no more'. But as Christian doctrine was formalized, so the equation of sin with death was consolidated, and with it came an emphasis on the blackness of sin which is not found in the Old Testament. Near the turn of the fourth century CE St Augustine speaks of '*nigritudo peccatorum*' – the blackness of sins – and St Jerome of '*nigredinem vel varietatem peccatorum*' – the blackness and variety of sins. The emphasis on the blackness of sin continues through the many centuries of Christian faith. Charles Spurgeon in the nineteenth century preached in his Tabernacle that 'spiritually we are blind . . . unable to behold the blackness of sin'. It is through the Christian emphasis on the blackness of sin that the large abstract concept of 'blackness' developed, which has come in our time to be grand, vague and portentous, combining suggestions of despair, evil and the infinite. The ancient world had not known 'blackness' in that sense.[12]

Spurgeon's reference to a blackness that we cannot see is apt, for the colour of sin would have to be called a mental colour, a head-colour. Whether sin is black or red – even scarlet or crimson – we do not see it with our retinas. Sin's colour exists in inner space, in that mental domain where sights, words and thoughts overlap. In this space one will 'see' colour, even when no colour is mentioned: if someone says, 'Think of a London bus', one has an impression of scarlet, whatever the reason for mentioning the bus. When William Blake says, in 'The Sick Rose', that the invisible worm 'has found out thy bed of crimson joy', again we see red (and so know that he is speaking of a red, not a white, rose), though he is thinking mainly of the luridness of sex in secrecy – that is, of exhilarating sinfulness – and not of bloodstained sheets. But though in a sense we see these head-colours – even with an impression of glare or vividness – their optics obey different rules from those of actual sight. These colours do not, for instance, cancel each other, or mix to make a composite colour. On the contrary, they coexist, and in the same location. Sin did not cease to be red when it became also black. Through the centuries of Christian denunciation of pleasure one would often have to say that sin is not the less luridly red for being black, and is not the less black for being often blood-red.

Though the stain of sin, whether red or black, is not a stain that our retinas see, the idea that sin was a black stain on our being inevitably had a consequence for the people who actually are, visibly, black. The curse fell especially on Ethiopians. The ancient world did not have a problem with skin colour: it simply understood that the further south one's homeland was, the darker one's skin would be burned by the sun. But for Christian preachers, searching for images, examples and metaphors, the temptation was irresistible, and the 'Ethiopian' became at once the image and the demonstration of sinfulness. For the Ethiopian was black from the curse laid on Ham, a divine punishment laid on sin, and this curse was equated with the blackness of sin, though all Genesis says is that Ham's descendants will always be servants (9:25).

Nor does the Christian back-projection of blackness stop at Ham, or Cain, or indeed Adam, since it followed that if evil and sin were

20 Sébastien Leclerc, 'St Benedict scourging a monk who is being led astray by a black demon', etching from the *Vita et miracula sanctissimi patris Benedicti* (1658).

black, then the Devil and his devils were also black, and had been since their own Fall. The Epistle of Barnabas of the fourth century CE refers to the Devil as 'the Black One', and the lesser devils who figure in Church history will often be called 'a black demon', as though their colour were taken for granted. In a lively engraving to the *Life* of St Benedict, Benedict scourges a monk who is being literally led astray by a small, impish demon, who is black (illus. 20). In pictures the Devil is not always black: he and his minions may be green, or red,

21 Duccio di Buoninsegna, *The Temptation of Christ on the Mountain*, 1308–11, tempera and gold on wood.

or have a blotched skin resembling the sores of the plague. But often also the Devil is shown as black, in images that have a further cruel corollary for Ethiopians. For not only were Ethiopians thought black from ancient sinfulness – as descendants of Ham – they also provided a standard comparison when describing the Devil. In the apocryphal Acts of Bartholomew, of the third century, a demon who has hidden in a temple is brought to light, and is 'like an Ethiopian, black as soot'. In an early stage of the temptations of St Antony, around the year 300, the Devil appears to Antony 'as a black boy'. A fellow desert saint who had visited Antony, St Macarius the Younger, saw demons 'like foul Ethiops' flying round a group of monks. In the fourth-century *Conferences* of St John Cassian the comparison is regular and abusive too: the Devil appears to Abbot John of Lycon 'in the shape of a filthy Ethiopian'; Abbot Apollos sees a young monk tormented by a devil in the form of 'a filthy

Ethiopian . . . aiming fiery darts at him'; and an esteemed elder sees that a young monk breaking stones is assisted by 'a certain Ethiopian' whom he recognizes as the Devil. The association of devils and devilry with Ethiopians was to continue for a thousand years, and when the medieval tradition of illuminated manuscripts developed it became a frequent practice, from the thirteenth century on, to represent both demons, and the torturers and executioners of Christ and Christian saints, as men with black skins and negroid features.[13] In Duccio di Buoninsegna's painting of the temptation of Christ on the mountain-top, the Devil being dismissed by Christ looks (except for the wings) like an elderly, naked black African man (illus. 21).

It hardly needs to be said that the denigration of Ethiopians was not the purpose of Christ, or of his first Apostles. The several Christian creeds said that Christ died for all men, and the Acts of the Apostles record how Philip the Evangelist 'preached Jesus' to 'a man of Ethiopia, an eunuch of great authority under Candace queen of the Ethiopians' (8:27–35). The Ethiopian invites Philip into his chariot, and when they come to a body of water he asks to be baptized, 'and they went down both into the water, both Philip and the eunuch; and he baptized him' (8:38). Augustine, too, said that Christianity was to embrace 'the Ethiopians who lived at the ends of the earth'. Ethiopia had one of the most ancient of the Christian churches.

It was nonetheless difficult for the early Christian teachers to negotiate such a text as the Song of Songs. 'I am black, but comely, O ye daughters of Jerusalem, as the tents of Kedar, as the curtains of Solomon' (1:5) – the 'but', it should be said, comes from the Latin text, *'nigra sum sed formosa'*. The early Church Father Origen, at the turn of the second century, touched on the racial question lightly, even charmingly: 'If you repent, your soul will be "black" because of your former sins, but because of your penitence your soul will have something of what I may call an Ethiopian beauty.'[14] Origen also said it made no difference whether one was born among Hebrews, Greeks, Ethiopians or Scythians, for God created all men equal and alike. In the following centuries, however, the prejudicial weight of Christian blackness grew, and for St Bernard of Clairvaux, writing in the twelfth century, the light poise of Origen was unavailable. When Bernard comes to blackness, he begins a mighty labour of exoneration and compensation. 'It is better that one be blackened for the sake of all "in the likeness of sinful flesh", than for the whole of mankind to be lost by the blackness of sin.' It is clear from the phrasing here that he is working towards a comparison of the Bride of the Song with Christ, and he goes beyond traditional iconography – and beyond probability – when he says that Christ on the cross became visibly black. 'What did the eyes of the beholders see but a man deformed and black, his hands splayed out on the cross as he hung between two criminals?' One would think that if Christ takes on our blackness, then blackness is ennobled. But black for Bernard is still 'the abject hue that indicates infirmity'. The Bride will not be black in Heaven, for Bernard's black Christ says, of his life after death, 'But shall I still be black? God forbid! Your beloved will be fair and ruddy, strikingly beautiful, surrounded by roses and lilies of the valley.'[15]

Bernard honours the Bride because, in her blackness, she anticipates Christ. He is clearly emancipated from the gross identification of Ethiopians with sin. Nor does he, as his sermon proceeds, insist that blackness must signify sin. Rather he moves, by subtle steps, through an ascent among more sacred blacknesses. 'There is another blackness', he says, that of enduring penance in sorrow for one's sin. Then, 'there is also the blackness of compassion, when you condole with a brother [whose] trouble fills you with gloom'. Again, 'there is the blackness of persecution, to be regarded as a most noble adornment.' This brings him to a further black which had always perhaps been his destination – the black of church vestments – which allows the Bride to be identified with the named Bride of Christ, the Church. 'The Church glories especially in . . . this dark covering from the curtains of her Bridegroom.' The black robes of monks and priests are the black curtains of Solomon's temple, and in the celebration of a marriage at once material and spiritual, the Church is identified with Solomon's Ethiopian beloved. Having come so far, the sermon ecstatically soars to the blood-red black of breathless passion.

> To be discolored by the sun may also mean to be on fire . . .
> Christ the Sun of justice had made me swarthy in colour,
> because I am faint with love of him. This languor . . . makes
> the soul swoon with desire . . . Why do you term swarthy one
> who yields only to the sun in loveliness?

Given Bernard's eloquence, it is not surprising that his celebration of the Song of Songs is often cited in discussions of the teasing

'Black Madonnas' that can be found in some medieval European churches, some of which may date back to the thirteenth century. It is hard to make a true general statement as to how far these very ancient images of the Virgin, which often are of wood, are black from exposure to fire, dirt, damp, candle smoke or other damages of time – or from the addition, at some date, of pigment. Their colour is not always as black as soot, though they can be of a deeply dark brown. In the church at Altötting in Bavaria, the odd blackness of the small wooden figure is set off and emphasized by a vast, glittering glory of gilded church ornament – seen here, appropriately, through the shimmering tinsel of a Christmas tree (illus. 18). But no medieval evidence survives of a commission to make or purchase a Black Madonna, nor is there substantial reason to associate the Black Madonnas with Isis or other old, dark goddesses, as is sometimes done. It is perhaps best simply to record that the Black Madonnas are not new: they have long been called 'black', and their blackness has been no obstacle to their veneration. On the contrary, the blackness has, if anything, added to the sense of their sacred mystery, and to their reputation for assisting miracles.

To return to St Bernard, though he alludes to black vestments, he himself, as a Cistercian, would have worn white – robes whose paradisal whiteness he might have associated with lilies of the valley, a flower which evidently, like the rose and the palm, grows in heaven as on earth. It was other orders, such as the Benedictines, and their reformed brethren the Cluniac monks, who wore black – the Benedictines having done so since the fifth century. But Cistercians too wore a black scapular – a kind of black pinafore – over their white robes, in recognition of the Benedictine origin of their order. By St Bernard's time, moreover, black was established as a liturgical colour, to be worn during Advent, Lent and on days of affliction; white was worn for Christmas, Easter, the feast of the Conversion of St Paul and the consecration of bishops.[16]

The founders of religious orders have seldom specified dress colours. Nor did St Benedict require the brethren to wear black. But one duty of the monk was to mourn, both for the killing of Christ and for the sinfulness of man, and to seek atonement for human evil. Early monasticism moved towards black, the traditional colour of mourning and penitence, and by the end of the first millennium different styles of black habit were widely adopted by the Roman, the

Coptic and the Orthodox churches. No single fixed meaning for the colour black was instituted by the Christian church, but the values of colours were discussed among the communities; some orders were to wear brown or grey. In an exchange of letters, St Bernard himself, a white monk in a black scapular, debated colours with Peter the Venerable, a black monk of the Cluniac order. Peter and St Bernard agreed that white was fit for the joy of church festivals, while black was the colour of grief, humility and abject penitence, and so more suitable – Peter urged – for everday wear by contrite Christians.[17]

The etching by Alphonse Legros of a monastic refectory was made in the nineteenth century, but shows the life of the black habit as it had existed for a millennium (illus. 22). The season may be Lent, since the sole dish on the table carries a fish; the nosegay in its small vase may be Canterbury bells, which symbolize faith. One monk prays, or says grace before eating. The monk next to him claws his stomach, perhaps from the pangs of fasting, though he could be sunk in religious melancholy. With his black eye sockets and hairless tonsure he resembles a skull, a memento mori for his brothers. His neighbours, however, are talking calmly, perhaps of divinity or monastery gossip. The standing monk, whose turn it is to serve, is not over-interested, while the monk with his back to us reads from a Bible or a breviary. Their austere quarters and simple fare and furniture are more than clear. An oil lamp flares in the draught near a Christus, whose face is sunk in shadow.

Beneath the monk's robe, of black or dyed wool, a second black garment was sometimes worn, not of sheeps' wool but of goat-hair. In the Old Testament both prophets and people put on sackcloth and lie in ashes when consumed in lamentation; and sackcloth was made from black goat-hair. In the Book of Revelation, when the sixth seal is opened, 'the sun became black as sackcloth of hair' (6:12). Under the name *cilicium* (later 'cilice'), from Cicilia in Asia Minor where black goat-hair was plentiful, the hair shirt quickly found a place in early Christian asceticism. As St Jerome recorded affectionately, when the young St Hilarion entered the desert waste near Gaza, only fifteen years old and a smooth-cheeked, thin and delicate youth, he wore nothing but a shirt of sackcloth beneath a cloak of animal skin. As St Jerome knew from his own hair shirt, sackcloth caused constant pain and abrasion. Never shown and seldom laundered, the true black dress of remorse and atonement, it might on death be revealed, its black weave clotted with dirt and dried blood, and possibly crawling with vermin, like the hair shirt found on the body of Thomas à Becket.[18]

In time Christian black, which began in humility, came to represent the harsh and even deadly authority of the Church. The Dominicans, the 'Black Friars' who came to staff the Inquisition, were known by their black cloaks and hoods, and they were an order whose founder, St Dominic, *did* require a covering black garb to be worn (over a white habit).[19] But the origin of Christian black lay in the death of Christ, and not only in his sacrifice but in the darkness of the Passion itself, when Jesus cried in torment that God had abandoned him, and the earth quaked and the veil of the Temple was rent, and 'there was a darkness over all the earth . . . and the sun was darkened' (Luke 23:44–5). In many painted crucifixions the figure of Christ is spotlit – often sentimentally – against that black darkness. In the *Crucifixion* of Matthias Grünewald, however, there is no special lighting (illus. 23). Behind Christ there is indeed black darkness, and the landscape is dim as in an eclipse or twilight, but Christ and those mourning for him share a low-key residual daylight. He has died, it seems, in pain and despair, and the scarred body may have started to decompose. The humiliation and misery of His death is there, and his mother appropriately wears not blue but black.

Later Christ rises, attended by white angels, and He sits beside the Father in white glory now. But Christianity never forgot that

22 Alphonse Legros, *La Réfectoire*, 1862, etching.

depth of abandoned darkness: rather, it was cherished, and distinguished clearly from the blackness of sin. From the first centuries Christianity has preserved the tradition of a sacred darkness or blackness. The darkness represented the deprivation of the soul, yet also it could be identified with excessive light and brightness. God Himself was both blinding light and darkness. In the Bible the Lord 'made darkness his secret place' (Psalm 18:11), and when he climbed Mount Sinai to receive the Commandments, Moses 'drew near unto the thick darkness where God was' (Exodus 20:21).

In Christianity the mystical darkness is best known from the *Mystical Theology* of 'Pseudo-Dionysius', written around 500 in the Middle East. The divine mysteries rest 'in the brilliant darkness of a hidden silence [pouring] overwhelming light'. These contradictions are echoed, with an eloquence of human need, in the fourteenth-century English text *The Cloud of Unknowing*: 'And therfore schap thee to bide in this derknes as long as thou maist, euermore criing after him that thou louest.' Such loving longing is most famously described by the sixteenth-century Spanish priest now known as St John of the Cross in his poem 'The Dark Night of the Soul':

> One dark night,
>   fired with love's urgent longings . . .
> I went out unseen,
>   my house being now all stilled . . .
> O night more lovely than the dawn!
> O night that has united
>   the Lover with his beloved,
> Upon my flowering breast . . .
>   all things ceased; I went out from myself,
>   leaving my cares
>   forgotten among the lilies.

'The Dark Night of the Soul', the poet says in his own commentary, is a 'substantial darkness' that 'acts upon the soul . . . as fire acts upon a log of wood', at first making it 'black, dark and unsightly' and transforming it at last to be 'as beautiful as fire'. 'For the nearer the soul approaches to [God], the blacker is the darkness which it feels . . . and thus, that which in God is supreme light and refulgence is to man blackest darkness.' It is nonetheless a darkness in which – as in the Song of Songs – the Lover and the divine come together in a peace within human understanding.[20]

One may ask how this vision may still speak to us. The twentieth-century painting *Christ of St John of the Cross* by Salvador Dalí can be criticized for its melodramatic perspective – looking down on Christ from above, as He hangs in absolute solid blackness (illus. 24). The composition is however based on the drawing which St John of the Cross himself made, where again we look down on Christ's head from above (and to one side). The effect of hiding Christ's face – as with any painted figure seen from behind – is to question his identity. In the Dalí one may well wonder, is this Christ – this young man with the modern haircut? Or if the crucifixion is that of St John, may this be St John himself, on his cross? But that is unlikely, since St John of the Cross was in holy orders and had a tonsure. Nor is humanity represented here, to be redeemed by the sacrifice, whereas Grünewald showed grieving people aware of their need, their outline touching the outline of Christ. Dalí, by contrast, shows two fishermen occupied with their tackle; the water may be the Sea of Galilee, but they seem unaware of Christ above them. Perhaps He hovers in their future, for the powerful keel of their boat continues upwards into the stem of the cross.

Nor does the notice on the cross bear the inscription 'INRI' (Iesvs Nazarenvs Rex Ivdaeorvm), which is common in paintings of the Crucifixion and may be seen in the Grünewald. Dalí's notice is blank. This, then, is not the King of the Jews. It may not be Jesus; he may not redeem. He is perhaps modern man, or some of us, in a spiritual – not material – crucifixion (for we see no nails). We do not know if he is alive or dead. We do not know if this is the blackness within which God dwells, or whether it is – as Christ Himself cried – the blackness of absolute abandonment. There is ultimately an ambiguity in blackness: it may be emptiness and loss; it may be power in hiding.

23 Matthias Grünewald, *The Crucifixion*, 1510, tempera on panel.

24 Salvador Dalí, *Christ of St John of the Cross*, 1951, oil on canvas.

25 Muhammad with his daughter Fatima and son-in-law Ali, illustration to the Siyer-i Nebi, 1595.

FOUR

Black in Society: Arabia, Europe

IT SEEMS THAT the colour which we wear externally has a relation to the colour that our inner self may be. For it was only after the soul was found black in its sinfulness that whole polities began – slowly – to welcome black into their general dress, and at large into their 'material culture'.

It was not only in Christendom that this slow move from inner to outward occurred. On the contrary, society's change of colour did not occur first in the Christian world but in the world of another faith: Islam. Here, too, the worship of a single God was reflected in an emphasis on light versus blackness; and here too blackness was both the colour of sin and the colour of the most holy things.

In Islam, as in Christianity, faith became 'material' in the use of white and black cloth. Muhammad (*c.* 570–632) wore sometimes white robes and sometimes black on his military campaigns. His armies flew both white and black flags, which might be inscribed with sacred texts. The principal flag under which they fought was plain black, with no symbol or inscription of any kind. It was known as Al-'Uqab, the eagle, and derived from the flag of Muhammad's own Quraish clan – which also was solid black, and probably earlier had an eagle in its centre.

The use of an eagle as a battle standard goes back further than the Roman legions: in the sixth century BCE the conquering armies of the Persian emperor Cyrus had marched behind an eagle. But an 'eagle' that appeared as a solid field of black would seem to have another name: Death. For black had long been the colour of mourn - ing in Arabia, and was also – as further East – the colour one showed when riding out with one's affiliates to avenge an injury. The black flag of Muhammad, however, also offered salvation,

provided one surrendered and was converted. The original banner
was said to have been made from the head-cloth of Muhammad's
wife Aisha.[1]

Muhammad's warriors wore a black head-dress, and when Muhammad conquered Mecca, he wore a black cape and black turban. His
favourite colour, though, was said to be green. He liked to wear a green
cloak and turban – green as the silk robes and cushions of Paradise.
About black he had divided feelings, for he also called it 'the colour
of Shaitan [Satan]', and he disliked the morosely mournful use of
black. When a mother brought her child to be named, and the
child wore a black shirt, he said, 'If he wears such clothes throughout his life, he will weep until he dies.' He forbade the use of some
black clothes, saying they should be burned, and black dye on hair
(other colours were allowed). Black could represent sin, death, imper-
fection, and Muhammad told a story of his own childhood: that when
he was three or four, playing in the countryside, two men in white
robes came up to him with a golden bowl full of snow. They cut open
his chest and found and removed a black spot from it; then they
cleansed his heart with snow and replaced it. Since then, in Islamic
tradition, the phrase 'black spot' has referred to the centre point of the
heart – not necessarily with a dark connotation.[2]

In a sixteenth-century illustration to the Turkish epic the Siyer-i
Nebi, Muhammad wears green, with a black lining or undergarment
(illus. 25). He stands in the centre of a golden flame, and his face,
which should not be drawn, is veiled in white. His son-in-law Ali
wears the black robes of their clan, the Quraish, with the green turban that was later to mark those who had made the sacred pilgrimage
to Mecca. Muhammad's daughter and Ali's wife Fatima stands
behind them in a blue gown, but is veiled like Muhammad and has
her own golden flame. The killing of Ali, in the disputes that followed
the death of Muhammad, initiated the great schism in Islam, and
Shi'a Muslims have worn black since that time. Other divisions of
Islam have made a strong use of black, sometimes to show their alli -
ance with the Shi'as. In a Turkish miniature, also sixteenth-century,
Muhammad, whose face again is veiled, wears black robes and turban, while the first four Rightly Guided Caliphs who succeeded
him wear deeply dark or black robes (illus. 26).

On the battlefield black banners had a messianic as well as a
punitive value. On the Day of Judgement, when the Mahdi leads the

26 The prophet Muhammad (centre) and his successors, the first four Rightly Guided Caliphs: Abu Bakr (632–4), Umar I (634–44), Uthman (644–56) and Ali ibn Abi Talib (656–61). From a Turkish miniature of the 16th century, gouache on paper.

holy army out of the East, he too will fly a plain black banner. Male descendants of Muhammad wear black turbans today.

BEHIND THE BLACK banners of Islam were the other black cloths, coarse and fine, of Arabia. Central to Arab culture for many centuries was the loose-woven fabric of black goat hair from which tents were made (illus. 27). The goat-hair tent had probably originated in Mesopotamia, and spread later to Mongolia, Iran and Arabia. In the heat of the desert it has a perfect amenity. The open sides allow the constant movement of air, while the loose weave of black hair gives a dappled shade. The black fibres, absorbing the sun's heat, warm the air above them, which rises, drawing more air in through the sides of the tent and making a constant breeze. If and when it rains, the goat fibres swell and block the spaces, making a gigantic black umbrella.

The same cooling principle works with dress. One is told one should not wear black in the sun. But the black robe or *thawb* which Bedouin women wear, or wore until recently, is of very loose weave – often of the most airy, light cotton gauze – and is so large it must be gathered in folds (illus. 28). If you hold one from a balcony it reaches to the ground. The *thawb* is light though large, and in recent

27 Bedouin tent of black goat's hair, Palestine, 1890s.

86

28 The *thawb* is a deliberately voluminous cotton-gauze overgarment worn by some women in the Arab world. This example, from Oman, is elaborately embroidered and ornamented.

years its science has been examined. The loosely folded layers hold the heat at a distance, while – as with the tents – the outside layer heats, drawing air in and up through the loose weave. In other words, one wears black in the desert because it is cool, and it is cool because it is hot.[3]

Black in Arabia, when it does not stand for death, is the colour of wonderful coolness – of the deepest shade, where life may be enjoyed. For the sun there is the blinding, bleaching enemy of life. Black is good also for goats, though their hair is not loose, because short-wave radiation (heat) cannot penetrate so far into black hair as it can into white.

Professor Tarif Khalidi of the American University in Beirut has kindly supplied me with a summary of the senses of black (from the *swd* root) in the most celebrated dictionary of classical Arabic, the *Lisan al-'Arab* by Ibn Manzur (who died in 1311). Black may refer to things that are precious, especially in a desert: 'the two blacks' are dates and water. Also, as elsewhere, black can refer generally to bad things: 'black hearts' refers to enemies, and a 'black word' is one that is ugly. The word 'black' can also be active visually, in a way that makes sense in brilliant sunlight: so a distant figure is 'black', as is a large crowd, or a large, dense forest. As with the forest, black is perceived as near to green, and the villages that make the country-side round a city may again be called black. The 'crowd' sense can extend to large majorities of other kinds, including great wealth, as in the remark that someone has much *sawad*. The words and idea of blackness have then in Arabic a play of antitheses that is comparable with, though different from, European usage. Black can carry the same sense of secrecy as our 'in the dark'; and the phrase 'black and red' is a way of referring to everyone: that is, both Arab and non-Arab.

Black is the colour especially associated both with sin and holiness. In the eastern corner of the ancient granite shrine in Mecca – the Kaaba – is the Black Stone, still set where Abraham placed it. It was white when it fell from Heaven, in the time of Adam, but long ago was blackened by the sins of men. It was an object of pilgrimage before Islam, when the Kaaba housed the idols which Muhammad swept away. And still it is an object of reverence to the slowly wheel-ing multitudes who file each year into the Great Mosque in Mecca, and kiss the Black Stone if they can reach it. Thanks to modern photo - journalism, it is a familiar sight: a huge cube of stone, draped (from a date later than Muhammad's) with a jet-black pall (illus. 29). As the armies of Mecca, like those of Rome, used to follow an eagle, so also Mecca has its own 'lapis niger'.

Black has various religious values in Islam. In the Qur'an, when Allah tells his angels he is going to create man, he says he will create a mortal 'of black mud fashioned into shape'. And in later Islamic mysticism, just as in Christian mysticism, it was believed that the blackest depths of night both hid, and represented, 'the Light of the Absolute'.

Passage through this mystical 'night of power' – the night of 'black light' in Sufi teaching – is allegorized in the legend of Muham -mad's 'night journey'. On the winged white beast al-Buraq, who is 'larger than a donkey but smaller than a mule', Muhammad flew one night to the temple in Jerusalem. There he found Abraham, Moses and Jesus, who asked him to lead them in prayer. The angel Gabriel then conducted him through the seven heavens and into Paradise, where he spoke with God, who told him of the importance of regular prayer. With the mercantile expertise of the Quraish, and acting on the advice of Moses, Muhammad persuaded God to reduce the number of daily prayers from fifty to five. He then returned

29 The Kaaba, The Grand Mosque, Mecca.

on al-Buraq to Mecca. The subject is popular in the Islamic art of the Persian miniature, where Muhammad may be seen, again with a veiled face and sometimes wearing black robes, riding on al-Buraq, who has a human head with black hair – like the heavenly angels who accompany them.

In the later history of Islam, the whirling dervishes may, as their white skirts fly, achieve a divine inner stillness that is at once dark and dazzling: some dervish sects are clad, and spin, in black.

THOUGH WORN FOR coolness in the desert, and recognized as the colour of devotion, still black was the colour of death and revenge. When Muhammad's grandson Husain was defeated and killed at Karbala in 680, the Shi'a formalized their wearing of black as the colour of permanent accusatory mourning. Ever since then, on the Day of 'Ashura – the anniversary of Husain's death – Shi'a men may strip to the waist, otherwise wearing only black, and flog themselves with whips or chains, or cut themselves with knives and let the blood run freely.

The larger flowering of Arab black was still to come. This occurred when the Abbasid family, who descended from Muhammad's

youngest uncle, al-'Abbas, took up the mantle of Shi'a Islam. They
did so to win Shi'a support in their campaign against the Umayyad
Arabs, whose Caliph ruled in Damascus. They adopted the black of
the Quraish and of the Shi'a, and in 747–9 they rode to fight the
Umayyads flying black banners, with a strong messianic implication.
Their black was accusatory and vengeful on their own account also,
because they not only – while allied with the Shi'as – mourned 'Ali,
the son-in-law of Muhammad, but also their own leader Imam
Ibrahim, who had died or been killed in an Umayyad prison.[4]

When the Abbasids first rose against the Umayyads, they draped
their buildings in black, gathering in the mosque in black clothes
and black turbans, black banners in their hands. On their victory
black became the colour of their insignia and ceremonial dress. They
established their own, Abbasid, caliphate in 750, and in 762 moved
the capital from Damascus to Baghdad. From Baghdad their conquering black armies rode out, westwards, eastwards, northwards,
southwards, until, by 850, their dominions extended from Spain
to Persia, and included all the north coast of Africa.

Not everything was black, for this is the world of levitating carpets and rich-coloured silks, of green-domed mosques, of veiled
maidens and sherbets and thieves hiding in pots, which we know
from the stories of Aladdin and Ali Baba. The autocratic harshness
of the caliphate is reflected at the beginning of the *Thousand and One
Nights*, where a monarch who finds that his wife has been unfaithful decides that he must take a new, virgin bride every evening, and
kill her the next morning to preserve his honour. But it was also
a society in which, more so than under the Umayyads, a non-Arab
or a person of humble birth could rise to high rank in the service
of the caliph. There was some reflection of a society of opportun-
ity behind the fantasy-rise of Aladdin and Ali Baba from poverty
to princeliness (though the idea of a djinn, a genie in a bottle who
will do everything for you, sounds like the ultimate dream of
slave-ownership). It was a society – a civilization – in which Greek
and Latin texts circulated widely in Arabic, and in which the dis-
ciplines of science, philosophy and medicine flourished. The art of
making paper was introduced from China. Baghdad became the
centre of world trade, with the endless arrival of caravans and feed-
ing the bazaars with perfumes from Arabia, glass from Syria, pearls
from Persia, grain and linen from Egypt, hardwoods from Asia,

spices from India, silks, porcelains and peacocks from China and slaves from Byzantium.

Still the ceremonial colour was black. On significant days Abbasid towns were hung with black drapes. The caliph himself principally wore black and gold; often he wore a long black jubbah with a turban of black silk brocade. On honoured individuals he would bestow a black turban, and black garments decorated with gold inscriptions. The vizier, his first minister, wore black robes (as king's ministers later did in Europe), and the vizier's officials themselves wore black. As later in Spain, black was the prescribed colour for court dress – which included a tall, conical black hat in the Persian style. In courts of law the qadi – Islamic judge – wore a black cloak and black conical hat. Religious teachers wore black cloaks and turbans, and the learned more widely wore black gowns. And, as later in seventeenth-century Holland, black garments – of materials cheaper than silk – were worn at lower social levels. As we know from the *Thousand and One Nights*, a Kalender – a mendicant – was known by his 'coarse black woollen robe'.[5]

This was however (as later in Victorian England) a world of men's black, for while women were supposed to be decently covered, they were not lost to sight in enveloping gowns that were shapeless and black, in the way that Islamic culture later required. They wore veils, but also waistcoats and trousers of muslin, cotton and silk, often richly patterned and embroidered. In decorations and furnishings rich colours were valued – deep reds, gold, deep indigo blues, as well as the prized colour called 'sandalwood'. Above all, green had a role in Islamic culture not matched by any single colour later in Christendom. It was the favourite colour of Muhammad and also perhaps of God, since it was the colour of Paradise. Green was naturally attractive in a desert land, and the green of an oasis, as it appears in the distance, can be of a wonderful deep turquoise. Green was the colour of the turban one wore after making the hajj, the pilgrimage to Mecca. For a brief period, in 817, the Abbasids themselves made green the official colour for robes, insignia and ceremonies. The violation of tradition was resented, however, and in 819 black was reinstated.[6]

It is also true that, as in other, later societies, the grand and cere - monial use of black coexisted with the popular association of black with bad luck and bad omens, with death and with misery. A convicted criminal might have his face blackened with soot. Ambiguous beings like djinns might be black, either in their limbs or when first appearing as a twisting column of vapour. Black was the despised colour of hard, sun-scorched labour. Again, there was in Abbasid society – it is clear from the *Thousand and One Nights* – a substrate of anti-black (that is, anti-African) colour prejudice. The lover of the adulterous wife of the Sultan, mentioned earlier, was (in Burton's translation) 'a black cook of loathsome aspect', while the Sultan's brother presently discovers that his own wife has been unfaithful with 'a big slobbering blackamoor . . . a truly hideous sight'. For all that, the Nubian infantry was an honoured division of the caliph's army. The Egyptian historian Al-Maqrizi later reported that when the caliph's African armies marched out, formidable in their black turbans and black tunics, the whole force of them appeared as 'a swelling ocean of blackness'.[7]

THE CALIPH WAS a spiritual as well as a temporal leader, and his black robes claimed religious authority. The Abbasids circulated an apocryphal hadith, or saying of the Prophet, that the Archangel Gabriel visited Muhammad wearing a black robe and black turban, saying, 'This is the dress of the rulers who will descend from your uncle al-'Abbas.'[8] The Prophet then prayed for al-'Abbas and his descendants. Christian black dress also could be divinely inspired: the robes of the Dominican Black Friars were said to have been revealed to St Dominic by the Virgin, in a vision.

One must, I think, ask – though I do not know that it has been asked – what contribution the black fashions of Arabia may have made to the later steady growth of black in the West. Many later practices occurred first in the caliphate: for instance the use of black by monarchs, first ministers, officials and law officers; by the learned and by merchants; and by many of the citizenry and the soldiery too. It cannot be said there was a sudden imitation, for the use of black in Europe spread slowly over centuries, and mainly spread in those centuries when Abbasid power had shrunk. But the prominent use of black continued in Islamic countries after the Abbasids, and for many centuries Islamic civilization was a large fact in European consciousness. In the year 800 Charlemagne sent envoys to open relations with the Abbasid caliph Harun al-Rashid, who made them wait a month before giving them audience. Harun al-Rashid is famous still for presiding over a high phase of Islamic civilization; among other distinctions, he opened the world's first free public hospital. Islamic medicine was thought the best in the world, and a European physician of any ambition would seek to be trained by Islamic doctors. The caliphate was the centre of trade between East and West, and Muhammad's tribe, the Quraish, were both the guardians of Mecca and the dominant mercantile force in Islam. They were known by their black dress, and one cannot but wonder whether their style contributed to the black style of European merchants. For in Europe, by the early Middle Ages, black was thought of as the customary wear of merchants; and merchant black did not derive from church or university. Venice in particular had extensive trade with the Middle East; her patricians were rich traders, not aristocrats of noble kidney, and were known for wearing their black 'togas' constantly.

If the bazaar was one area of possible influence, another was the battlefield. The military use of banners and flags had expanded, in Islam, far beyond the precedent of the Roman battle standard. The Western use of banners was slower to expand, though in legend, Charlemagne raised the sacred banner of the Oriflamme when he rode into the Holy Land. In Europe the use of banners grew especially in the twelfth century, when knights began to wear their banner on their person as well – as a 'coat' of arms – with a matching design on their shield, and on the housing of their horse. European banners were not all-black, as their Muslim precedents sometimes were, but black ('sable') was one of the six leading colours in European heraldry. Creatures which are far from black – for example lions – may be black in their heraldic form, and in a certain sense the black 'eagle' banner returned. When the Roman Empire split, the Eastern Empire of Byzantium increasingly adopted as its emblem an eagle with two heads – as also, later, did the Holy Roman Empire. When carved in stone this eagle had to be stone-coloured, but in medieval heraldry it is most often black. Its wingtips and claws may be seen in a later illustration (see illus. 57). As the Holy Empire faded, the two-headed black eagle found a new home in the banner of Austro-Hungary and later figured, minus one head and oddly holding a hammer and sickle, in the arms of the First Republic of Austria. In the erstwhile Eastern Empire, meanwhile, it became an emblem of the Orthodox Church, and so entered the flag of imperial Russia. It is not of course surprising that empires should be depicted as eagles, since the eagle is emperor of the sky, but since most eagles are not black, it is interesting that in many cases this emblem of supreme power became black.

As to Western adaptations of what had been Islamic black, the principal channel of influence would have had to be through Spain. The Spanish, with the Portuguese, already had a native taste for black. This was related to their care of black goats, sheep and cattle, whose hair and wool they wore. Black usages were consolidated when a large part of Spain was conquered and governed by the Abbasid caliphate. It should be said that the occupying Islamic population was mainly composed of Umayyad Arabs, who later threw off their Abbasid governors; the Umayyads sometimes used white ceremonially where the Abbasids had used black. A black emphasis remained in Islamic-Iberian culture, however, and evidently survived the eventual defeat of Islam in Spain. Spanish citizens continued to be noted for their black, a usage which harmonized with the increasing use of black by the Catholic Church. Much black was already worn in Spain, then, even before the black fashions of Burgundy arrived in the Spanish court in the early sixteenth century. This occurred when, in 1516, Charles of Luxemburg, Duke of Burgundy, became King Charles 1 of Spain, and Emperor Charles v of the Holy Roman Empire. He brought with him the rich court black of Burgundy, and thereafter Spain was key in propagating black through Europe.[9]

Islamic black, in other words, was a component in Spanish black, which in the sixteenth and early seventeenth century was the active genius in Europe's black. One should not discount a possible eastern contribution to the black style of Burgundy itself, for Burgundy was active in the crusading wars with Islam. John the Fearless, who was known for his black dress, had been a leader in the war against the sultan Bayezid 1. When he was killed by the French in 1419, his son Philip the Good acted as the heirs of Muhammad had acted: he wore black ever afterwards in a perpetual mourning for his father that was grimly accusatory and promised revenge. Many in his court followed suit, changing black dress from a distinguished but occasional habit to the high fashion of royalty. Not that Philip was necessarily following eastern precedent, for his grandfather, Philip the Bold, also wears black in portraits, as Europeans of social distinction were increasingly tending to do.

Cultural contact did not prevent the Saracens – as they were called – from being demonized, or from being seen as scarcely human. The prominence of black in Islamic culture, together with its southern provenance and partly African armies, must have contributed to the widespread belief that the skin colour of all Saracens was black – and if not black, blue. Both visually in the illuminations and verbally in the texts of romances, Saracens are regularly represented as black or blue, as were giants, monsters and devils. In the fourteenth-century romance *The King of Tars*, war is fought against 'Sarrazins bothe blo and blac'. The sultan of Damascus, who marries the daughter of the king of Tars, is however simply black, the daughter herself being 'as white as fether of swan'. The couple's union is so unnatural that they cannot bear a human child, and the princess is delivered of a shapeless lump without limbs or features. Fortunately racial difference is secondary to religious difference, and on being given a Christian baptism, the lump becomes a bawling, beautiful human baby. The sultan is so moved that he converts to Christianity, and when he in turn is baptised his skin colour switches from black to white.

His hide, that blac & lothely was,
Al white bicom, thurch Godes gras.

The later life of the young family is militantly Christian.[10]

Our own Black Prince may have been swarthy, but the likelihood is that he was (after his death) called black because he rode to war – as his French enemies noted – '*en armure noire*'. It became a practice for quality armour to be coated with black lacquer, at once for style and to protect it from corrosion, as one may see in knightly portraits from the fifteenth and sixteenth centuries. If the crusaders who fought the Saracens sometimes were (literally) knights in shining armour, they often also were knights in shining black armour. In an illumination in the Luttrell Psalter, we may see a blue Saracen being unhorsed by the red lance of a black Christian knight (illus. 30). The knight's horse, it should be said, is also blue, while the Saracen bears on his shield the black head of an African man.[11]

In Europe, then, the use of black was spreading, and an account should be given of its native growth.

❖ ❖ ❖

30 A Christian knight fighting a Saracen, illuminated page from the Luttrell Psalter (*c.* 1320–40).

IN THE CHURCH in Europe, the increase of black had been slow. Though shirts of black goat-hair had been worn (unseen) since the third century, and the dress of hermits and monks tended to black in the sixth and seventh centuries, the vestments used in church services were light in colour and often white. They had survived from Roman civil dress, and become 'vestments' when civil fashions changed while they did not. They included, in the fourth century, the alb, a long linen shift based on the Tunica Alba that Roman senators wore, and the pallium, a rectangular white drape such as the Greek philosophers, and perhaps Jesus too, wore as they taught. The long-sleeved white dalmatic was worn in the first century by decadent youths in Rome and in the fourth century by bishops. After 500, in the higher ranks especially, rich colours were added: reds, violets, greens, not to mention cloth of gold. Embroideries and jewels multiplied, together with fringes, cascades of tassles and headgear that could resemble a crown.[12]

Such robes were for church services on high and festive occasions. For lesser services, and both in processions and in daily wear, parish priests and bishops often wore – from at least the sixth century – the *cappa nigra*, the 'black cape' of the Church. This was woollen, black, bell-shaped and body-length. It was not itself a 'vestment', but it gave protection from the cold both inside draughty churches and outside too (it was also known as the 'pluviale').

It was only at the start of the second millennium that the black cassock evolved, as one now might think of a 'cassock' – not a cape, but a long, loose, all-round garment complete with hood. It was almost always black. During services it was worn beneath other vestments; otherwise it was the public daily wear of priests. Popes, cardinals and archbishops sometimes wore cassocks that were white, scarlet or purple (respectively), but the black cassock said, at large, 'Christian priest'. It carried into the world the grave, ascetic and penitential implications which the black habit had by then carried for centuries in monasteries, though well-to-do canons and clerics would have their cassocks lined with fur. In hard weather the *cappa negra* was worn over the cassock.

Worn so generally, the cassock (and cape) made black the colour of other activities besides prayer and penance, for the daily business of the Church, early in the second millennium, included education, medical and social care, and a widening range of administrative functions. Through the eleventh and twelfth centuries the Church provided the bureaucracy within the emerging nation states, since it had a near monopoly of literacy, education and intellectual expertise. This sense of the priesthood survives in our words 'clerical' and 'clerk', which refer both to the clergy and to the keeping of written accounts.

Within the Church, learning became more privileged – and more necessary for a career – as canon law was elaborated, and skills in logic and disputation were honed. In towns the children of the better-off would be taught by monks and nuns in schools attached to monasteries and cathedrals. During the twelfth century the well-to-do began to found academies on their own account and to hire priests to teach in them. By such means universities began, in time winning formal recognition (Paris in 1150, Oxford in 1167, Cam - bridge in 1209). Teachers were in holy orders, and the students also wore black clerical robes and were often tonsured. At an early point the cassock was open at the front, allowing freer arm movement, and thus became the black academic gown.[13]

Students let their hair grow if they returned to civil life, but if they became lawyers or physicians they continued to wear the black gown of the academy. So the gown came to represent not so much faith as long-trained, authoritative expertise – in short, professionalism. The law, physic and the Church itself became known as the 'long-robed professions'. On ceremonial occasions the grandeur of expertise was flaunted – for instance, a doctor of medicine in Paris would wear a red cope with an ermine cape – but daily wear was a black gown, more or less fine.[14]

The Church itself, in its power, grew more militant. In 1215 (more formally in 1233) the Black Friars, the Dominicans, were founded. They were not to grieve and pray in monasteries but to go into the world, evangelizing and educating – with the harsh support of the secular arm, should that be necessary. They participated in the eradication of the Cathars and became a principal order in staffing the Inquisition. Their greatest power was to come in the fifteenth century, when a Dominican prior, Girolamo Savonarola, established a theocratic republic in Florence which he governed with passionate severity. In the four years from 1494 to 1498 games were forbidden, books and paintings were burned, and everyone was required to wear dark or black clothing. Though, as a Dominican, Savonarola wore a white cloak beneath his black cloak and hood (the white signifying his immortal soul), he arranged his dress, in the portraits of him that survive, so only the blackness shows round his shrewd, hawkish, purist's face.

His theocracy failed, and if there was much black, there had also been much colour in the medieval world. In the fourteenth century the short jerkin had come in, and on their newly visible legs men wore hose of different colours – one leg red, one black, or one leg blue, one yellow – ending in preposterous pointed toes which might curl round and be attached to the knee. Women's shoes also had pointed toes, sticking out beneath the hem of fur-trimmed gowns which might again be parti-coloured, blue down one side and red or white down the other. These were young fashions: their elders wore gowns which could be richly damasked, but also could be sober and dark.

Mid-century, the Black Death began. It was called black because its symptoms could include black spots, and black necrosis of the extremities, but it was black also in its deadliness. Very roughly one-third of the people in Europe died, each in three or four days of increasing pain while the swelling buboes oozed pus and blood. Grotesquely, the plague doctors who attended the sick looked themselves like carrion birds: their wide hats and long waxed coats were often black, while their face masks were shaped like the cruel beak of a bird, with red-glass eyepieces. The beak contained aromatic herbs to counter the smell of death and the bad air that was thought to carry infection. Their care must have helped, for they were well rewarded, but it can have given little comfort to see that dark figure bend down as though to peck you.

The grief, and the trauma, must have been profound, but it is clear that not everyone was thrown into mourning, since in the following decades there was a multiplication of sumptuary laws preventing the ignoble from wearing – for instance – scarlet trimmed with ermine.[15] Black was not forbidden, and those who had not only survived but prospered could beat the sumptuary legislation by wearing, for example, the finest black velvet. In this way the sumptuary laws assisted the fashion for black, and those merchants who already wore black could, as their wealth grew, wear ever more expensive blacks, as we see from their portraits in the side-leaves of altarpieces given to churches. Their faces are serious, and doubtless they gave sincere thanks both for life and for success. It may also be that the Black Death had a long- if not a short-term effect, for though fashions were bright in its immediate aftermath, they darkened slowly through the early decades of the fifteenth century, while a grotesque celebration of death was elaborated in pictures and carvings of dancing skeletons, who accosted rich and poor, and kings, popes and farmhands, leading them all to the grave. In Pieter Bruegel the Elder's *The Triumph of Death*, of the following century, Death assails man in a thousand forms, including regiments of skeletons – as well as plague, warfare and every sort of accident (illus. 31). But especially Death emanates from the curious black tower or vessel in the centre of the picture, with windows like goggling eyes. Fire and black birds rise from it, a giant black insect hovers, while frolicsome black Deaths lean from its sides, and even wave to us as if they enjoyed the excursion.

As to the fifteenth century, as the decades passed, it became ever less smart to wear clothes like Joseph's coat. It is not surprising if darker fashions weighed on aristocracies in a world prone to apocalyptic epidemics, where priests in black had power over the soul as physicians in black had power over death, while lawyers in black had power over goods, which one had bought from merchants in black with money one had borrowed from bankers in black, who offered at interest the loans which caused families, and royal families, to be increasingly engulfed in debt. At a fifteenth-century wedding in Florence the bride might wear black velvet worked with gold

31 Pieter Bruegel the Elder, *The Triumph of Death*, c. 1562, oil on panel, detail.

thread. Other ladies might wear rich dark damasks, while men wore black and gold tunics with hose that were part red, part black.[16] Dark tones and black were increasingly the signature of wealth managed with probity and foresight, and of discreet possession of the goods of this world. In the courts of kings, also, colours were deepening. It was in this context that the court of Burgundy made its move into black, and Charles of Luxemburg and Burgundy brought court black to Spain.

Europe was then ready when, through the later decades of the sixteenth century, the midnight black of Spain – gleaming with golden trophies ferried from the New World – spread its influence through allied states in Italy. Black became the smart wear of serious, handsome young men as they coolly posed for portraits, their fingers poised on books of verses (illus. 32). The black doublet in Bronzino's *Portrait of a Young Man* is sumptuous in its material and elaborate cut, though the detail is hard to make out in the assured, daunting, even blackness.

From Spain black spread also to those states with which Spain was most often at war, England and the Netherlands. In those wars Christendom was divided ferociously against itself. Interests alligned with one persuasion or another, the choice being between Catholics

32 Bronzino (Agnolo di Cosimo di Mariano), *Portrait of a Young Man with a Book*, late 1530s, oil on wood.

in black on one side, and on the other Lutherans in black and Calvinists in black.

IF I HAVE been brief on the expansion of black in Europe, it is because I was lengthy on the subject in an earlier book, *Men in Black*. I have tried to avoid repeating details. We can see how the currency of black had grown and diversified by the early seventeenth century if we follow the painter Peter Paul Rubens on the journey he began in

1628, when he believed he could make peace between the hostile powers of Spain and England.[17]

Rubens was one of the great masters of colour in Western painting, second (if second) only to Titian and equalled (if equalled) only by Delacroix and Monet. But often he wore smart black in the Spanish style, both as a gentleman (he began early to give himself a sword in self-portraits), and because painters, like musicians, were likely to wear black, as the colour of dedicated expertise in an art. But at the time of his mission he wore a plainer style of black, since he was in mourning for his wife Isabella. The diplomacy was in part a distraction, though he also evidently believed, perhaps vainly, that he could affect political events. It is not surprising if a painter who loved the body as he did should hate war (this was the period of the Thirty Years War, from 1618 to 1648) and seek to broker peace. He lived in the Spanish Netherlands – Flanders – where the gentry wore Spanish black, as did the priesthood, especially the ubiquitous Dominican Black Friars. A plainer black was worn in the neighbouring country Holland, where the rapidly prospering merchants were Calvinists.

At this time, Rubens was 51 years old. He was briefed for his mission by the Spanish viceroy in Antwerp, the Infanta Isabella, an aunt of Philip IV of Spain. She too would have looked sombre as they conversed, since following her husband's death she had joined the Order of the Poor Clares, and wore the black head-dress and habit of a nun. Rubens needed to be accredited by the Spanish court, and travelled to Madrid, where the nobles wore grand black and the citizens plain black, as also again did the many priests, monks and nuns. Likewise the penitents who would pass in black processions, with eye-holes in their drooping hoods; they carried black flails to scourge themselves.

The black style of the Spanish and Italian aristocracies would have been familiar to Rubens from his earlier travels, when he had painted (among others) the young Genoese noble Giovanni Carlo Doria in a high-crowned black hat and shining black armour, leaping towards us on a prancing horse (illus. 33). The Spanish court itself was more uniformly black than on his previous visit, since the complaisant and pleasure-loving Philip III had been succeeded by Philip IV, who made black the official dress colour at court. We can see his lantern-jawed, guarded, Habsburg face in portraits by Velázquez.

Velázquez also wore black, as we know from self-portraits; he and Rubens climbed the hill above the Escorial together.

Rubens's principal discussions were with Philip's first minister, the Count-Duke of Olivares. He too wore black, as we know from the portrait that Rubens made of him, wearing a fur-trimmed black gown over a plain black doublet. In different portraits by Velázquez we may see now the sobriety, now the splendour of his blacks (illus. 34). Black was suitable to him because, as Rubens remarked drily in a letter, Olivares lived like a monk 'and had in his room a coffin in which he would lie while *De Profundis* was being sung for him'. Olivares let Rubens wait weeks and months for full instructions, for while it was the custom to use famous painters as unofficial ambassadors – they had access to monarchs – they could not be thought noble since they worked with their hands.

Rubens travelled through France to take ship for England. The tone and style set by French tradition, and by the Bourbon monarchy, was lighter and more colourful than that of Spain, especially since France just then was seizing the leadership of young fashion from Italy. Her young gallants wore bright-coloured capes, and belts of coloured ribbons tied in bows. In France black was worn by merchants and often by artisans, by the learned as well as the clergy, and by the Protestant Huguenots. The first minister of France marked Rubens's passage. Though, unlike Olivares, he was a churchman, he did not wear black but red, since he was Armand Jean du Plessis, Cardinal-Duc de Richelieu.

At Dunkirk the artist boarded the English man-of-war *Adventure*. In London Rubens stayed with Balthazar Gerbier, sometime agent to the duke of Buckingham, in a large house near Charing Cross, close to the old Water Gate which still stands near the Thames. At one point Rubens fell into the Thames when a galley taking him to see Charles I at Greenwich was overturned. Charles Stuart may well have worn black satin when Rubens did see him, since he favoured the colour (in 1634 he had in his wardrobe ten suits of black satin to seventeen in other colours – cinnamon, fawn and green). The negoti - ation of a peace made some progress, though Charles troubled Rubens by his overriding concern to get help from the king of Spain in recovering British possessions in the Palatinate. The conversation would have been in Italian, the lingua franca of the time, since Rubens did not speak English, but had excellent Italian from earlier travels.

33 Peter Paul Rubens, *Giovanni Carlo Doria on Horseback*, 1606–7, oil on canvas.

Matters were referred to the king's council, and consideration took many months. It was fortunate for Rubens that the English Parliament was at the time suspended by Charles, for it was domin - ated by Calvinist Puritans who would oppose a peace with Catholic Spain. Had the parliamentarians met, they would have worn black, not merely out of Calvinism, but because by that date parliaments, senates and seigneuries, like gatherings of elders and aldermen,

34 Diego Velázquez, *Portrait of Gaspar de Guzmán, Count-Duke of Olivares,*
c. 1625, oil on canvas.

generally wore black throughout Europe. Probably Rubens did not know that Richelieu had dispatched an agent, Furston, to contact leading Calvinists, assuring them that, though a Catholic, he had the highest regard for them, and trusting they would exert themselves to prevent a peace between England and Spain.

In the streets of London Rubens would have seen many styles, some in crimson, green, white and gold after French or Italian fashion. There were the black coats and black, steeple-crowned hats of the sectaries. Young aristocrats were brilliant in black velvet and satin, with radiant ruffs or intricate lace, just as Rubens's pupil, Anthony van Dyck, had painted them when he had been in London. A pining lover conned a sonnet, dressed in funereal black. On very many heads of both men and women he would have seen black felt hats made from beaver fur, and he himself wore one – or several – which we see in his self-portraits (they hid a receding hairline). Some ladies wore a 'gibeline', a kind of pom-pom on a stem, jutting upright like a mushroom on their foreheads: this often was black.

Behind the people, many house-fronts had black-stained beams. Inside the Gerbier house itself, the walls may have been hung with leather panels embossed in gold: these were normally black or red (in Antwerp, in Rubens's house, they were red). There may have been cabinets and a harpsichord made from ebony, with ivory inlay. The frames of mirrors, and of pictures on the walls, would have been of ebony (or, in a poorer house, of blackened whalebone). If Rubens sat with the Gerbiers, while they played on woodwind instruments to beguile a rainy evening, the instruments would have been turned (literally) in black cocuswood from the Caribbean.

While in London Rubens met a compatriot from the Netherlands, the inventor and alchemist Cornelis Drebbel, who may have shown to Rubens the underwater boat he was in the process of inventing. It consisted of a longboat with a superstructure housed in canvas, with canvas sleeves surrounding the oars, the whole being coated thickly with the age-old black protector, pitch.

Cardinal Richelieu dispatched a diplomat, the Marquis de Châteauneuf, to urge the English against the folly of an Anglo-Spanish peace. In spite of this, eventually, Rubens's efforts found success. A formal exchange of envoys was agreed, and Sir Francis Cottington and Don Carlos Coloma travelled in opposite directions across Europe, timing their journeys so they would arrive in the foreign capitals on the same day. Don Carlos was received in the new-built Banqueting House designed by Inigo Jones in Whitehall, all white fluted columns and pilasters. It is likely that many of those present wore black, given the importance of the event; there was some confusion when the cartwheel ruffs of the ladies, which were extremely wide, began to crush each other in the not-wide doorway of the Banqueting House.

It was from this hall, whose ceiling was later decorated by Rubens with paintings representing the peaceful reign of James I, that Charles I took his final walk in 1649: through a space where a window had been removed, stepping onto a platform which was raised high so his execution could be seen. As we know from the contemporary portrait by Edward Bower, Charles had worn black, and a tall black hat, throughout his trial (illus. 35). At his execution, too, he wore black.

That, however, was after Rubens had gone. Before he left, Rubens presented Charles with his great painting *Minerva Protects Pax from Mars*, or *Peace and War*, which hangs now in London's National Gallery. In it, Pax, or Peace, squeezes a bare breast so as to direct milk into the mouth of a cherub, while behind her the goddess Minerva, in a black-lacquered helmet and black breastplate, presses the war-god Mars to depart. His armour and shield are also stained black, as was the fashion, while the Fury Alecto who leads him on is dark-skinned with black hair (which Rubens, a fair man, seldom painted). Though he loved light and colour, black returns to his canvas when he contemplates war. In a later, more pessimistic painting, not only is the armour of Mars stained black, but also Europa, or Europe, who tries vainly to restrain him, is herself dressed in mourning black.

His mission done, Rubens returned with honours to his home in Antwerp, and to his two surviving sons, Albert and Nicholas. He resumed his regular life, where he painted every weekday, and on Sunday, the day of rest, drew designs to be engraved on wood or copper – the black-and-white department of his art. At the end of 1630, aged 53, he remarried. His bride was the pretty, plump, fair-haired Hélène Fourment, then sixteen. He painted her many times, sometimes naked as Venus, and at other times in the smartest of rich, noble dresses, which often are black. In *Hélène Fourment with a Carriage* the billowing black dress, worn with a black hat and trailing black veils, is almost all one can see (illus. 36).

35 Edward Bower, *Charles I at His Trial*, 1648, oil on canvas.

Most intimately and most famously, Rubens painted Hélène naked except for a large black fur in *Hélène Fourment as Aphrodite* – as it is called – of 1638 (illus. 37). The thick, black fur must have had a luxurious softness, for Hélène sensitively fingers it, inviting us to feel it too. The soft black beauty of it complements her beauty, though her bright but reserved eyes suggest that, however lovely, she also is a thoughtful person. But though sumptuous, the fur is very black, and one may wonder whether its darkness includes an acknowledgement of mortality – hers, ours, but also that of Rubens

36 Peter Paul Rubens, *Hélène Fourment with a Carriage, c.* 1639,
oil on panel.

himself, for he was ill with arthritis and gout and had only two years of life remaining. There is some enigma in her bright look, while the first finger of her right hand points into the darkness behind her. Not that the intimation of death – if any is present – seems either macabre or depressed: the darkness is there, it peacefully bides, coexisting with the tender warmth of love here and now.

For blackness was no longer confined to picture frames. It had, in Rubens's lifetime, entered painting itself: in the work of a painter six years his senior, who was active in Rome when Rubens, as a young man, had gone there to study – Michelangelo Merisi, from the town whose name was to become his own, Caravaggio.

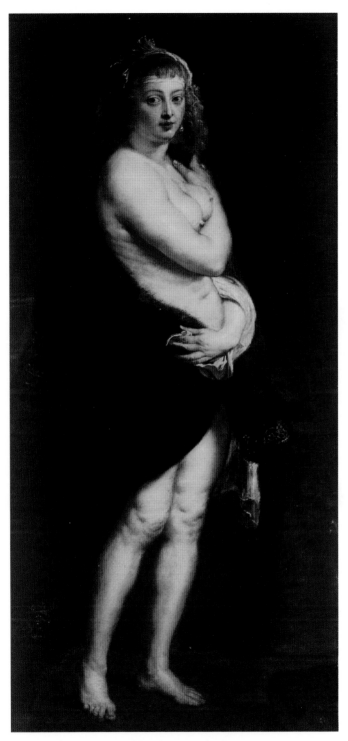

37 Peter Paul Rubens, *Hélène Fourment as Aphrodite*, or *Het Pelsken*
(*The Fur*), 1638, oil on panel.

38 Caravaggio, *David Victorious over Goliath*, late 1590s, oil on canvas.

FIVE

Two Artists in Black

PERHAPS FASHIONS IN art should not follow dress colours. But if dress fashions do relate, however indirectly, to a dominant colour that we find within ourselves – and if artists may be the sensitive centre of a culture – then it should be no surprise that the colour black rose to power in art in the years that saw the high point of the black style in dress. One artist in particular was the conduit of this change, and his innovation was quickly imitated.[1]

Michelangelo Merisi was born near Caravaggio, near Milan, in 1571. When he was six northern Italy was ravaged by the plague. His father and two grandparents died in one night, and some of his late, dark paintings of the deaths of saints may recall that epidemic. Though he seems to have made a slow start in his apprenticeship, by his early twenties he was famous in Rome, not only for his low-life studies of cheating gypsies, but for the dramatic way in which he painted figures, close-up and firm-fleshed but with the face and part of the body spotlit, while other limbs disappeared in solid darkness. The effect was intensely theatrical – perhaps to our eye cinematic – and also highly artificial, since we almost never see people in such an absolute contrast of light with dark. The reflectiveness of human skin means that it is hard for one part of a face to be bright as day while the other part is dark as night. A contemporary said that Caravaggio painted his studio black to make such visual drama possible. He would have needed also to arrange a single, brilliant light-source, perhaps the midday sun admitted through a tiny aperture. The extreme contrast of tone lent itself to the expression of crisis, of terror or wonder, and so to the representation of miracles, or the death by torture of saints.

Though other artists had painted night-scenes – lit sometimes by a luminous Christ-child – Caravaggio had invented, or perfected, a new kind of image, which ever since has been identified with the Italian term *chiaroscuro* (literally 'light-dark'). His style of deep contrast may be seen in innumerable later paintings, engravings, photographs and films. He did not jump in a single picture from even tones to this new intensity, but in some early paintings, like the teasing *Sick Bacchus* of 1593–4, some shadows are as near-black as the background. Four or five years later, in *David Victorious over Goliath* of the late 1590s, most of Goliath's gigantic form is lost in blackness (illus. 38). Only one giant hand, a massive shoulder and the cut-off head with Caravaggio's face are strongly lit. Goliath – and Caravaggio by implication – are half made of darkness.

Not all his scenes are executions or Christian miracles, but again, when he paints pagan gods and young saints as beautiful boys, the background will be dark towards black. If he paints Bacchus (against the dark background), the young, fat, sensual god will have thick, jet-black curls and be crowned with grapes as black as his eyes, while he twists into a love-knot the black ribbon that holds his robe (illus. 39). With his other flushed hand he raises to us a Venetian goblet containing wine so deep-red it is nearly black – and is black in the nearby decanter. The piled wicker basket in front of him includes lustrous black plums, black figs and black grapes, while blemishes darken on the brighter fruit (as they do in Caravaggio's early still-life *Basket of Fruit*).

In life, as in art, Caravaggio was a dark figure, and those who knew him found blackness in his person. The Roman barber-surgeon Luca described him in 1597:

> a stocky young man, about twenty or twenty-five years old, with a thin black beard, thick eyebrows and black eyes, who goes dressed all in black, in a rather disorderly fashion, wearing black hose that is a little bit threadbare, and who has a thick head of hair, long over his forehead.

The head of hair and eyebrows were also black, as we see in the drawing of him, aged 25, by his friend Ottavio Leoni. As to his clothes, black was fashionable at the time, but young fashionables could wear other colours, while Caravaggio wore only black. He wore the same black clothes to rags, so if he seems now dandy, now tramp, he also is an early example of the artistic person known for their dramatic

39 Caravaggio, *Bacchus, c.* 1597–8, oil on canvas.

black outfit (as later artists have been, from Baudelaire to Johnny Cash). Clearly he liked black: the chest in which he kept his 'ragged' clothes was covered with black leather, and he kept a knife in an ebony chest. He also acquired – perhaps for protection as well as company – 'a black dog that was trained to play various tricks, which he enjoyed immensely'. He called the dog Corvo ('Crow').

The black he wore had several values. Though as a young man he was housed in the palazzo of an art-loving cardinal, he also lived a violent street life, going about by day and especially by night with young sword-toting rowdies, in a world where black cloaks were ubiquitous. As the affidavits show, they were worn not only by Caravaggio but by both the victims and the witnesses of his street violence. Black cloaks were worn also by the papal constables – the *sbirri* – who several times arrested him. They wore them for the same reason that black was worn by thieves (who also blackened their faces): because it made them invisible in the night.

Clearly Caravaggio was drawn, as we would say, to the dark side. As a favoured protégé of Cardinal del Monte, living well among demure boy-musicians and doe-eyed castrati (whom he painted with tender sensuality in *The Musicians* and *The Lute Player*), he might have seemed well provided for. Did he need to strut the streets with a sword, trading virile insults ('*cornuto fottuto*' – fucked cuckold – was a favourite shout) and getting into knife fights between the tavern and the brothel? Matters may have been darker. It is not just that his bisexual passions included boys and prostitutes (it appears): he may have played the pimp for the Fillides, Annas and Lenas who posed for his Virgins, Judiths and St Catherines.

It may be that without his immersion in street life, he could not have painted his biblical figures with that weathered, soiled, scarred actuality which gives his art its hard punch of the real. But his attraction to violence seems also addictive. He was arrested for breaking a dish into a waiter's face, for '*deterpatio portae*' or house-scorning (which was normally done with rocks and excrement), and for attacking an enemy from behind at night and giving him a head wound with (in different acounts) a dagger, a pistol or a hatchet. Repeatedly the fights left him injured (so his sword had to be carried for him, as he limped through the streets, by the boy-model Cecco who was said to share his bed). The brawling also injured his name with the cardinals and abbots who paid for his altarpieces. He sounds as though he had a condition like Tourette's, but in a physical form, so he could not stop himself from lashing out disastrously, both with words and with the nearest jagged object. It must be said that in the transcripts of police interrogations, he is uncowed and unforthcoming: he is sardonic and contemptuous. Clearly he was a formidable person whether he had a knife or a brush in his hand. His behaviour may suggest to us pathology, though to him it may have felt like original sin. For he paints miracles and crucifixions with manifest conviction – like the disciples at Emmaus realizing with wonder that the beardless young man eating with them is Jesus. In his immortality Jesus is younger than he had been when he died. On the wall behind him a large shadow resembles a cloak, except where, above his head, it is like an opaque black halo.

One must be wary of equating the dark pigments a painter uses with the 'black' – the bad – elements in his subject or in his life. But Caravaggio does demonstrate how the life-values, death-values and art-values of black may hang together inextricably. In *The Flagellation of Christ* it is hard to read the dense black shadows that occupy three-quarters of the picture space as other than the darkness of evil being done (illus. 40). We see Caravaggio's hallmark realism in the awkwardness with which the exhausted Christ sags towards us, and again in the savage effort with which the right-hand torturer lifts his knee and heaves, straining to tighten Christ's bonds. The left-hand torturer, who holds a flail in one hand and Christ's hair in the other, looks in part demonic, though he also has the energetic snout of a hooligan. The torturer in the foreground wears a dark sleeveless jacket and, as in other Caravaggios, this foreground black leads the darks in the picture, scaling back through the black hair of the left-hand torturer and the dark, shadowed column to the darkness behind them, which seems opaque, spaceless, solid – as if it spoke and said, here is the final pit of callous sadistic cruelty. But also it has the black of fear, of pain in expectation, for the flagellation is still to begin: Christ's body is as yet unscarred.

It is a very similar darkness, however, which, in a different picture, surrounds St Jerome, painted as a bony, white-haired old man writing busily with a skull beside him, and which again surrounds the young St John the Baptist, turning nearly naked to us, seen as a distinctly attractive young man. Both John and Jerome wear – or fail to wear – loose shapeless robes of that splendid red which is Caravaggio's one touch of sumptuous colour: it may be the red of martyrs' blood, but is also triumphal, the colour of ultimate spiritual victory. Blackness reads here as the intensity, the solemnity, of Christian spirituality; at once sacred, profoundly penitential, and possibly mystical. The darkness has the same value in more anecdotal paintings, like *The Madonna of Loreto* (illus. 41).

The legend illustrated here is almost ludicrous: it was believed that the holy house where Mary lived in Nazareth flew miraculously to Italy in the year 1294, landing in the woodlands east of Rome. The cult was derided by Protestants, and few of the thousand pilgrims who made the journey each year (in the final stages on their knees) can have met the Virgin in person, but that is the miracle that has occurred for this elderly couple. The scene has a quietness,

40 Caravaggio, *The Flagellation of Christ*, 1607, oil on canvas.

41 Caravaggio, *The Madonna of Loreto*, 1604, oil on canvas.

as if they have come not to an altar, but to the street entrance of a good but plain house, where the Virgin herself has come to meet them, not in a visionary incandescence of light, but as an actual if noble nursing mother answering a night-time knock on her door (though her naked child looks not newborn but two or three years old). The picture has the reality of daily life, but is surreal too – for why should these visitors be down on their knees? But how should the Virgin answer a street door? If a prostitute modelled for her, the trade does not show in her fine-featured face. She acknowledges the couple, whose hands, raised as if in prayer but slightly parted, express reverence and wonder. We see the man's bare, muddied feet – they are the nearest thing to us – and the elegant, long-toed feet of the Virgin, bare feet being, in Caravaggio's work, the signature of a sacred subject.

There were many blacks in Caravaggio's world, and we cannot give a single value to the dark-to-black pigments that swamp his picture-space. In person he seems the embodiment of opposite extremes, or of the violent vacillation between extremes. He is like a character by Dostoevsky, at once the greatest of sinners, but also a tormented saint. He was not, in that period, unique in his extremity. Andrew Graham-Dixon emphasizes the importance, as an influence on the young Caravaggio, of figures like Carlo Borromeo, the cardinal-archbishop of Milan in the 1570s and '80s. He was a Pope's nephew, and his rapid rise in the Church was widely attributed to favouritism. When young he spent lavishly on horses and hounds, but his style even then was severe, with all of his 150 servants dressed head-to-toe in black velvet. This may sound like the black of high princely fashion, though with hindsight we see that it presages Borromeo's latent spirituality, which later showed with charismatic effect when he led processions dressed in black sackcloth, with a rope round his neck, carrying the heavy black cross which bore the Holy Nail. According to a Jesuit priest who witnessed these processions, he was sometimes accompanied by a thousand flagellants, and his bare feet bled on the hard stones of Milan.

The colour black is ambiguous, and values can reverse as one studies a Caravaggio. He had an intellectual life – he corresponded with Galileo – but we do not know whether, in asking prostitutes to model for the Virgin and the saints, he was turning with truculence to the women he knew, or whether he was thinking of Mary Magdalene and of the insistence of Jesus that her faith could equal anyone's. Time after time his paintings were rejected by commissioning priests because of the low-life character he gave to biblical figures. In a later painting of the dinner at Emmaus there is an elderly disciple who looks not merely poor and meek, but like an old lag who has done time for house-breaking. Caravaggio will savagely paint savagery; and also will echo the distinctly anti-wealth charitableness in several remarks of Jesus Christ.

He spent his last young years on the run, having killed an enemy in an arranged confrontation between two bands – swordfight at the OK Piazza, as it were. From Italy he fled to Malta, an island which had its own black theme. The native Maltese were 'little less tawnie than the Moores'; the wives of the citizens wore 'long blacke stoles, wherewith they cover their faces' while those governing the island, the Knights of St John, wore at all times a long black robe with a white, eight-pointed 'Maltese' Cross. The knights were flogged if they dressed irregularly. They had been founded as a crusading order – originally they had cared for the sick in Jerusalem – and it is clear that their austere militarism appealed to Caravaggio. The admiration shows in his portrait of the order's grand master, Alof de Wignacourt, grizzled and spartan in black-varnished armour (illus. 42). His black helmet is carried by a page in black, on whose pale, responsive face the brightest light in the picture falls.

The portrait, and Caravaggio's conduct, so pleased the grand master that he obtained a papal dispensation to make Caravaggio himself a knight of the order. Clearly Caravaggio still had his Renaissance genius for wheedling gifts from patrons. Within a month he was arrested, following a brawl in which another knight was shot. He escaped from his cell with a rope-ladder, fled Malta, and *in absentia* was stripped of his knighthood. The Black Knights of Malta were on his trail, however, and it was the knight whom he had attacked on Malta, the Conte della Vezza, who led the final assault on him. He was waylaid in a Naples street and held down so that he could be deliberately wounded in the face. His injuries, which may have damaged his sight, contributed to his death nine months later at the age of 39.

It is clear that he saw himself as a sinner, and late in life he said his sins were not venial but mortal. We do not know how guilty he may have felt for his presumptive sodomy – though we know it was

42 Caravaggio, *Alof de Wignacourt with His Page*, 1607, oil on canvas.

not possible then to feel relaxed about an active bisexual life. The penalty for sodomy was beheading, and this judicial fact must have some bearing on the seven or more beheadings that he painted, in which the cut-off heads of Goliath, Holofernes, John the Baptist and Medusa are (in five or more cases) clear self-portraits. Cut off, or nearly cut off – for he likes also to show the blood dripping or gushing as the blade saws resistant sinew – the strong-featured head, with black curly hair, hovers on the boundary of death and life, one eye glazed, one glinting. The blade will be held – and the head held out to us – by a beautiful young woman or (most often) young man. Given the historic taboo, and the penalty, this style of self-portrait looks compulsively, even suicidally, confessional. In most cases the darkness behind the beheadings is as solidly black as any he painted – *all* we see may be the youth, the sword, the thickly dripping head – and it is possible that Caravaggio lived wildly and violently, and painted with both innovative genius and religious zeal, while believing that he himself was damned. The blackness in his painting, when not sacramental, may be the blackness of damnation.

SINCE SPAIN ALREADY had a strong black tradition, it was natural that Caravaggio's inventions should have an impact on Spanish artists. Ribera (who was to spend most of his life in Italy) painted Prometheus tipping and flailing, luminously naked against dark rocks, while a coal-black eagle takes a peck. In the oeuvre of Zurburán more than one spotlit Hercules strides within a deep-black cave to cudgel swarthy malformations. The great Velázquez paints boys, Infantas, street-traders, with rich ochres and richer blacks. John Ruskin was to call Velázquez 'the greatest master of the black chords . . . his black is more precious than other people's crimson'.[2]

In the Netherlands Caravaggio's reputation was relayed by, especially, Rubens. One might have thought Rubens, with his love of transparent, luxurious colour, the last person to enthuse over Caravaggio, but his admiration was intense and practical too. In 1607 he urged his Italian patron, the duke of Mantua, to buy Caravaggio's *Death of the Virgin* after it was rejected by the Carmelite fathers of Santa Maria della Scala. The duke's Roman agent was struck by Rubens's care for the transport arrangements: 'Sr Peter Paul Rubens . . . in order to preserve it from injury, is having I know not what sort of case constructed' of timber and tin. Thirteen years later, established as 'the prince of painters' in Flanders, Rubens led the campaign to buy Caravaggio's *Madonna of the Rosary* for the Dominican church in Antwerp.[3]

Though the acclaimed genius of colour, Rubens will also use deep chiaroscuro and dark-to-black backgrounds, as in his *Last Communion of St Francis of Assisi*. His black still differs from that of Caravaggio: it is a positive colour, not deep shadow, in energetic play with his reds and bronzes, his deep greens and blues, and with his light hues of pale rose, pale turquoise and pale gold, which find their way even into his flesh tones. Rubens's black, one might say, is bright.

Through Rubens especially, the influence of Caravaggio's tenebrist style was transported to the Netherlands, encouraging a school of young dark painters who became known as the Caravaggisti, both in Flanders and in neighbouring Holland. Younger, more independent artists further refined the play of chiaroscuro. Vermeer in particular manages the effect of a single light source within a dim or dark room. It is very likely that he used a camera obscura (a darkened box or compartment in which a single aperture focuses the scene, just as in a camera) to help him capture real-life extremes of perspective and shadow. Thus an officer in a large black felt hat, sitting close to us with the light beyond him, becomes a giant, near-black silhouette; we look past him to the much smaller figure of the woman he is talking to, who gently handles a delicate glass. Vermeer comes even closer than Caravaggio had to the kind of 'close-up' image, with a steep perspective and strong light-and-dark, which was to be the new way of European imaging – consummated 200 years later with the invention of photography. As is often said, his pictures resemble (and of course have inspired) stills from films.

In his *Woman Tuning a Lute* the chair and cloak look huge because they are close to the peephole of the camera obscura (illus. 43). The blacks and darks are strong in the picture, behind the curtains, in the further chair, in the lute itself and the shadowed gown of the girl. But what is most striking is the subtlety and sharpness of her look. It is the best painting I know of a quick eye movement – a glance – so we wonder whom she has heard arriving out in the street, or whether, after all, she is gazing keenly inwards, at the fine note she hears as the string rings in tune. In her mouth there is a hint of hope or pleasure, though she has a serious, pale face. The entering light is cold and grey, but warm-to-gold where she sits. The painting intrigues: it invites us to notice the rapid impulse inside her, but at the same time preserves her solitude and privacy, for we stay outside her. Vermeer does not, as a nineteenth-century artist would have, invite us in to tell her story. The dimnesses and darknesses in the room have a depth – as she too does – which we respect from a small but sympathetic distance.

However, it was above all another Dutch artist who developed – indeed who, by Vermeer's time, had already developed – the dark

43 Johannes Vermeer, *Woman Tuning a Lute, c.* 1665, oil on canvas.

innovations of Caravaggio, so much so that his name became a byword for powerful blacks, both in his foregrounds and in his depths of shadow. In portraits by Rembrandt the sitters nearly always wear black, half merged into the shadows behind them, while their serious eyes may also be black – literally so, a black disc of paint. Like Caravaggio, Rembrandt restricts himself often to the palette of Apelles, working mainly in black, white, red and yellow – through many earth-colour richnesses of burnt umber, burnt sienna and burning gold, while his blacks often could be said to be warm.

The prominence of black cloth is not surprising, since bolts of fabric, and yarn, were a large part of Holland's international trade. A special committee of the Drapers' Guild certified the quality of blue and black cloth before attaching the small lead seal of approval.

Rembrandt painted a group portrait of six of these Staalmeesters in clothes and hats of the deepest black, perhaps with a witty pleasure in seeing a person wear the goods he also guarantees.[4] Again, in *The Anatomy Lesson of Dr Nicolaes Tulp*, there is clear pleasure in the fine, jet-black clothing worn by Dr Tulp, and by all but one of his seven colleagues or pupils (illus. 44). Their blacks, and snow-white pleated collars, contrast beautifully with the grey-green pallor of the cadaver, whose flayed fingers flex as Dr Tulp plucks the tendons. Black here has not so much the bourgeois worth of the Staalmeesters: rather, it signals the dedicated scholar, in transit, we might say, between the devotion of the priest and the concentration of the scientist. The dark background is neither gloomy nor spiritual: rather its opacity returns us to the foreground – it gives us no option but to focus on the figures. The sitters may be Calvinists, but black here is secular. The effect is common in Rembrandt, but can be seen in other Dutch portraits, by for instance Jan Lievens.

A proviso must be made, for if one looked only at portraits by Rembrandt, one would think everyone in Holland wore black all the time. Clearly this was not the case, since in genre scenes showing

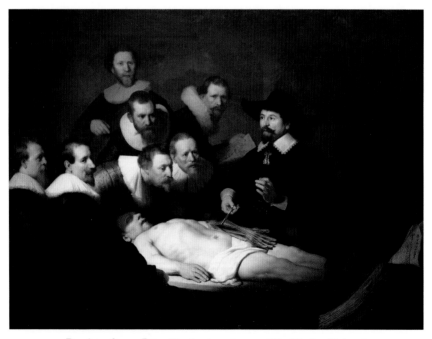

44 Rembrandt van Rijn, *The Anatomy Lesson of Dr Nicolaes Tulp*, 1632, oil on canvas.

streets, fairgrounds and taverns the main colours are buff and brown, or the deeper sorts of green and blue (though in almost every picture someone will wear black). And when Rembrandt himself paints a kind of genre-scene – the greatest genre-scene of all, *The Night Watch* – his militia is in various colours. The leader, Captain Banning Cocq, wears black velvet with a scarlet sash; his lieutenant is luminous in buff, white and gold; while the lead arquebusier wears a crimson doublet and breeches. Others wear different blue-greys and browns.

Black was worn especially for responsible occasions, like a meeting of the deacons of a church, or of the officers of a trading guild, or of the rectors of a charitable institution. Clearly, posing for a portrait – especially a portrait by Rembrandt – could have a comparable importance. Black is of course compatible with the Calvinist or Mennonite faith, with its emphasis on solitary, contrite prayer; at the same time, a quality black quietly shows one's wealth and standing. But black also suits the steady seriousness with which Rembrandt's sitters gaze back to us. Seeing their gravity, we might think again of the Protestant ethos – the bleak churches with no stained glass, a cosmos stripped of saints and seraphim. But their seriousness may have had a more immediate source. Portrait painters will speak of a problem in their occupation: that as time passes the subject goes inert – the eyes dull, the body slumps – so, when painting the face at least, the artist must talk them back to life. It may be that Rembrandt's own voice, and weighted gaze, caused his sitters to return the same look to him; so they face, as he faced, the serious side to life, especially after his bereavements, and quarrels with women, and his catastrophic bankruptcy and fall from fashion. Though we do not hear his words, we see the face his sitters saw when we look at his own self-portraits – where again he seems to think, and not only about tone and texture, but about the ways in which men and artists stumble, as well as about when and where to scumble.

As to his dark backgrounds, they may be simply that – a foil to the foreground – as when he paints a neutral black behind a snub-nosed kitchenmaid leaning on a window-sill. In his early work he could be facile, adding black to turn up the emotional pitch. He used the same elderly model for St Paul, St Peter (in prison), for *Jeremiah Lamenting the Destruction of Jerusalem*. This old man, who may have been a relative, has a lean, lined, long-nosed face; he looks pensive, weary, seasoned, kindly – and very little like a Hebrew prophet, or early-Christian evangelist. The drama – the pretence of intensity – is made by the exaggerated chiaroscuro. Here we see the soft side of Rembrandt, and may recall how pious bourgeoisies love to reward sentimental art.

I realize I may seem arbitrary in this chapter in attributing different meanings to the black backgrounds, in different paintings, which may in themselves be nearly identical flatnesses of paint. But we do give the dark a different value if we see in front of it a child's face in a window-frame, a person who looks deeply depressed, or a frolicking skeleton. Similarly the choice is partly ours when we read blackness as receding space, or as enclosure. In Rembrandt's *The Abduction of Proserpina*, the entire right-hand side of the painting is black or near-black against the strong sunlight that falls on Pluto, who thrusts his hand under Proserpina's skirt while the needle-toothed lion-face on his chariot grimaces into the darkness (illus. 45). We could say the blackness is simply blackness, and still we associate it with Pluto's Underworld and death, while the bright light on Proserpina, as she pushes and claws the rapist's face, is life and spring in defeat.

More hideously eloquent is the blackness engulfing *The Blinding of Samson*, in which a determined soldier screws a Javanese 'kris' with a rippling blade hard into Samson's eye socket, while Samson's foot, flying up in the air, clenches its toes in the extreme of agony (illus. 46). Other soldiers lug Samson's chains with a desperation equal to his rage to be free, while a soldier in red with a brutish face pokes a halberd at Samson's other eye with the look of a lout goading penned cattle. Delilah makes away with sparkling shears, holding high the chestnut mist of Samson's hair. Blackness surrounds them: it could be the dark of blindness, or of atrocity (that word coming from the Latin *ater*, black). Or we might ask where events are occurring, for we seem not to be in a house or a tent but in a cave: a round, dark hollow with a round entry also, through which light enters – not unlike an eye socket with the eye taken out. In which case the darkness would indeed be blindness, though we see all too clearly the destruction of sight.

THE BLACK ON Rembrandt's canvases is lamp-black, made by pounding with linseed oil the greasy soot of burned tar. Rembrandt's mastery extended to another black, that of ink. 'Indian ink' was

45 Rembrandt, *The Abduction of Proserpina*, c. 1632, oil on panel.

available then, though Rembrandt preferred not to use it for drawing; he liked the warm tones of bistre and brown ink. But his etchings are not printed in sepia; they are made with thick black printing ink (which might be of burned vinewood, bound in gum arabic and linseed oil, with iron or copper sulphate as the drying agent).

If we pause to follow Rembrandt through the successive blacks of the etching process, we shall see him hold up a copper plate, polished on one side. He waves its underside over a candle flame until it warms. Then he strokes the plate with a cake of semi-transparent stuff which melts across the metal. When this has cooled and hardened – it is the 'etching ground' – he waves the plate again, shiny side down, over the tip of the candle flame where smoke begins. When the metal is black with soot, he lays it down, takes a needle set in a wooden handle, and begins to draw in the night-black surface. He works in the negative, exposing the copper in thin, shining lines which will later print black. Unlike the copper itself, which an engraver must dig with a burin, the etching ground offers no resistance. It is like drawing with a biro on waxed paper, so the most perfect control of the hand is needed. But he is Rembrandt, he has that.

When the drawing is made, he lowers the plate into a tray of shallow acid. Blinking at the fumes, he strokes the sunken plate with a feather, removing the tiny bubbles which gather along the lines as they are eaten – 'etched' – by the acid. Then he takes the plate out, cleans it and inspects the thin lines the acid has bitten. He – or an apprentice – warms the plate over the candle again, and rubs hard into it a thickly concentrated printing ink. On the hot metal the dense ink liquifies, and runs into the etched grooves, so the whole plate is shining black with ink. Now once more he cleans the plate, with rags from the bench beside him, while a pile of blackened rags grows on the other side, perhaps in a basket. Again he holds up shining copper, with the lines of half-congealed ink glistening in the grooves. Only now can he lay it on the bed of the press, and on top of it a dampened sheet of paper, and on top of that blankets to spread the pressure. He screws down the press to its hardest thrust, then unscrews it, and rolls the blankets back. Very carefully he peels back the paper, and lays it on the bench. Finally he sees the 'etching' – where, in places, the densest-woven webs of line

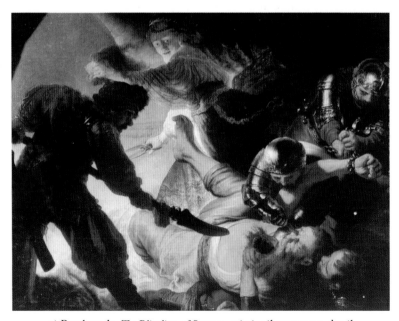

46 Rembrandt, *The Blinding of Samson*, 1636, oil on canvas, detail.

47 Rembrandt, *The Omval*, 1645, etching.

build people, things, in lustrous black. To make another print, all the inking and wiping must be done again – well, the apprentices may do that.

Inspecting his print, he may take pleasure again in the way each etched line, fine as an eyelash, has exactly the fluidity, the delicate curl, which it had when he drew it with his needle. In engraving proper there is not that sensitivity, since one pushes against resisting metal – which is why engravers first began to use etching, as a short cut toward the finished print. Also that is why he will etch, not engrave. So one shallow hairline makes the surface of water, another clumps leaves, while a handful of firmer, square-set lines give the back of the man who stands on the riverbank (illus. 47).

In this art, his genius is sure. No etching is maudlin, as his painted crucifixions have sometimes been. He loves black paint and he loves rich colour: but in ink on paper he never fails (see illus. 63).

SINCE 1455, WHEN the Gutenberg Bible began to be printed, black-and-white has filled the world: in black clothes and white ruffs, in chequerboard floor tiles, in house-fronts of plaster with beams stained black, in harpsichord keys of ebony and ivory, but above all in black ink on white paper. In hand-bills, broadsheets, books and above all endless Bibles, together with woodcuts, 'dutchwork' pictures – that is, copperplate engravings – and etchings that pretend they *are* engravings: for those who cannot read can see, so every eye drinks black and white. Often the lines could not be delicate, for hundreds of copies must be printed; but firm lines may have beauty too, like the beauty of an elegant, spare, clean penmanship.

It was part of Rembrandt's downright genius to foreground the material stuff of art, so we see the latent visual pun – the visual equivocation – which gives pictures life. We see an etched line curve on paper, and it grows and waves like grass in a breeze. Or, in his oil paintings, we relish a kneaded thick impasto, and also read it as the frogging of a cloak. In *A Woman Bathing in a Stream*, Hendrickje's white shift is brushed with nearly dry paint, so we see the paint-crust on the canvas, and at the same time see light cotton – which she raises, stepping gingerly forward, up to her calves in water (illus. 48). She has a soft but also hesitant smile as she tests her footing on what may be a riverbed. But would a riverbank be piled with drapery? The water is too big to be a bath in a house. Nor could she appear nearly naked at a quayside, though there seems to be masonry behind her legs. We meet her in an imaginary space. The water, on the picture's right side, extends we do not know how far; and this water is black.

'Black water' can have sombre meanings, as it does in the tales of Edgar Allan Poe, but in pictures water's blackness may represent depth, and also its odd, fugitive materiality. Water can smother us, or disperse into the finest spray. Also black water is clear water, for dust or scum would catch the light. Black water has no boundary: we are unsure of its surface and cannot plumb its depth. In *A Woman Bathing in a Stream* the colours are warm earth-colours, while Hendrickje's exposed skin invites us to feel the delicious coolness. In this black water there is nothing sinister: it has the darkness of the strangeness of its nature as an element.[5]

It was a different black water that Caravaggio had painted in his *Narcissus* (illus. 49). Though is it water? The surface is flat and hard as glass – but black glass, and thick, or solid to a depth. Or might it

48 Rembrandt, *A Woman Bathing in a Stream*, 1655, oil on panel.

be a heavier fluid, more inert, like mercury? In it this young man contemplates, breathlessly, a shadow-figure who looks back. Mirrors, too,
when Caravaggio paints them, are black as if made of obsidian. See
a reflection, his art says, and you will meet a shadowy doppelgänger:
not the self you know but your occluded self, obscure with menace.
As if the psyche – he might say the soul – were a pothole of black
water, and far from transparent.

49 Caravaggio, *Narcissus*, *c.* 1598–9, oil on canvas.

And for an uncanny encounter in Rembrandt's art, there is the portrait of his close friend the melancholy poet Jeremias de Decker (illus. 50). The painting is strange because it is *so* black, so we only partly make out the edges of hat and coat against the blackness everywhere. An arrowhead of shirt-collar is brilliant white, and warm light touches a third of Decker's face, with its sombre, sad, good-willed expression. But the shadow of the hat-brim falls oddly on his right eye, across the iris below the pupil (and his left eye is dark), as though he stood just beyond the border of sight. Decker was dying, and died before the picture (a gift of friendship) was finished. Black here

50 Rembrandt,
*The Poet Jeremias
de Decker*, 1666,
oil on panel.

is death, but death seen in a still grief, as one gazes after a friend who
has already 'passed over', and who for a little may mutely look back
from within the shadow that takes him away.[6]

The question has been asked whether Rembrandt was a melancholic, and showed this when he painted himself with shadow
blacking half his face.[7] One resists this idea, I think: he seems too
much to relish the substantial stuff of life, even when he paints his
own broad, subtle, doughy face. But Jeremias de Decker was known
for his melancholy, in his life and in his verse. It perhaps is time –
or overdue – to turn from black surfaces to the primal 'black stuff'
within us. *Melan choly*, the Greeks called it: black bile, which also is
melancholia.

51 Albrecht Dürer, *Melencolia I*, 1514, engraving.

SIX
Black Choler

THE COLOUR BLACK has been identified with frightening things
beyond our power – the darkness of the night, the Devil, evil. But
also, from ancient times, there has been a powerful will to find a
blackness not only outside us, but inside us also. Sin, in the Bible, may
be called a stain, which makes it sound external. But the stain is on
our soul, not on our body: in other words, it is within. Apart from
sin, for many hundreds of years there was another black substance
discovered inside us. The Greeks called it *melan choly*, the Romans
atra bilis. In England we first called it 'black choler' from the Greek,
and later 'black bile' from the Latin. But we still use the old Greek
name when we speak of 'melancholy' or 'melancholia'. This is now
another name for clinical depression, but for the Greeks, too, black
bile could cause depression, as well as other deformities of body
and mind.

One may speak of a will to find blackness within, because black
bile is an invention, and its blackness another imaginary colour, like
that of sin. For there is no black bile. The only black substance a physi-
ologist will find in the body is clotted blood. But for 2,000 years
physicians and scientists believed, or rather knew, that black bile
not only existed, but could control our well-being. Their ideas were
not only theoretical. They made dissections, more often of animals
than of people, and probed the look, smell and even the taste of the
things they found. Black bile was one of the body's four 'humours'.
The others were not elusive: they were blood, which was red and
plentiful; and phlegm; and yellow bile. This is the bile we know by
its burning, gagging bitterness if even a few drops rise to our throat.
Our liver produces up to a litre of it per day; as a digestive fluid it
breaks down fats and releases the vitamins soluble in them. Bile can

be of different colours: brown, acid yellow, green as grass. It can also be dark, in vomit, but it is not black.

Black bile was found, in other words, because of a powerful wish to find it. There needed to be four humours, because it had been known since Pythagoras that the universe was ordered by fours. There were four elements (earth, air, fire, water), and four qualities (dry, cold, hot, wet), and four domains (earth, sky, sun, sea). The philosopher Empedocles explicated this order, building on separate earlier ideas as to what the fundamental form of matter might be: the candidates had been water (Thales), air (Anaximenes) and fire (Heraclitus). The new fourfold order must extend to the human body also, and the breakthrough is recorded in a text, 'Of the Nature of Man', which is attributed to a practising Greek doctor, Hippocrates (*c.* 460 to *c.* 370 BCE) or to his son-in-law Polybus (fl. *c.* 400 BCE). In this text the humours were formalized, and aligned with the elements and the qualities, also the four seasons and the four ages of man (and incidentally with the four colours of Apelles). Phlegm was white, and cold and wet, and nearest to winter and water; blood was red, and hot and wet, and nearest to spring and air; yellow bile was hot and dry, and nearest to summer and to fire; and black bile was cold and dry and nearest to autumn and to earth.[1]

The humours were said to determine our temperament, and we still use words reflecting this system if we call a person who is too positive 'sanguine' (overactive blood), or an unresponsive person 'phlegmatic' (excess of phlegm), or an irascible person 'choleric' or 'bilious' (overactive yellow choler) or a depressive 'melancholy' (overactive black bile). Of these four humours, black bile was the most dangerous. For while blood, phlegm and yellow bile were tied to particular dispositions and illnesses, black bile could have a catastrophic effect on one's mood, one's character, and one's fate. It had an intrinsic morbidity, and its pathology was thought to cover stuttering, ulcers, epilepsy, hallucinations and depression. The excess of it caused lunacy, and self-destructive activities ranging from suicide to bad marriages. Again, in these effects, one finds a will to see things as they 'ought' to be: because black bile was black it must cause diseases, and a cause of diseases would – surely? – be black.

In the understanding of black bile, as it worked within us, morbidity and blackness were tied together. In Greek the verb *melancholan* – as it were, to be black-bilious – became synonymous with *mainesthi*, to be insane. The madness of the melancholy person might be raving lunacy – or it might be moral lunacy. Plato thought a tyrant must be a melancholic. In the rationalist age of Plato and Aristotle the god-inflicted rage of the tragic heroes was reinterpreted as mental illness, and Hercules and Ajax were judged melancholics. The question of insanity was complicated, however, because it was also believed that frenzy could be a transcendental and visionary state. Black bile might cause insanity and psychopathic crime, but at times could break into revelation, even genius. An author known as the Pseudo-Aristotle compared the different effects of black bile to those of wine; he makes it sound like an alcoholic secretion of the body.

Lunacy, suicidal depression, criminal violence and revelation were the extremes, and the wise man sought to regulate the danger-ous swing of the humours. If too cold, black bile could lead to impotence, and if too hot, to sexual hyperactivity. A bland diet was recommended, and unexciting conversation. The view that darkness would allay the black fumes gave way to an early form of seasonal affective disorder therapy, recommending rooms filled with light.

The Greek understanding of the humours was accepted by Rome, and it was a Greek doctor who settled in Rome (in 162 CE) who advanced the theory of black bile. Galen examined the dark fluids he drew from the body, and concluded that there were two black biles: 'One is like the dregs of the blood, very thick and not unlike the dregs of wine. The other is much thinner and so acid that it eats into the ground.' The former, he decided, was a concentrated, degener-ated, black form of blood (as undoubtedly it was), while the latter was a toxic, burned form of yellow choler, black from combustion. It may be that both of these were distempered blood, but the effect of his discovery was to increase the unique morbidity of black bile, since it became now both the morbid humour as such, and the morbid form of another humour. His analysis was extended by the great Persian physician Ibn Sina ('Avicenna', *c.* 980–1037), who specific - ally argued that black bile both existed in its own right and also could be the scorched, degenerated form of each of the other humours: it could be yellow bile 'when burnt to ashes . . . phlegm when burnt to ashes . . . blood when burnt to ashes . . . natural melancholy when burnt to ashes'. This meant that we now had not one but five forms of black bile within us: one natural, four 'adust' or combusted, and all of them deleterious.[2]

Galen himself had made diagnosis easier, since he argued that heat made men tall and cold made them short, while moisture made them fat and dryness thin. A thin, short, black-haired, swarthy man was liable therefore to an excess of black choler, and care must be taken that he did not self-harm, or harm others. Thus, by a different path from the Christian understanding of sin, a new shadow fell on people of a dark complexion, who need not be Africans; they could be Celts. A tall, well-fleshed, fair-haired person with a rosy complexion was likely to be both fit and noble.

Nor would black bile, and the blackness of sin, stay forever separate, and in medieval theology they became united. Before the Fall, St Hildegard of Bingen (1098–1179) explained, the bile in the human body could not have been black. Even Adam's gall 'sparkled like crystal and shone like the dawn'. Black bile originated in the breath of the serpent, such that the moment Adam ate the apple, his blood curdled and blackened 'as when a lamp is quenched, the smouldering and smoking wick remains reeking behind'. Then Adam's 'gall was changed to bitterness, and his melancholy to blackness'. In sexuality also, St Hildegard explained, black bile had lethal consequences, since it caused the melancholic to be 'a sadist driven by hellish desire: one who runs mad if he cannot sate his lust, and, simultaneously hating the women he loves, would kill them by his "wolfish" embraces if he could'.[3]

The symptomatology of black bile had grown complex: depending on the humour in which it originated, and whether it was too hot, cold, moist or dry, it could produce lethargy or mania, taciturnity or loquacity, workaholism or paralysis, insomnia or stupor and anorexia or gluttony (showing in obesity or emaciation); it could make one a voluptuary or an ascetic. Though elaborate, the symptomatology gave a good accommodation for the 'bipolar' dimension of melancholia.

This systematic and vastly imaginary science is wonderfully revelled in by Robert Burton in his *Anatomy of Melancholy* of 1621. His huge, encyclopaedic book is a patchwork of quotations and learned allusions – restated with demotic vigour – for he had read everything both within and beyond his subject (reading the Arabs in Latin), back to Hippocrates and before. Needless to say, the colour that recurs is black, since melancholy, in all its forms, derives from the 'depraved humour of black choler'. Black choler itself is 'cold and dry, thick, black, and sour'. Physical signs of melancholy include skin that is 'black, swarthy'; a stool that is 'hard, black'; black spots on the finger-nails; and blood that is 'corrupt, thick and black'. The excess of black choler may originate in the liver, or in 'black blood drawn from the spleen', or in 'the black blood about the heart', or elsewhere again (he cites also the brain, womb, small intestine and the abdominal wall). But wherever it originates, the transmission is direct. From that 'infla-mation, putridity' 'black smoky vapours' arise. These 'fuliginous and black spirits' ascend to the brain, where they darken perception and thought. He cites Galen's view that 'the mind itself, by those dark, obscure, gross fumes, ascending from black humours, is in continual darkness, fear and sorrow'. Colour vision is affected ('to melancholy men all is black, to phlegmatic all white, etc.'). Melancholy may then in turn bring on other diseases, like 'black jaundice'.[4]

Burton certainly participates in the superstition (on the one hand) and the crude materialism (on the other) which were part of the old understanding of melancholy. He accepts that melancholy may be sent by the Devil ('if it is from the devil, the sufficient sign is that it turns the humour to black bile'). He also accepts astrological argu-ments, quoting Melancthon and noting that a man born under Saturn may be 'sullen, churlish, black of colour'. Superstition combines with materialism when Burton discusses – at length – the risks of eating black foods. He warns against 'black meat', like the flesh of hares ('melancholy, and hard of digestion') or of 'fenny fowl' ('as ducks, geese, swans, herons, cranes, coots . . . their flesh is hard, black, unwholesome, dangerous, melancholy meat'), against 'bread that is . . . black . . . causing melancholy juice and winds', and against black drinks, such as 'thick, black Bohemian beer' and 'all black wines . . . as muscadine, malmsey, alicant, rumney, brown bastard, metheglin'. He warns against drinking black standing water, though he notes that it is good for washing horses.

Burton had a purpose in marshalling these diverse symptom -atologies. They were the evidence and ammunition for his primary diagnosis of a continent, a world, gone melancholy-mad. For so he read the political blundering of the Stuarts and their darlings; the wanton militarism of the nation states, who in his lifetime began the Thirty Years War; and the self-inflicted terrors of both Catholic and Calvinist 'enthusiasts' who decided, with wild wailings, that they were damned for eternity. Burton is clear too about the fundamental character of melancholy as in the mindset of an individual: melancholy consists of 'fear and sadness, without any apparent occasion'. Melancholy may be manifest in extreme delusions – for instance, the belief that one is a shellfish, or that one's legs are made of glass – and Burton remarks several times that melancholics may 'see, talk with black men' (not Africans, but hallucinated black figures). But his thinking is sound at the centre, for he does include, together with picturesque lunacies, states and ideas which we too would associate with true depressive illness. He says melancholics

> cannot avoid this feral plague; let them come in what company they will . . . they are weary of their lives . . . often tempted, I say, to make away with themselves . . . they cannot die, they will not live . . . they dream of graves still, and dead men, and think themselves bewitched or dead . . . *Anno* 1550, an advocate of Paris fell into such a melancholy fit, that he believed verily he was dead.

One might put this beside a more recent description of being 'racked by melancholia . . . an abyss of sorrow . . . a life that is unlivable . . . wan and empty . . . I live a living death'.[5]

The *Anatomy* includes a psychological theory of depression. It was not hard for Burton to pursue this line of thought, since it was believed that the body would secrete black bile in response to emotional hurts, ranging from bereavement to disappointment in love. It was also thought that black bile could collect in the system, and poison the mind, as a result of physical inactivity. Both idleness and solitary, sedentary occupations were dangerous, as was life in a monastery, a convent or an Oxbridge college – something Burton understood, since he was an Oxford college librarian for the four decades of his adult life. He said contemplation 'dries the brain'. He notes, as current psychology would, that melancholy may arise in 'such as are born of melancholy parents'. Also that melancholy may result from 'immoderate Venus in excess . . . or in defect': that is, from too much sex or none at all. He cites Valescus, saying that Venus omitted 'makes the mind sad, the body dull and heavy', and Avicenna, saying of Venus 'moderately used . . . that many madmen, melancholy, and labouring of the falling sickness, have been cured by this alone'.

Nor are all his blacks negative, for he notes the sexual charge of black. Of all human beauties, he observes, the greatest is in the eyes, and 'of all eyes (by the way) black are most amiable, enticing and fairest'. He cites Homer's celebration of the black ox-eye of Juno and quotes Ovid's praise of his mistress for her black eyes and her black hair. Julius Caesar, he notes, was 'of a black quick sparkling eye', adding that (as Averroes had said) 'such persons . . . are the most amorous'. Writing of lovesickness, or love-melancholy, he cites Aelian Montaltus, 'for if this passion continue, it makes the blood hot, thick, and black', and he describes the burned and blackened organs observed by Empedocles during the dissection 'of one that died for love' ('his heart was combust, his liver smoky . . . roasted through the vehemency of love's fire').

The Anatomy of Melancholy was first published in 1621 and though already large was expanded again for each of the four editions that followed, up to Burton's death in 1640. We might call it a runaway bestseller, and it clearly responded to what was both a fashionable and a serious interest of the time. Though Burton mentions many hundreds of books, one he does not mention is William Harvey's *De Motu Cordis*, published seven years after the *Anatomy*, in 1628 in Frankfurt, and launched in the city's annual book fair. We know it by its title in translation, *Of the Motion of the Heart and Blood in Animals*. In it Harvey recorded the calculation he had made – which no one had made in 2,000 years – as to the weight in fluid ounces of the blood which the heart pumped out, each hour, to the extremities of the body, where it was assumed to evaporate. 'Now, in the course of half an hour, the heart will have made more than one thousand beats . . . Multiplying . . . by the number of pulses, we shall have . . . one thousand half ounces . . . a larger quantity . . . than is contained in the whole body.'[6] For so much blood to vanish at the fingertips and toes, and be replaced from new food eaten hourly by the hundredweight, was clearly impossible. It followed that blood must be recycled. Harvey studied the means and route of this circulation, and from his investigations especially there followed the slow collapse of the old physiology, and with it the medicine of humours, which had been 2,000 years in the building.

Not that Harvey found no blackness in the body. He notes in his preface that the blood found in the ventricles of the heart on dissection is 'black in colour and coagulated', and again in chapter Five he refers to 'thick, black and clotted blood'. He refers respectfully to 'the divine Galen' and uses the old language, referring now to blood that is 'hotter and more spirituous', now to blood that is watery or 'thick and more earthy'. But the black stuff in the body is blood: there is no more black bile.

IF BLACK BILE ceased to control behaviour, the name 'melancholia' survived; as did melancholia itself, the condition we call depression. In 1516 – long before the new medicine, and a hundred years before Burton wrote – melancholia as a mental state had been the subject of a major masterpiece. And in art, as in life, 'melancholia' was to flourish for further whole centuries, with a recurring reference to the colour black.

In Dürer's copperplate engraving *Melencolia I* (the spelling is Dürer's), a large, handsome woman sits slumped in despondency, idly holding a geometer's compass, while unused tools – a plane, a saw, a hammer and nails – lie round her (illus. 51). And the skin of her face is dark or black. It may be that it is not always seen as black because one could say her face is deeply shadowed. But the shadow on her face is deeper than the shadow on her dress, and the contrast between her cheeks and temples, and the white of her eyes, make it clear that she is dark-skinned. Her features are European, not Indian or African: she is black from the rising fumes of Black Choler, as melancholics were said to be, and the blackness shows most in her face, the window to her mind or soul. That soul is not well: she is marked by despondency and perhaps ill will. She could be said to scowl, to be sullen.

I make a point of her mood, because in criticism she is sometimes romanticized. Erwin Panofsky describes her thus: 'her gaze, thought-ful and sad, fixed on a point in the distance, she keeps watch, withdrawn from the world, under a darkening sky, while a bat begins its circling flight'. The elegiac tone makes her sound like a Pre-Raphaelite maiden, though her look is surely more discontented, even baleful? Robert Burton, who (of course) knew Dürer's print, described her as 'a sad woman leaning on her arm with fixed looks . . . surly, dull, sad, austere'. Nor is it clear that she is, as Panofsky says, 'thinking hard'. Her excess of black bile could be a symptom, not a cause, of her darkened state of being, for this engraving has always been felt to touch the mystery of real depression. One could say it shows the ill will of the deeply unhappy.[7]

It does not help, in other words, to sweeten Dürer's asperity with hints of tragic nobility, for the print has various elements of contradiction, negativity and the grotesque. Meteors were portents of sudden dire disaster, and the meteor in this print blazes at our eye, itself like an eye of rage. The bright rainbow above could be a blessed sign. It is clearly an arc from a perfect circle, perhaps marked by the compass that Melancholia holds; it suggests colour in this black-and-white plate, and God's covenant with the new world after the Flood. And the sea beneath it has risen in flood, as seas were known to do when meteors fell. But what a contrast between the head-on fury of the meteor itelf and the inert, leaden weight of this dead-flat water. Its waveless, rippleless, stagnant surface could remind us of the dead seas – sterile and hopeless – in the late paintings of L. S. Lowry. From over this sea, perhaps out of the meteor, there flies towards us, not a bat, as Panofsky says, but a snake-rodent, a flying deformity, with 'Melencolia I' blazoned on its bat-wings: its snake-tail writhes, its blind rat-head snarls as it shrieks. It is the horror-face of melancholia – and stands then in a strange relation to the grand Melancholia who fills our sight. For she is an angel (or a 'genius'), with her fair hair and flowing robes and those lustrous white wings which Dürer has chosen to give her, and which no earlier picture of Melancholia had. With their aid, one would think, she could soar to a height, though maybe they are mainly present to show that she cannot or will not fly. The wings oblige us to compare her with the bat-winged abortion in a kind of visual syllogism. For it is Melancholia and she is Melancholia: they are aspects of one thing.

Dürer's double vision shades towards the surreal. Some angel this, sunk in lethargy and resting her cheek not on the palm of her hand but, as Panofsky notes, on a plump, clenched fist. The beautiful, sharp-edged Dürer light – the white, cold, north-European light – is in her clothes, her wings, her hair and in the victor's wreath of cress and laurel which she wears, but her face is black; the blackness seeming more a metaphor than a medical explanation for her sterile stasis. One cannot but wonder if Dürer knew from the inside – in himself, in a parent – the state he draws from the outside here: the failure of will, impulse, art, which can befall us for reasons that stay obscure. There is an odd visual irony in the engraving – in the beautiful drawing, for instance, of the carpenter's tools in the foreground: the plane, the straight-edge, the jagged and vicious-looking saw whose spike is the nearest thing to our eye. And in the more-than-life-size metal pincers that advance from under her skirt as though she had, beneath voluminous taffeta, not only the pretty slipper we glimpse (through which we can count her toes) but also iron crab-claws, nipping.

Whose are these tools? Including the modern-looking claw-hammer, which again is distinctly bigger than life-size, if we follow the perspective. Does this strong-limbed angel, when not seized with melancholy, tie up her loose sleeves and bend to at a bench? Or does a giant carpenter live nearby, strong enough to lift the odd stone polyhedron (known as Dürer's solid) or the grindstone on which a sleepy cherub sits, as if it were the angel's baby – making a picture one could lightly read as a caricature of Venus on a loveless day, beside her winged child Cupid? Christ was born to the carpenter's trade, and died on a piece of carpentry. Does the ladder in the background lead to Heaven, or greatness – though how should the angel need it, since she has wings? For whom should the bell toll, that hangs un-rung on the wall, near the hourglass halfway through its hour? Behind Dürer's solid a flame flares in the crucible of an alchemist. In the foreground, clear white, is that image of perfection, a sphere; it could represent the world, or the great bright globe of God's Creation, with the stars in their spheres concentred inside it. The sleeping greyhound is drawn with the beautiful minute attention to living things with which Dürer always draws; Panofsky calls it a half-starved, shivering wretch, though one could also call the dog lean and fit for the chase.[8] But it sleeps, the cherub dozes, the world in this picture is asleep or frozen, except for the rat-snake-bat, and the angel, who looks ahead, expecting nothing, from that place (within life) where journeys halt, where values are cancelled or lost, and where art, craft and science fail, not from difficulty but from the enigma that may at any time swallow everything – depression, the paralysis and death of impulse. Dürer said the purse at her feet was riches, the key at her waist was power: that is their meaning, and they have no meaning; they are no use to her now.

A COMPARABLE IMAGE is Holbein's *The Ambassadors* (illus. 52). Here too, on a table, are accumulated artefacts representing science, art, endeavour: a globe (two globes), a polyhedron, a geometer's devices, a closed book – and a sundial, to set beside Dürer's hourglass. We do not find a tradesman's tools, nor would we, since the two figures shown are (most probably) a French seigneur and a French bishop. Rather, for leisured but active fingers, there is a lute – but a string is broken, cancelling the soundtrack of this image, like the un-rung bell in the Dürer. And all these images of discovery, progress and prosperity, and of worldly and ecclesiastical state, are qualified by the odd big narrow oval that slants not across but above the floor, which, if we study it from an angle which shrivels the picture, shows a clean but perhaps grinning skull.

The skull here is death. Melancholia need not fasten on the sense of death, and in Dürer's print the dejection and paralysis have a more elusive source. But also, as Burton noted, melancholia may manifest as a sense of death everywhere, or in the belief that, though alive, one is also dead. The Dance of Death was a popular theme, and Holbein made two series of woodcuts showing a vivacious, almost sinuous skeleton leading a soldier, a child, the Pope to death. One might adapt T. S. Eliot's lines on Webster, and say that Holbein was much possessed by death, and saw the skull beneath the skin, while breastless creatures underground leaned backwards with a lipless grin. In his painting known as *The Body of the Dead Christ in the Tomb* the emaciated, tortured corpse of Jesus lies stretched, as on a rack, in the claustrophobic low box of his coffin, with no hint of resurrection or salvation, while the sharp-nosed, dead-eyed head still has the corners of its mouth drawn back as in total pain and despair (illus. 53). The painting shocked Dostoevsky when he first saw it, and he stood riveted before it for twenty minutes, so his wife feared an epileptic fit; and Prince Myshkin, in Dostoevsky's novel *The Idiot*, says this painting could kill religious faith. Christ's hair is raven-black, the coffin-lid is black and blackness descends from it to graze the figure, while the feet touch, as if standing lightly, the jet-black end-panel which also could be endless space.[9]

In *Black Sun: Depression and Melancholia* Julia Kristeva speaks of crypts or tombs within the psyche, within which a distress or its sources are locked away in a kind of 'black hole', around which the melancholic organizes a life marked by the absence or avoidance of affect – of natural feeling. It is hard not to see the *Dead Christ* as such a crypt, in which a disabled self lies imprisoned. Kristeva connects

52 Hans Holbein the Younger, *The Ambassadors* (double portrait of Jean de Dinteville and Georges de Selve), 1533, oil and tempera on oak.

the dark turn in Holbein's art with his (apparent) embracing cynicism, his (rumoured) fitful dissipations, and the low level of affect in the record of his life: she suggests he met with a perfection of *style* his depressive inner emptiness, producing in the process an art of unique, austere beauty.[10] In *The Ambassadors* there is much blackness, together with colour, while the skull is both in the picture and in contradiction with it. It does not rest, but hovers at an angle, evidently feeling a different gravity from ours and lit by a different light-source. Considered as a head, it is shorter than the heads of the two standing figures, though as wide as the skull of a dinosaur. Everything about it says both that we all die and that death exists in a different universe, which makes our universe thin as a shred.

If we wanted to cite, in literature not art, a figure who unites Holbein's preoccupation with death with the broader melancholia

53 Hans Holbein the Younger, *The Body of the Dead Christ in the Tomb*, 1521, oil on wood.

of Dürer's image, we could turn to a famous literary creation. Prince Hamlet says:

> Alas, poor Yorick! [taking the skull] . . . My gorge rises at it. Here hung those lips that I have kissed . . . Now get you to my lady's chamber, and tell her, let her paint an inch thick, to this favour she must come. Make her laugh at that . . .

and also:

> I have of late, but wherefore I know not, lost all my mirth, forgone all custom of exercises; and, indeed, it goes so heavily with my disposition that this goodly frame, the earth, seems to me a sterile promontory. This most excellent canopy the air, look you, this brave o'erhanging firmament, this majestical roof fretted with golden fire – why, it appears no other thing to me than a foul and pestilent congregation of vapours. What a piece of work is a man! How noble in reason! How infinite in faculty! In form and moving how express and admirable! In action, how like an angel! In apprehension, how like a god! The beauty of the world, the paragon of animals – and yet to me what is this quintessence of dust? Man delights not me – no, nor woman neither, though by your smiling you seem to say so.[11]

One might wonder if Robert Burton had this speech at the back – or perhaps at the front – of his mind when he began his *Anatomy of Melancholy* (for he liked plays, wrote them in Latin, and quotes Shakespeare and Ben Jonson). His first paragraph reads:

> Man, the most excellent and noble creature of the world . . . the wonder of Nature . . . the marvel of marvels . . . a little world . . . governor of all the creatures in it . . . far surpassing

all the rest, not in body only, but in soul . . . created to God's
own image . . . But this most noble creature . . . O pitiful
change! is fallen . . . he is inferior to a beast; . . . How much
altered from what he was! before blessed and happy, now
miserable and accursed . . .[12]

That Hamlet is a melancholic is explicit in the play. Claudius says
'There's something in his soul, O'er which his melancholy sits on
brood', and Hamlet himself fears the devil is making fantasies 'out
of my weakness and my melancholy'. Hamlet conforms to the traditional representation of melancholy in his perpetual wearing
of black clothes, which, as he says, goes beyond the requirements
of mourning:

> 'Tis not alone my inky cloak, good mother,
> Nor customary suits of solemn black . . .
> That can denote me truly . . .
> . . . I have that within which passeth show,
> These but the trappings and the suits of woe.

The first illustration ever made for *Hamlet*, engraved by Elisha Kirkall
for Rowe's edition of 1709, shows what we might call a 'modern dress'
production (illus. 54). This was standard practice at the time, but also
Prince Hamlet, in his melancholy disorder, could easily seem a contemporary figure – in his black coat and breeches and his periwig,
which is shaded to look at least dark. Unusually for a gentleman he
wears black hose, one of which, as Shakespeare indicated, has been
allowed to fall down.[13]

The origin of Hamlet's melancholy is not made fully clear –
it was perhaps not fully clear to Shakespeare, though we can see
he knew melancholy, perhaps in someone close to him. Following
Freud, who surely had *Hamlet* in mind when writing his great
essay 'Mourning and Melancholia', we may speculate as to how
the death of a parent, for whom one has hatred as well as love,
may confound the psyche, disable 'affect' and spread malaise and
destruction, especially when perceived betrayal by the other parent fosters sexual disgust. Then life may seem not so different from
death – a sleep with bad dreams, as Hamlet says, saying also that it
is only the fear of such dreams that stops us from killing ourselves

54 Elisha Kirkall after a drawing by F. Boitard, frontispiece to *Hamlet* in Nicholas Rowe's edition of the works of Shakespeare (1709).

at once.[14] It is ludicrous to think like this – except that this is how melancholia thinks.

Not that Hamlet, the creation, can be reduced to a psychosis: of all the creations in anglophone literature, he is the one who comes nearest to seeming – as few literary figures really do – alive in the way actual people are alive. This is partly because his character, his motives, and his pathology too, are as complex and elusive as such things are in life. He is known best of all for his melancholy, and for being dressed – for all time – in black.

THE FIGURE – AND the mental image – of Hamlet assisted in what became a fashion of melancholy. When severed from its dependence on black bodily fluids, melancholy becomes entirely a thing of mood, disposition and mental state. Melancholy could then vary between a condition of inexplicable misery and a solitary, sad reflectiveness which might also be enjoyed.

Burton had recognized the attraction of melancholy: 'melancholy . . . is most pleasant at first . . . a most delightsome humour, to be alone, dwell alone, walk alone, meditate, lie in bed whole days'. It is this note which dominates John Milton's poem, 'Il Penseroso', which concludes:

> These pleasures Melancholy give
> And I with thee will choose to live.[15]

But still Milton's Melancholy has a black face. She is dark from excess of brightness, and in order to protect our sight: explicitly he says she is black and beautiful, to be compared with the loveliest princess of Africa:

> But hail thou Goddes, sage and holy,
> Hail divinest Melancholy,
> Whose Saintly visage is too bright
> To hit the Sense of human sight;
> And therfore to our weaker view,
> O're laid with black staid Wisdoms hue.
> Black, but such as in esteem,
> Prince Memnons sister might beseem,
> Or that Starr'd Ethiope Queen that strove
> To set her beauties praise above
> The Sea Nymphs, and their powers offended.

Milton is referring to Queen Cassiopeia (the mother of Andromeda, whom Perseus rescued, who must also have been black though often she is not in paintings). Cassiopeia was 'starr'd' when she was transformed into a constellation in the black night sky. Milton's Melancholy, who is now a goddess, is however of still nobler parentage, for she is the incestuous daughter of 'solitary Saturn' by his daughter Vesta – not that we should think her blackened by incest, since 'in Saturn's reign / Such mixture was not held a stain'. Saturn, as a god, was identified with melancholy, and melancholy with blackness: astrologically, melancholics were born under Saturn, and Robert Burton places the sign of Saturn, ♄, at the centre-top of his title page.

Confirming thoughts of darkness and night-time, Milton pictures Saturn 'oft' meeting with his daughter 'in glimmering bowers and glades . . . and in secret shades / Of woody Ida's inmost grove'.

Milton has been daring, so far, for a young Christian scholar. Evidently needing to restore respectability, he now covers her native blackness with the black habit of a nun.

> Come pensive Nun, devout and pure,
> Sober, steadfast, and demure,
> All in robe of darkest grain.

Gazing now to the skies in holy passion, she 'forgets [herself] to marble'. This could mean that Milton now forgets her black skin, as William Blake did when he chose this moment for his illustration to the poem (illus. 55). She does however still wear a gown which, Blake palely suggests, should be thought of as black. Milton himself does not imagine an austere cast of nun, since he says her robe of darkest grain is 'flowing with majestick train'. He also gives her a 'sable stole of cypress lawn / Over her decent shoulders drawn', and this stole again is lightly suggested by Blake, though we could hardly call it 'sable'. 'Cypress lawn' was the very best black linen, so Melancholy may seem to be still in transition between the nun and the royal personage she had been before. Her appearance, however, which has proved so unstable, is fading. Blake could be said to catch her last visual moment, before her metamorphosis into music – into the sweet, sad song of the nightingale, the darkness-loving bird. In moving to Philomel's ravishing song, 'most musicall, most melancholy', Milton comes to that concrete suffering of which melancholy is the distorted shadow. For, on hearing the name of Philomel, the reader must remember rapes, killings, cannibalistic revenge, cruel mutilation – all of which are distant now, within 'her sweetest, saddest plight'.

By this idiosyncratic route Milton comes to the relationship between melancholy and pain – real hurt, misery, the 'abyss of suffering' within a person. For wherever melancholy stands between diffused misery and philosophical pleasure, there is always a distance between melancholy and hurt. If there is a wound, it has been hidden or obscured; and if melancholy is pleasant, there is hurt in the hinterland. So Milton cries, later in the poem,

55 William Blake, illustration to John Milton, 'Il Penseroso', *c.* 1816–20,
pen and watercolour over black chalk.

. . . let Gorgeous Tragedy
In sceptred pall come sweeping by,
Presenting Thebes, or Pelops' line.

Presenting, that is, horrifically violent stories involving murder of
husbands, fathers, daughters, mothers, as well as incest, insanity

154

and self-blinding. The pain and horror are set back, however, when the tragedy is seen as 'gorgeous' and 'sceptred' – though the word 'pall' means Milton is still thinking of a funeral, and black drapes, however royal.

Through the poem Milton regulates the distance between off-stage pain and the pleasure of melancholy, above all by reference to music. For pain itself is beautiful and sweet when sung by Orpheus – 'such notes as . . . / Drew Iron tears down Pluto's cheek'. One could say Milton's melancholy is made of music, from the distant clink of the bellman to the crescendo Milton mounts at the close – 'let the pealing Organ blow, / To the full-voiced choir below'. But it is made of visual imagery too, and paradoxes of light and dark: he somewhat anticipates the 'darkness visible' of *Paradise Lost* when he speaks of a place

> Where glowing Embers through the room
> Teach light to counterfeit a gloom

or when, near the close, he imagines stained-glass windows 'Casting a dimm religious light' – casting, that is, light and dimness at once.

Though Milton was a classical scholar, there is no explicit reference in 'Il Penseroso' to the humoral medicine of the Greeks, and when he does refer to 'humours black' elsewhere in his work, it is in the later sense of 'humour' as a mood or prepossession. So in *Samson Agonistes* Manoa, Samson's father, says (with some echo of humoral diagnosis):

> Believe not these suggestions which proceed
> From anguish of the mind and humours black,
> That mingle with thy fancy. (ll. 663–6)

More at large, the imagery of black fluids runs through Milton's work, often likened – in a comparison that harks back to early descriptions of black bile – to the dregs of wine. At the bottom of the universe, when God creates the world in *Paradise Lost*, are 'the black tartareous cold infernal dregs / Adverse to life'. The tower of Babel is built where 'a black bituminous gurge / Boiles out from under ground' (and becomes one of Nimrod's raw materials). And when the rebel angels invent gunpowder, they dig in the soil of heaven until they find a 'sulphurous and nitrous foam' which they reduce 'to blackest grain'. It is presumably because gunpowder is black that the rebel-angelic artillery shoots 'black fire and horror with equal rage'. Black materials are found above all in hell, where they burn with black fire since there is no topsoil beside hell's river, 'sad Acheron of sorrow, black and deep'.[16]

For Milton the prince of hell, Satan, is not black, though traditionally the Devil had been black (Hamlet said, 'Nay, then, let the devil wear black, for I'll have a suit of sables'; iii.ii.30). We hear of Satan's spear, his harness and his shield, so probably we should imagine him – artists usually do – as a cross between a Greek and a Roman soldier, but gigantic. It may seem odd to call the Devil a melancholic – like calling Colonel Custer a paranoiac – since a fallen angel has reason to feel depressed. He is, though, a melancholic by Robert Burton's definition of religious melancholy: 'a sickness of the soul without any hope or expectation of amendment'. In that condition, one suffers 'the sense of . . . God's anger justly deserved' while 'the heart is grieved, the conscience wounded, the mind eclipsed with black fumes arising from those perpetual terrors'. Terror is not Satan's avocation, but Burton had said of religious melancholy, 'this desperate humour is not much to be discommended, as in wars it is a cause many times of extraordinary valour'. Milton's Satan certainly has valour, flying alone through Chaos, and declaring war on God and Creation. Critics speak of 'the high melancholy music' of his speeches, and the phrase is apt:

> Which way I fly is Hell; myself am Hell;
> And, in the lowest deep, a lower deep
> Still threatening to devour me opens wide,
> To which the Hell I suffer seems a Heaven.

The abyss through which he fell from heaven has reappeared within him, and is bottomless.[17]

The illustration by Gustave Doré cannot literally show Satan in his despair, since it is tied to lines in the poem which describe the 'Paradise of Fools', a dark wilderness on the outer edge of Creation which, when Satan visits it in Book iii, is still deserted (illus. 56). Later it will be filled by all those who build their hopes on vain, transitory, material things – among whom Milton includes religious 'enthusiasts',

56 Gustave Doré, illustration to John Milton, *Paradise Lost* (1667),
Book iii, ll. 473–4 (edition of 1882).

hermits, pilgrims, monks and friars. Burton had characterized severe
and deluded religious belief as 'religious melancholy', and Doré's
plate does seem to hold the darkness of self-inflicted terror, pain and
mania. The figure in the centre may then not be Satan, but some other
misguided leader in Milton's list (which includes Nimrod, who
according to some built Babel, and the philosopher Empedocles).
But in his armour, martial pose and royal diadem he is indistinguishable from Satan in the depth and fury of his anguish, and probably

is taken by many scanning this magnificent edition to be Satan at the heart of a teeming mental hell where sinners, demons and lunatic believers tumble pell-mell forever in a flying-falling darkness. Often in Doré's plates Satan is seen more or less in silhouette, as though a shadow fell wherever he flew, however bright the firmament. For Satan could also be called melancholic in the sense in which Pseudo-Aristotle used the term, when he called the destructive and self-destructive heroes of tragedy – Hercules, for example – melancholics.

Though melancholy, however, Satan is not literally black – except when, on his arrival in Paradise, he abandons his heroic form in order to advance 'like a black mist low creeping', as he seeks, through the 'thicket dank', the body of the Serpent. It is his incestuous child Death, by his daughter Sin, who is the ominous jet-black form in *Paradise Lost*, reviving – one might say – black's oldest value. Almost invariably, Milton's illustrators make Death a skeleton, because Death is Bones, but Milton's words are clear – and apt – for the towering, coal-black shadow-shape of Death:

> . . . The other shape,
> If shape it might be called that shape had none
> Distinguishable in member, joint, or limb
> . . . black it stood as night,
> Fierce as ten furies, terrible as hell,
> And shook a dreadful dart.[18]

Steadily through the poem, the light who was the prince of angels draws towards the blackness that already stands beside hell's gate his cherished son and shadow-self, and gift to man, black Death.

THESE THREE FIGURES – Prince Hamlet, the melancholy poet of 'Il Penseroso' and Milton's Satan – were to characterize the new vein of poetic melancholy, the melancholy consciously sought by English poets, which was to run through the following, eighteenth century and on into the Romantic age. Those poets, and their blacks, are for later mention, but in closing the present thumbnail biography of *melan choly* I shall note that melancholy was to change its hue – or rather, to add another colour to its spectrum. From the mid-eighteenth century the phrase 'the blue devils' gained increasing currency, meaning delirium tremens and the hallucinations of alcoholism. The sense of it broadened to feeling 'blue' – depressed – and in time it became 'the blues', a depressed mood, until that in turn was translated into wonderful, sombre music. But just as sin did not necessarily cease to be red when it became also black, so depression did not cease to be black when it became also blue, and the phrase 'black depression' has currency still. Famously, Winston Churchill called depression his 'black dog'. On the road ahead, then, are the black paintings of Mark Rothko, but I should turn first to the different black of the community which in time, with good reason, made 'the blues'. I should turn, belatedly, to Africa.

57 Lucas Cranach workshop, *St Maurice*, 1529, oil on wood,
left wing of altarpiece.

SEVEN

Servitude and Négritude

ALTHOUGH THE SOUTHERN European nations had a long acquaintance with Africa, there had, before the time of Shakespeare, been few representations of Africans in England. But for Shakespeare, and for his time, Africa had become important. Africa was to provide Shakespeare with the hero, and then the heroine, of two of his best-known plays; and in his work we see the picture of Africa that prevailed before the English entered the slave trade – which in time they came to dominate.

In general Shakespeare was alert to blackness. In his tragedies there is the sense – much more so than in ancient tragedy – of an impenetrable darkness which surrounds us closely. 'Come, thick Night,' cries Lady Macbeth, 'And pall thee in the dunnest smoke of hell.' 'Arise black vengeance from thy hollow cell', says Othello. There is the extraordinary line, said by Edgar, in *King Lear*, 'Croak not, black angel; I have no food for thee.' In *All's Well That Ends Well* there is a reference to 'the black gown of a big heart' (the image is of a cassock).

Shakespeare had moreover a marked interest in people – not Africans at all – who could be called black. In his early comedy *Love's Labours Lost*, Biron is teased about the looks of the girl he likes, Rosaline, 'By heaven, thy love is black as ebony.' He replies, 'Is ebony like her? O wood divine! . . . No face is fair that is not full so black.' Another friend ribs him, 'To look like her are chimney sweepers black.' Rosaline is however far from dark-skinned, since Biron also calls her 'a whitely wanton': but her hair, her eyebrows and her eyes are so black that he can see nothing else. Simultaneously he castigates, and celebrates, his helplessness before black beauty:

> And among three to love the worst of all,
> A whitely wanton with a velvet brow,
> With two pitch-balls stuck in her face for eyes.

What is most notable is the divided feeling Biron has about Rosaline's black eyes, as if their charm were so powerful that only explosive words would do. For pitch-balls were incendiary weapons. They were catapulted blazing into enemy strongholds, to incapacitate troops and ignite ammunition stores.[1]

With the same violence of divided feeling the poet, in Shake - speare's sonnets, writes of his beloved:

> For I have sworn thee fair, and thought thee bright,
> Who art as black as hell, as dark as night.

He is referring at once to her sexual conduct and to her colouring. For Shakespeare does not call his 'dark lady' dark, he calls her black. In sonnet 131 he says:

> . . . thinking on thy face . . .
> Thy black is fairest in my judgement's place.

And the following sonnet ends,

> Then will I swear beauty herself is black,
> And all they foul that thy complexion lack.

Unlike Rosaline, the Lady is dark-skinned – 'If snow be white, why then her breasts are dun.' Her hair is black – 'If hairs be wires, black wires grow on her head' – as are her eyes ('my mistress' eyes are raven black').[2]

We do not know if the Lady is of mixed race. What is clear is that both the sonnet-poet, and Biron in *Love's Labours Lost*, speak of their obsessive love with excited self-reproach, as though to love 'black' women were perverse and dangerous. Their own desire is suspect to them, though also irresistible, as if it drew them towards a forbidden zone, like the sheer cliff in *Hamlet* whose precipitous drop incites one to fall. These elements are again present when Shakespeare imagines his supreme, and North African, 'dark lady' in *Antony and*

Cleopatra. In the opening lines of the play, Cleopatra is called 'tawny', and she herself says of her skin colour:

> . . . Think on me,
> That am with Phoebus' amorous pinches black

That is, her skin is not merely burned black by the sun, but is bruise-black from the passionate lust of the sun-god (Phoebus). Like the Lady, she is irresistibly desirable and sexually promiscuous. She is called a 'strumpet', a 'triple-turned whore', the ex-mistress of Julius Caesar and Gnaeus Pompey who in 'hotter hours' had other lovers 'luxuriously [lecherously] picked out'. When he accuses her, Antony is perhaps unfair, since she does not cheat on him in the course of the play, and it is he who, when one wife dies (in Act I, Scene 3), immediately marries another one (in Act II, Scene 2). But dangerous Cleopatra is, destroying Antony absolutely, and herself in the process: her antics on battlefields make him lose his war with Caesar, and her pretence that she has died from grief causes him to kill himself. At the play's end she is many things: tender and grieving, mercenary, playful and courageous. She dies 'a lass unparalleled', pretending that the cobra whose bite will kill her is 'my baby at my breast'.[3]

One might say that Cleopatra dramatizes those particular preju-dices that Shakespeare (and his time) had about women: but she also dramatizes the derogatory prejudices that Shakespeare (and his time) had about Africans. Again we might say Cleopatra was hardly 'African', since she was Greek and at most north Egyptian. But Shakespeare has little to say of her Greekness, and when she describes herself as black, she sounds like one of those ancient black pharaohs whom Martin Bernal imagines in *Black Athena*.

Shakespeare's sense of geography has been called loose, and if we turn to his other play about a North African, we find that Othello, a 'Moor', is imagined as a black African man. Actually, in Shakespeare's time, the word 'moor', like 'blackamore', was applied broadly to Africans; it derives, via the Roman province of Mauretania, from the Greek *mauros*, meaning black (and *mavros* means black still in modern Greek). Othello is called a 'thick-lips' and 'an old black ram' (perhaps with an implication of tightly curled hair), though he is also thought of as a handsome man. The love between him and

Desdemona is, like that between Antony and Cleopatra, clearly based on mutual strong desire and admiration.[4]

If we put Cleopatra beside Othello, we can see the larger side of Shakespeare's idea of the African. They are both fit heroes for tragedy because they have a largeness, a grandeur of heart as well as libido; they have a natural authority, even a magnificence, and easily speak with a grand public eloquence. It is also true that they have no reflectiveness. They are not introverts at all, as Shakespeare's European protagonists are. And they can slip, without great difficulty, into violent savagery. Othello says of Desdemona, 'I'll chop her into messes', while Cleopatra tells her tortures as a recipe:

> Thou shalt be whipped with wire and stewed in brine,
> Smarting in ling'ring pickle.[5]

In the final account, both are victims of the unscrupulous European brain. Cleopatra is in part destroyed by the ruthless operation of Roman militarism, coldly controlled by the future Augustus Caesar; Othello is destroyed by a clever, manipulative European, who is twisted at the centre, neurotically jealous and eaten with grudges, and virulently colour prejudiced. The play *Othello* gives a sense of the difficulties of mixed marriages, even as it creates, at the start, a uniquely radiant picture of martial honour and heroism, in a black general, marrying for love a beautiful, good, white woman.

The narrow and nasty form of colour prejudice is voiced in Shakespeare's work. When the prince of Morocco fails to win Portia's hand in *The Merchant of Venice*, she says, as he leaves, 'Let all of his complexion choose me so.' And in the earlier play *Titus Andronicus*, the 'Moor' Aaron, who is again African, is both coal-black and evil in the most conventional way (though sympathetic when he snatches his child from an abusive midwife: 'Zounds, ye whore! is black so base a hue?').[6]

Shakespeare's attitude to Africa is mixed because he stands at just that point in history when attitudes were tipping towards greater degradation. For though the skin colour of Africans was widely associated with sin and even devilry, the perception of Africans in the later Middle Ages had not been solely negative. The Christian tradition itself privileged certain individuals. There was not only the Bride, black but comely, of the Song of Songs. From the thirteenth century, in European illuminated manuscripts, the Queen of Sheba was sometimes depicted as coal-black, and in the second half of the fourteenth century the custom had begun, in altarpieces, of letting one of the Three Kings – Balthazar – be an African. He is usually younger than or subordinate to the other, white Kings, and may be the last to reach the manger, but also he may be both handsome and majestic. Also, from the thirteenth century, St Maurice – the Egyptian commander of a Roman legion who was martyred for his Christian faith in 287 CE – began to be represented as African. In Cranach's painting of 1529 he wears the glittering full armour of the Late Middle Ages, and has something of the dandy in his crimson cap decorated with ostrich feathers (illus. 57). At the same time his sword is a spotless golden cross, while his cloth-of-gold banner shows the wingtips and claw-tips of the eagle silhouette, which in this context will call to mind both the actual Roman Empire in whose army Maurice served, and the later Holy Roman Empire whose soldier-saint he had become.

In Shakespeare's lifetime no English colonist owned slaves. An English sea captain, John Hawkins, had attempted to trade slaves in the 1560s, and been beaten off by the Spanish. The first slaves arrived in an English colony in 1619 (three years after Shakespeare's death), and the first permanent slave-trading English outpost was established on the West African coast in 1631 (at Kormantin in present-day Ghana). But the slave trade itself had existed since the beginning of the sixteenth century, practised by the Portuguese and the Spanish, and some characters in Shakespeare's plays do voice the racial prejudices which would facilitate slave-trading in Africans. Shakespeare himself, however, and a good part of his public, one would guess, shared in a more moderate outlook which dated back to the ancient world. One piece of evidence for this is the attitude to love between Africans and northerners. Even Aaron in *Titus Andronicus* is the loved consort of Tamara, queen of the Goths. The loves of Antony and Cleopatra, and Othello and Desdemona, stand in a grand continuity with Solomon's liaison with the Queen of Sheba, and his love for the Bride in the Song of Songs, and with the marriage of the Roman emperor Septimus Severus to the Syrian or Berber lady Julia Domna – as well as with Cleopatra's actual amours with Julius Caesar, Pompey and Mark Antony. Such matches were still great, and luminous, but their thrill could be touched by fear, as we see in the intermittent demonizing of the Lady of the sonnets.

There is a comparable doubleness in 'The Masque of Blacknesse', which Shakespeare's great competitor, Ben Jonson, wrote for performance at court in 1605, 'because it was her Majesty's will'. In the masque, Niger ('in forme and colour of an Aethiope') welcomes twelve 'negro' nymphs, his daughters, saying, 'in their black, the perfect'st beauty grows . . . their beauties conquer in great beauty's war'. Niger is joined in his welcome, however, by a white Æthiopia ('her garments white and silver'), who personifies the moon, said to have been worshipped in Ethiopia. She commends the English sun (and king):

> Whose beams shine day, and night, and are of force
> To blanch an Æthiope.

The black nymphs, it appears, may grow white after all. On the subject of Africa, Shakespeare, Jonson and their world hover precariously on the edge of a change for the worse.[7]

FOR UNDOUBTEDLY THERE is a correlation between the expansion of the slave trade and the increasingly degraded perception of Africans. It is not that the ancient world had no colour prejudice. In Talmudic thought, 'the curse of Ham' was blackness, passed on to all Africans through Ham's black son, Canaan. And in the Bible, in the Book of Numbers, we are told, 'And Miriam and Aaron spake against Moses because of the Ethiopian woman whom he had married: for he had married an Ethiopian woman.' But the element of colour-prejudice was fluctuating, and was not, in the Roman world, identified with slavery. The Romans had black slaves, and in the *Satyricon* of Petronius the principals consider escaping their troubles by covering themselves with ink, so as to be mistaken for Ethiopian slaves. But slaves in Rome were not necessarily Ethiopian, and might equally be Slavs, Celts, Germans, Gauls or Britons.[8]

As slavery developed in the English colonies, decade by decade through the seventeenth century, the standing of Africans was increasingly debased. In a sense the colonists also had white slaves, in the form of bonded labourers whose bonds could be inherited. But as the number of black slaves grew, and economic dependence on them increased, the conditions under which they survived deteriorated. At an early point the right to carry arms in an emergency was removed, though not from white bonded labour, and 'negro' women, unlike bonded white women, were required to do fieldwork. Miscegenation was viewed – and punished – with increasing severity, except in those colonies (like the Carolinas) where it was too frequent, and popular, to oppose. Africans were from the start identified by their colour, mainly using the Spanish word for black, *negro* (hence also 'negers', 'negars', 'negors'), though the English terms 'moore' and 'blackmore' continued. The colour coding of race-based slavery became more explicit after 1670, when the word 'negros' in administrative documents began to be replaced by 'blacks', and the words 'Christians' and 'English' by 'whites'.[9]

It is perhaps not surprising that the characterization of Africans became more derogatory as it became more completely the case that the slaves of the world were black Africans. For the whole process had happened before – centuries earlier – when, in the seventh century, Islam began its career of conquest. Slavery had existed in Arabia before Muhammad, but the vast colonial expansion which he inaugurated meant that many more slaves were drawn from deeper in Africa. Not all Arab slaves were African – Muhammad's slaves included Persians and Greeks – but as Islamic slaves became preponderantly African, so references to Africans became more derogatory. The Arabic word *abd*, which derived from the verb 'to serve', meant first a 'slave' regardless of race, then a slave who was black, and then, in colloquial Arabic especially, anyone whose skin was black.

In the home, Arab fathers could choose whether or not to recognize the children born to them by household slaves – and to make them members of their tribe – and it appears they hesitated to do this if the mother was black, though Arab homes might include many black slaves. Happily, enough Arab fathers did acknowledge their black sons for a school of black Arab poets to develop in the seventh and eighth centuries: they were known as 'Aghribat al-Arab' – the 'Arab crows'. Their attitude to skin colour could be apologetic, anticipating Blake's poem 'Little Black Boy' ('I am black, but O! my soul is white'): the poet Suhaym (whose name is a diminutive of 'black') wrote, 'though I am black of colour, my nature is white'. Or they may compare themselves with the precious spice musk: 'If I am jet-black,

musk is blacker', says Nusayb ibn Rabah. He was court poet to the
Umayyad caliph 'Abdel al-Malik, and fortunately had a genius which
more than made up for any stigma of skin colour:

> Blackness does not diminish me, as long
>   as I have this tongue and a stout heart, . . .
> How much better is a black, eloquent and keen-minded,
>   than a mute white.

After the eighth century the poetry of the Arab crows came to an
end, as black African converts to Islam came to use Arabic for their
scholarship and their own languages for poetry. The Arab slave trade
continued, however, and was little affected by Western abolitionism.
It was still substantial in the 1950s, and is not dead now.[10]

THOUGH THE ENGLISH made a late start in trading slaves across
the Atlantic, their slave-fleet expanded, and by the mid-eighteenth
century the slave trade was dominated by the English.

Even before the trade involved England, the English especially
had been struck by the foreignness of Africans. It is likely that the first
'negroes' appeared in London in 1554, brought there 'till they could
speak the language' so as 'to be a helpe to Englishmen' in trading
with 'negroes' on the African coast.[11] The blackness of these 'blacke
Moores' was especially problematic because very few Englishmen
had ever seen an African. The main supposition (following classical
ideas) was that Africans were scorched black by the sun, though it
was sometimes argued that tropical heat 'floated' black bile to the
surface of the body. The new voyages of discovery had however
made these arguments more difficult, since peoples were found –
in the New World especially – who lived in the same latitudes but
were not black. In his essay 'Of the Blackness of Negroes', Sir
Thomas Browne dismissed the solar argument, since the equatorial
sun had not made African animals black: as he pointed out, 'lions,
elephants, camels' are not black. He also dismissed as ludicrous the
classical belief that Africans were scorched when Phaeton stole the
chariot of Phoebus, lost control of it and burned the earth. What he
had noticed – as an observant physician – is that skin colour is hereditary, so that mixed marriages produce a mixed skin colour. He also

speculated on pathology, observing that 'it is not indisputable whether [black skin] might not proceed from such a cause and the like foundation of Tincture, as doth the black Jaundice'. He dismissed the superstition – first recorded by Herodotus – that the sperm of Africans was itself black, though he did claim that the

> sperm of Negroes . . . being first and in its naturals white . . . upon separation of parts [there arises] a shadow or dark efflorescence in the out-side; whereby [their births] are dusky.[12]

Browne did not accept that black skin was God's punishment for the children of Ham – an idea that was mocked by others in the early seventeenth century. The ecclesiastical controversialist Peter Heylyn derided 'that foolish tale of Cham'. To others this tale seemed less foolish, since it explained both Africans' blackness and their fitness for servitude. Noah had said, 'Cursed be Canaan; a servant of servants shall he be unto his brethren', and Jeremy Taylor could preach, in the mid-seventeenth century, that Ham's dishonouring his parents 'brought servitude or slavery into the world'. The jurist Sir Edward Coke claimed 'That Bondage or Servitude was first inflicted for dishonouring of Parents: For Cham [was] punished in his Son Canaan with Bondage.'[13]

Undoubtedly because the idea was convenient, Africans were increasingly seen as 'degenerated and debased below the Dignity of Humane Species'. They were described as living like beasts, and within the growing trade were bought, sometimes branded, penned and flogged off, like cattle. In 1651 the Guinea Company had instructed Bartholomew Howard 'to buy and put aboard you so many negers as yo'r ship can cary, and for what shalbe wanting to supply with Cattel, as also to furnish you with victualls and provisions for the said negers and Cattel'. As they were increasingly treated as inferiors, so they were judged to be inferior, until their very inferiority became an 'obstacle' to their ever being free. As Thomas Jefferson put it, as late as 1787, in his *Notes on the State of Virginia*,

> I advance it therefore as a suspicion only, that the blacks . . . are inferior to the whites in the endowments of both body and mind . . . This unfortunate difference of color,

and perhaps of faculty, is a powerful obstacle to the emanci-
pation of these people.[14]

Assisted by such views, the slave trade expanded through the
later seventeenth and eighteenth centuries, reaching its maximum
volume at about 1760. By then British ships were carrying over
40,000 Africans to the Americas each year, in a trading triangle
which ferried arms and industrial goods to Africa, slaves from Africa
to America and the Caribbean, and the products of slavery (sugar,
cotton and tobacco) back to the home ports of Bristol and Liverpool.
The conditions of travel are perhaps best recorded by an African
American author. In his *Interesting Narrative* (1789) Olaudah Equiano
describes a childhood trip to Barbados:

> The stench of the hold [was] intolerably loathsome . . . The
> closeness of the place . . . added to the number in the ship . . .
> brought on a sickness . . . of which many died . . . This
> wretched situation was again aggravated by the galling of
> the chains, now become insupportable; and the filth of the
> necessary tubs, into which the children often fell, and were
> almost suffocated. The shrieks of the women, and the groans
> of the dying, rendered the whole a scene of horror . . . One
> day, when we had a smooth sea and moderate wind, two of
> my wearied countrymen who were chained together (I was
> near them at the time), preferring death to such a life of
> misery, somehow made through the nettings and jumped into
> the sea.[15]

The trade was accompanied by criticism, as well as by rational-
ization. Some Quakers and dissenting groups condemned slavery
as un-Christian in the seventeenth century, and in 1688 came Aphra
Behn's protest-romance, *Oroonoko; or, The Royal Slave*. Behn was
not concerned only with the freedom of Africans: she celebrated
also their 'perfection' of body and mind, and since the novel
became an international bestseller, it shows how far from colour
prejudice the seventeenth and eighteenth centuries could go, even
as the slave trade flourished and expanded. It is true she makes
Oroonoko more beautiful than other Africans, in recognition of his
status as an aristocrat, adding that 'his Face was not of that brown

rusty Black which most of that Nation are, but a perfect Ebony, or polished Jet'. She also says that the old king of the country has 'many beautiful Black Wives: for most certainly there are Beauties that can charm of that Colour'. Oroonoko's beloved is 'a beautiful Black Venus to our young Mars; as charming in her Person as he, and of delicate Virtues'. So far as I know, this is the first use of the phrase 'black Venus'.

The criticism made in the eighteenth century had more intellectual muscle. Adam Smith denounced the ways in which 'those nations of heroes' ('the negroes from the coast of Africa') were subjected 'to the refuse of the jails of Europe'. On a visit to Oxford, Dr Johnson proposed a toast 'to the next insurrection of the negroes in the West Indies'. The poet William Cowper, a friend of William Wilberforce, returned to the attack in poem after poem, playing nature's 'black complexion' against black evil ('the black-sceptred rulers of Slaves'). Finally, as abolition approached, he imagined a 'Slave Trader in the Dumps' (1788) offering at auction the thumbscrews, jaw clamps, padlocks, bolts, ropes ('supple-jack') and chains that accompanied his 'pretty black cargo of African ware'.[16] The same year, the humane artist George Morland, who in his English pictures showed the agricultural poor, depicted the anguish of slavery in a painting called *Execrable Human Traffick; or, The Affectionate Slaves*. The work later became a popular anti-slavery print, under the title *The Slave Trade* (illus. 58). Both versions represent the pain of separation of two African brothers, one of whom is taken in slavery by white men in white (one brandishing a cane) while the other is allowed to stay. In another painting, *African Hospitality*, he shows Africans helping shipwrecked Europeans ashore and giving them comfort, refreshment and directions; we cannot tell whether these Africans have any knowledge of the slave trade.

It has to be said that a robust opposition to slavery could coexist with a derogatory view of Africans. The philosopher David Hume was 'disgusted' with the 'unbounded dominion' of slave-owners', but also found himself 'apt to suspect the Negroes to be naturally inferior to the Whites'. Others were willing to mock comprehensively the ideas of good and bad skin colours, and of better or worse races. In Germany Johann Gottfried von Herder wrote, 'The Black has as much right to consider the white a mutant, a born vermin, as the white has to consider him a beast, a black animal.' The 'negro' might

58 J. R. Smith, *The Slave Trade*, 1835, hand-coloured engraving, after George Morland's painting *Execrable Human Traffick; or, The Affectionate Slaves* (1788).

say, 'I, the black, am the original man. I have taken the deepest draughts from the source of life, the Sun.'[17]

Many decades were still to pass before the practice of slavery by the West came, officially, to a close. The photograph shown here of an African American family was taken in 1862 – after the American Civil War had begun (illus. 59). It was titled *Five Generations on Smith's Plantation, Beaufort, South Carolina*. The plantation owner has a name, but the five generations do not. Evidently the photographer, who was white (he was Timothy H. O'Sullivan), did not try hard get his camera straight, but apart from that the wooden hut leans precariously. The poverty is evident, and so is the solidarity of this 'nuclear' family, who plainly spend their small earnings on items that reflect their sense of self-respect and of a right to style, such as a smart waistcoat or blouse – or a family photograph. The older man has not bothered with finery, and we can see that he survives from still harder times.

Sadly, too, the slow abolition of slavery through the nineteenth century brought only a qualified freedom to Africa itself. It has been argued that, disinterested as abolitionist campaigning had

59 *Five Generations on Smith's Plantation, Beaufort, South Carolina, 1862.*

been, abolition had advantages for Britain, which was quicker than its competitors in moving beyond the 'plantation economy'. The financial interest now lay in the colonizing of Africa itself. As a consequence, the snatching of Africans to sell them elsewhere was succeeded by the acquisition of the lands where they lived. Africans now could work at home, but again for foreign masters.

Colonialism too could be seen as iniquitous in the eighteenth century. Dr Johnson had called the colonists in North America 'European usurpers' and William Cowper had asked in *The Task* (in 1785!), 'Is India free . . . Or do we grind her still?'[18] Herder, Johnson and Cowper could speak in these terms because it could still be argued, and on biblical authority, that all men were created equal. The cruel irony for Africans was that, as the nineteenth century and abolitionism progressed together, the idea of 'equality' receded, not merely in economic practice, but in the intellectual world. Charles Darwin was to say, in *The Descent of Man*, in a passage that is perhaps too often quoted, that

> at some future period, not very distant as measured by centuries, the civilised races of man will almost certainly exterminate, and replace, the savage races throughout the world. At the same time the anthropomorphous apes, as Professor Schaaffhausen has remarked, will no doubt be exterminated. The break between man and his nearest allies will then be wider, for it will intervene between man in a more civilised state, as we may hope, even than the Caucasian, and some ape as low as a baboon, instead of as now between the negro or Australian and the gorilla.[19]

It is important to say that Darwin stood strongly apart from the racisms – and the 'darwinisms' – of his time. In his encounters with tribal peoples he was repeatedly struck by 'how similar their minds were to ours', and in *The Descent of Man* itself he argued that the black races had bred themselves black through many millennia of sexual selection because of the beauty that black skin can have. Nonetheless the passage quoted cannot but be taken to mean that for Darwin, in at least some of his thinking, the African 'negro' and the Australian aborigine belonged to the earliest surviving stage of human evolution.

In other ways also, nineteenth-century science was to cooperate with popular prejudice. Before Darwin published his view of evolution, J. J. Virey had argued, in his *Dictionnaire des sciences médicales* (1834), that the genitals of African women were different, larger and more inflammatory than those of European women. A further twist of research associated African women with prostitutes, since prostitutes were said to have a primitive physiology. In 1893 Cesare Lombroso found numerous proofs that 'phenomena of atavism are more frequent among prostitutes than among ordinary female criminals'. Prehensile feet were unusually common in prostitutes, and 'the obsessive obesity of prostitutes' was 'perhaps of atavistic origin'. He noted that 'Hottentot,

60 From Cesare
Lombroso and
Guglielmo Ferrero,
*La donna deliquente:
La prostituta e la
donna normale* (1893).

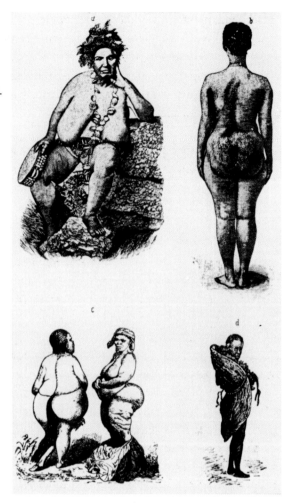

African, and Abyssinian women when rich and idle grow enormously
fat, and the reason of the phenomenon is atavistic'. He then argued
that the fatty features of Hottentot women, including their buttocks,
were a throwback to an earlier, more animal fattiness. In one illustration he juxtaposes an Ethiopian prostitute lethargically holding a
tambourine (a) with three views of the buttocks of Hottentot women
(b and c, illus. 60). Comparing criminals, he found prostitutes to be
less intelligent than premeditating murderers, for 'to kill in an explosion of bestial rage is compatible with the intelligence of a Hottentot;
but to plan poisoning demands a certain ability and astuteness.'[20]

Medical theory was hardly more helpful. In 1799 Benjamin
Rush, a signatory to the American Declaration of Independence,

published his lecture arguing that 'the Black Color (as it is called) of the Negroes Is Derived from the Leprosy'. In evidence he claimed that leprosy was the most 'durable' of the hereditary diseases, and was 'accompanied in some instances by a black color of the skin': in particular, in the form of leprosy known as the 'black albaras', 'the skin becomes black, thick and greasey'. He further noted that many Africans had leprosy; that leprosy could also cause whiteness of skin, and there were albinos in Africa; that negroes, like lepers, were insensible of pain and had 'strong venereal desires'; and that leprosy could cause swollen lips, depression of the nose and thickly matted hair. It should be said that Rush was a dedicated physician and an ardent abolitionist. He wanted to help, and asked, 'Is the color of the negroes a disease? Then let science and humanity . . . discover a remedy for it.' All he could offer, however, were his observations that some lightening of skin could be produced by fear, by bleeding and by the application of 'oxygenating muriatic acid' or 'the juice of unripe peaches'.[21]

The 'science' of Benjamin Rush did not win wide assent, but it did cooperate with other arguments of the time, for instance that dark skin was related to syphilis, which also was a form of leprosy. For syphilis, like leprosy, sometimes darkens the skin, and depresses the nose, which may again be depressed in a syphilitic birth. It thus came to be argued that syphilis was not brought over from the New World by Christopher Columbus, but had spread to Europe in the later Middle Ages, coming up from Africa, where it had long been ubiquitous – because of the lawless sexual appetite of Africans. Once again a parallel was made between Africa and the brothel.[22]

Given such readings, in some of the science of the time, it is not surprising that the main popular image of Africa was of darkness and blackness, extending beyond skin colour. Darkness becomes a cliché in the titles of books, for instance in Henry Stanley's *In Darkest Africa* (1890), Wilson S. Naylor's *Daybreak in the Dark Continent* (1905), James Stewart's *Dawn in the Dark Continent; or, Africa and Its Missions* (1902) and, of course, Joseph Conrad's *Heart of Darkness* (1902). As James Stewart's title indicates, the light was that of the Gospel, though this light merged, in broader usage, with that of colonial civilization. When Sir Harry Johnston designed the postage stamp for British Central Africa (now Nyasaland) in the 1890s, he depicted a white cross on a shield which was itself half

61 Harry H. Johnston's design for a postage stamp for British Central Africa, 1890s.

black, half white (illus. 61). A tiny replica of Britain's coat of arms sits in its centre, while the heraldic 'bearers' are two jet-black Africans – decently clad in long white skirts – one bearing a spade, one a pickaxe. Actually the Africans are drawn quite carefully, with more care than could show when copied on a stamp. But if these Africans are not slave labour, still they are labour and nothing else. The motto on the scroll reads 'Light in Darkness' – the light being that of Christian British colonialism, and the darkness that of Africa and Africans, as benighted in soul as they are black in body.

One might say that darkness is an absurd image for a continent whose sunlight is blinding, with extensive deserts, grasslands and wetlands, and one cannot but suppose that the 'darkness' of Africa is 'coloured' by the black skin of Africans. Africa itself did have some black features: for instance, the river Niger, which, Mungo Park noted, was 'remarkably black and deep', being called by the Mandinka 'Bafing, or Black River'.[23] The illustrations showing Africa, in Euro - pean books of the nineteenth century, are highly stereotyped. We see the dark depths of jungles, or the deep shade of palm trees, in which the limbs of Africans are hard to separate from the black trunks and

62 Illustration to
Herbert Ward, *Five
Years with the Congo
Cannibals* (1890).

branches, so it seems they are black-skinned for reasons of camouflage (illus. 62). Being benighted, they are most active at night –
where again their blackness is the perfect camouflage – though they
do become visible when dancing wildly, lit by a fire, to the howls
of the witch-doctor and the beat of savage drums, while a crouching
figure turns the spit which skewers their supper, which may consist
of other Africans or the odd lost Christian European.[24]

TO TAKE UP the issue of skin colour, it would not now be thought
that black Africans or Australian aborigines are survivors from an
earlier stage of human evolution than are we ourselves. And though
Darwin himself was sceptical about the influence of climate and the
sun, he does, in *The Descent of Man*, touch on what now would be
thought the most important factor affecting pigmentation. In an
addition to the second edition of 1874, he notes that 'as Dr Sharpe
remarks . . . a tropical sun, which burns and blisters a white skin, does
not injure a black one at all', and goes on, 'whether the saving of the
skin from being thus burnt is of sufficient importance to account for

a dark tint having been gradually acquired by man through natural selection, I am unable to judge.'[25] It would now be thought that it is precisely because of its protective value that a high concentration of melanin has survived or evolved in those peoples who have lived for many hundreds of millennia under the most intense solar radiation – such as the peoples of equatorial Africa, South Asia and northern Australia. It is clear that in Africans, and in northern Australians, dark-to-black skin has survived or evolved independently, since – in their genetic ancestry – they are more distant from each other than Africans are from Europeans.

As to race, it would now be said that though movements of populations can yield contrasts, in the long perspective of evolution one cannot draw distinct boundaries between one race and another, since if one had travelled the world at a period when people stayed longer in the same habitat, one would find 'racial' features changing very gradually as one progressed from one environment to another. It used to be said that Egyptians were of a mixed ancestry, and their skin colour varied depending whether they had more ancestors from a light-coloured race at the mouth of the Nile, or from the Nubians of the upper Nile. As it now appears, there never were two distinct races. The Nile is the longest river in the world – more than 4,000 miles – and as one travels up its length from the Mediterranean through Egypt, South Sudan, Sudan and into Uganda and Kenya, which span the Equator, one finds a slow gradient of darkening skin colour, together with an increase in other features thought of as African. Nasal passages shorten to breathe a thicker, hotter, more heavily humid air, while bodies grow more elegantly tall and thin because extra-long calves and forearms dissipate body heat quickly. That gradient exists now as it did in the time of the Romans, of the Greeks, of the ancient Egyptians and Nubians, and for very many millennia long before then. The invasions that Egypt has suffered – from the Assyrians, Persians and Greeks, and later from the Mameluks, Turks, French and British – were not invasive enough to leave a visible change. In sum, the simple understanding in the ancient world that skin colour darkened as one went further south because people were burned more black by the sun was nearer to the truth than later, more 'racial' explanations.[26]

Putting 'race' to one side, one might take up the application to Africans of the word and idea of 'black', given that 'black' is identified, in many cultures, with soiling, accursedness and the threat of death. Simply as a colour description it is not exact, since most Africans are not jet-black. The old colonial literature drew many distinctions, which can have a grotesque sort of connoisseurship: so Stanley said 'the Wahumba . . . have clear ebon [sic] skins, not coal-black, but of an inky hue', and noted too that '"black" skin could have a tone as light as copper'.[27] It is not of course hard to understand why words for 'black' might be innocently applied to Africans, and Africans themselves will use such words for one people or another. But manifestly the 'blacking' of Africans is not always innocent. Colour-words can be used as a means of *othering*, of making the Other more 'other'. When Native North Americans are called 'red', or Chinese 'yellow', they sound more distinctly as though they come from another race – or another planet. People in the West do not call foreigners 'brown' in the same way, because brown is not an exaggeration: foreigners may *be* brown, as Westerners try to be in the summer.

In other words, the point of calling people 'red', 'yellow' or 'black' is that no one really is quite those colours, and use of the colour-words intensifies the foreignness. And if 'red' and 'yellow' can become prejudicial, how much more so will 'black', having associations ready to hand with death, misery, malignancy, guilt and supernatural evil? Calling Africans black has made it easier to call them animals, children, idiots, demons, prostitutes, lepers and syphilitics. Words for 'black' have assisted in a kind of psychic dumping in which bad things are driven from us and fastened onto Africans. For no other people on Earth has been so continuously, and so diversely, traded, flogged, shackled, branded, mutilated, slaughtered and variously abused as have Africans; and our naming of their dark skin 'black' has made it easier for this to happen.

To see the inner consequences of black-naming one need only look in the North American 'slave narratives', where Africans speaking only English take the word 'black' to themselves. Distinctions between Nuba, Masai and Kukuyu vanish, 'red' Fulanis from the Sudan no longer call 'Wolofs' black; rather there is one race, the 'blacks'. The word 'black' is still used generally for any bad thing, such as 'black hearts' or 'the blackest perfidy', or the question of whether the Devil is 'as black as he is painted'. And the bad sense of 'black' then plays against – but also with – skin colour when the ex-slave 'Aaron' remarks in his narrative, 'No matter if the slaves were as bad as they are black . . . ', and again when the Right Reverend Richard Allen of the African Methodist Episcopal Church humbly says, 'We do not wish to offend: but when an unprovoked attempt is made to make us blacker than we are . . . '. The black/bad play is recurrent through the slave narratives, adding an extra negativity to a situation that already is colossally disadvantaged, and which is then compounded by the abusive use of 'black' by whites. When 'Aaron' infuriates a white woman by calling her 'honey', she calls him a 'damned black scoundrel'. She hollers for her husband, who shouts, 'What have you been doing to my wife, you dam'd black scoundrel, you?' If Aaron were Chinese, or a Native American, the white couple might or might not call him a damned yellow or red scoundrel, but if they did the abuse would be weaker because 'yellow' and 'red' have none of the maledictory force of 'black'.[28]

The situation is more harsh again because slaves and ex-slaves inherit the picture of their oppressors as 'white'. Slave-owners did not have to be called white: Olaudah Equiano claimed that when he first saw the slave-traders, he was struck by their 'red faces'. But white, with black, has been internalized, so 'Aaron' says his heart is white, and William J. Anderson ('twenty-four years a slave . . . whipped three hundred times!!!') says the hearts of the white masters 'must be far blacker than the negro's skin'. Thus the relation of slave to slave-owner is continually re-described by using the most extreme colour contrast with which humanity has agreed to name its best and worst values.[29]

To take a testimony nearer to our time: in his first book, *Black Skins, White Masks* (*Peau noire, masques blancs*, 1952), the black Algerian psychoanalyst Frantz Fanon speaks of a 'neurotic society', of a communal 'inferiority complex': 'the Negro enslaved by his inferiority, the white man enslaved by his superiority, alike behave in accordance with a neurotic orientation'. Nowadays, he says, 'the first encounter with a white man oppresses [the Negro] with the whole weight of his blackness.' In a prose that is also a poetry of anguish he speaks of

> All this whiteness that burns me . . . I walk on white nails . . . So I took up my negritude, and with tears in my eyes I put it together again . . . A feeling of inferiority? No, a feeling of nonexistence . . . I feel in myself . . . a soul as deep as the deepest of rivers.[30]

He is speaking not of slavery but of colonial coexistence, which 'has created a massive psychoexistential complex. I hope by analysing it to destroy it.' Destruction is difficult, however, because of the totality of the equation of the African with all black and bad things not only in the workaday world but in all the realms of mental and cultural life:

> In Europe the Negro has one function: that of symbolizing the lower emotions, the baser inclinations, the dark side of the soul. In the collective unconscious of *homo occidentalis*, the Negro – or, if one prefers, the colour black – symbolizes evil, sin, wretchedness, death, war, famine.

Even return to a purely African life is miserable. If 'the educated Negro . . . wants to belong to his people . . . it is with rage in his mouth and abandon in his heart that he buries himself in the vast black abyss'.[31]

IN AFRICA, BEFORE white people came, black had a double value comparable to its value in other societies as the colour of elegance, and of death. The old practices have been recorded, and in part continue. Certainly black was and is associated with sickness and death. A medicine man may suck a small black pellet from the body of his patient, and show it moving mysteriously in the palm of his hand. It may in fact be black beeswax and move because of fine hairs projecting from it, but also it *is* the sickness – the pain and the curse – there for all to see. In the lower Congo mourners would smear their bodies liberally with a greasy black pomade made of burned peanuts and charcoal, and also rub black ashes into their bodies and their clothes, and sometimes roll in black ashes so as to be black everywhere. Such usages may be the ultimate origin of mourning black, which later became black clothes.[32]

As to how blackness came into the world, it was said in the lower Congo that when the son of the first woman died, she was commanded not to look on him until he was revived by God. She could not wait, and looked, and as a result her son stayed dead; thus death came, and her descendants, in punishment, were stained black. The myth offers a parallel not only to the story of Orpheus and Eurydice, but also to Genesis, where again the first wrong is blamed on the first woman, who brings in death with the colour black.

But though black could be bad, it could also be good, even curative. Medicinal charms might be black, like the 'Black Stone', which is now sponsored by the Belgian missionary society, the White Fathers. In alternative accounts it is actually an animal bone, or is cooked from herbs: it is credited with the unique ability to absorb snake venom. And black is often also beautiful. There is a Xhosa proverb, 'It is the seed of the umya', said of any person who is thought extremely beautiful. The seed of the umya – a species of wild hemp – is like a small, jet-black bead. Traditional practices, which continue today, include the cosmetic use, in Sudan and the Congo, of black pomades and body paint. The whole body or one side of it, or the head and some limbs, may be painted with black, geometric patterns, not as war-paint but with a ceremonial, magical or festive purpose. Nuba women in Sudan have used *hara* (pounded specularite) to make themselves 'surpassingly beautiful with the *hara*'s blackness', and among the Ndembu in Zambia young women might enhance their beauty again by blackening their vulvas with the soot of burned tree-bark. Among the Ndembu, women with very black skin have been considered the most desirable, and Victor Turner reports that black is also associated with a good marriage. If the bride is pleased with the frequent intercourse on the bridal night, she gives a secret signal to her ritual instructress, who collects *malowa*, black alluvial mud, and scatters a little of it on the threshold of every hut in the village.[33]

More at large, black stones and black glass have been used for beads. Black haematite and soapstone have long been used for sculpture, and for many centuries ebony has been carved into figurines and masks, often with that extraordinary freedom of stylization which was to be inspirational for twentieth-century sculptors like Henry Moore. Black paint was used prominently, decoratively, on shields, boats and fabrics made from tree-bark. Jet-black cattle were valued – and highly prized – because of their beauty.

Given all that black Africans have suffered, following their contact both with Arabs and with Europeans, there was a need for the ancient and present beauty of blackness to be reasserted – and by Africans. That reassertion has come in the twentieth century, with increasing force in the last many decades, and it would be fatuous for me to rehearse this great change. I shall refer to an early stage,

the *Négritude* movement which was founded in the 1930s by franco -
phone Africans living in Paris. The key figures were the dramatist
Aimé Césaire from Martinique and the Senegalese poet – and later
president – Léopold Sédar Senghor. The politics of the group were
Marxist, but its central thrust lay in its assertion of African values, and
in the work of Senghor in a celebration of black beauty. As in 'Black
Woman' ('Femme noire'):

> *Femme nue, femme noire*
> *Vêtue de ta couleur qui est vie . . .*
>
> . . .
>
> *Fruit mûr à la chair ferme, sombres extases du vin noir . . .*
>
> . . .
>
> *. . . les perles sont étoiles sur la nuit de ta peau . . .*

> (Naked woman, black woman
> Clothed in your colour which is life . . .
>
> . . .
>
> Ripe fruit with firm flesh, dark ecstasies of black wine . . .
>
> . . .
>
> . . . pearls are stars on the night of your skin . . .)

Curiously he treats her colour as clothing, though that perhaps is a way
of distinguishing her beauty from an essential self that is not colour-
bound. In any case her clothing is as alive as she is, since the word
vetue concentrates into *vie*, as her *perles*, shining like stars on her skin,
slide into the word for the skin itself, *peau*, and again the *fruit mur*
– the ripe fruit of her beauty – contracts to *ferme*, her firm flesh.
The 'black wine' he mentions might be red wine, though since he
speaks elsewhere of black milk and black blood, the wine may *be*
black, and a direct metaphor for African life and ecstasy. I do not
know that I can better illustrate the theme (in realist art) than with the
tender etching Rembrandt had made of an evidently tall and slender
negress 300 years before, in 1658 (illus. 63). Within the context of
Western art her posture and her exposure together make her a reclining Venus. More immediately from daily life, and from Africa, a
beautiful photograph taken around 1900 shows a Swahili woman
fixing the hair of another, with the aid of a comb of black African
hardwood (illus. 64).

63 Rembrandt van Rijn, *Reclining Negress*, 1658, etching.

64 A Swahili
woman fixing
another's hair,
c. 890–1920.

Wine is, however, a French much more than an African product, and the poem is in French – the colonial language. Later generations of African and Afro-European writers have criticized Senghor for cooperating with the colonial culture: indeed the whole drive of *Négritude*, in asserting 'black' values, has been seen as too simple a reversal, an inversion, of white takes on black. Fanon in his later classic, *The Wretched of the Earth*, scarcely uses the word 'black', and speaks of the need of the ex-colonies to 'turn over a new leaf . . . work out new concepts, and try to set afoot a new man'. The set of mind that makes an issue of colour, black or white, positive or negative, he casts behind him when he writes, 'We must shake off the heavy darkness in which we were plunged.'[34]

Even so, *Négritude* was an important moment, and had passion as well as an idea. Senghor's remark that 'Emotion is black as reason is Greek' is often quoted, but perhaps simplifies his larger argument that black culture reflects deep and beautiful parts of a common heritage with which European culture has lost touch. Perhaps all a white writer in an ex-colonial country can do is to recognize the retort that Africa gave to its colonists when it chose to speak its own values in its own voice, but in their language (which, by the way, is the language of England's own colonial invaders, whom, unlike the Africans, we never expelled). Nor is Senghor's asserted *Négritude* a simple quantity: he is not thinking of mixed parentage or now-fashionable hybridity when he writes,

J'ai vu le soleil se coucher dans les yeux bleus d'une négresse blonde

(I have seen the sun set in the blue eyes of a blond black girl)

A blonde black girl with blue eyes could not exist in actuality (hair dyed blonde notwithstanding), but in language she can – in the volatility of contradiction. Her black, then, is a mental colour, like the black of sin that is also crimson. The contradiction does not cancel itself, since it works a paradoxical magic, equating beloveds both black and blonde. It is not for her colour that the beloved is loved, beautiful as she is, both black and blonde. And to assert black as a colour is to assert other colours too, for if there were only black, black would not be a colour.

White still is a negative in his black-white play. Paris in the winter snow is '*la mort blanche*', and the white sun ('*le soleil blanc*') shines

over the cemetery that was colonial Senegal. He calls his own books
'*blancs comme ennui*', white like boredom. These dark plays with white
contrast with other paradoxes where blackness is brightness – as
in '*l'éclat sombre de ta gorge*' (the dark brightness of your throat), or
in his lover's '*peau de nuit diamantine*' (skin of diamantine night),
or again in '*Nuit d'Afrique, ma nuit noire, mystique et claire, noire et bril-
lante*' (Night of Africa, my black night, mystical and bright, black and
shining). So his opposites equate, and open distances, depths. Like
Fanon, he speaks of a black abyss, though the darkness of it must also
be hot, potent and dangerous since he speaks '*aux mines d'uranium
de mon coeur dans les abîmes de ma Négritude*' – 'from the uranium
mines of my heart in the abysses of my Négritude'.[35]

65 Hyacinthe Rigaud, *Louis XIV*, 1701, oil on canvas.

EIGHT

Black in the
Enlightenment

BY A POIGNANT visual irony, the main goods produced by black slave labour were white luxuries – first sugar, then increasingly cotton. Cotton, white as only cotton can be, was also worn in the hot months both by slave-owners and slaves.

The contrast of dark and light was to loom large in the slave-trading century and a half, from 1650 to 1800. The dark values of the sixteenth and early seventeenth centuries were retreating as the sombre power of Spain shrank. The power of blackness, which until then had grown steadily through history, waned. The new bright tone was set by the Sun King – Louis XIV – in France (illus. 65). In his portrait by Rigaud, he wears a silver coat with much white linen and lace at the wrist, and a white ermine cape with much lace (and gold) at the neck: but especially we notice that his vast blue train, embroidered with gold fleurs-de-lys, is turned voluminously inside out and shows endless ermine, lifted in a flourish of royal exposure to exhibit – as though they were naked beneath silver trunk-hose – his shapely legs in spotless white hose, in the posture of a dancer about to lead. For Louis liked to dance, both solo to the applause of his court, and in leading the revels as he led the nation.

This was a new, light monarchy. Louis' palace of Versailles, built in the 1660s and '70s, is of cream stone on the outside and white stucco, richly gilded, on the inside; it was filled with light from the many large windows, reflected again by the many large mirrors. The statuary was mainly white marble – though the black statue of a 'slave' (wearing a classical shift) may be found in the occasional niche. His courtiers wore, with much lace, colours ranging from strong red to salmon, deep blue to azure, the ladies being largely in white. His soldiers, too, extending his power through the Old and New

189

Worlds, mainly wore white uniforms (and sometimes blue – red was avoided, as the colour of the British).

We call the style of this period, especially at its high point in the early eighteenth century, 'rococo' (probably from 'rocaille', rockwork with artificial stones). Its piety can be seen in the voluptuous white-and-gold extravagance of the Wieskirche in Bavaria (of the 1740s and '50s), where the sensual swerve in the bodies of the carved Church Fathers is repeated in their swooning eyelids, and in the lascivious lips given to St Jerome. Its imperial grandeur is radiant still in the vast Winter Palace of the Tsars in St Petersburg – all white, pale blue and gold, the dream-palace of a society based, if not on slavery, on something little different in the form of Russian serfdom. With its many columns and curling cornices, the style is clearly a light take on Greek temples. As the mood of the century calmed, the plain style of those temples came more to the fore, until it seemed that no mansion or church, no bourse, corn exchange or customs house had a claim to respect if it failed to be fronted by a pediment with columns (or at least pilasters). Domestic interiors were light, with a lacy tracery of white-painted mouldings crossing panels painted white, or light blue, or pale grey-green.

Pursuing the white theme, one might speak of porcelain (known as china because it originated in China) – the teapots and figurines, the fragile china baskets. Plates were thin to translucency when held to the light, unless painted (lightly) with roses and tulips, or a Chinese threesome crossing a bridge. Simpler white cups were used in coffee-shops, where men talked money as they scanned the new white news-papers, while smoking in slender white clay pipes the tobacco raised in the New World by slavery.

As to fabrics, large imports of cotton came late in the century, for the principal cloth draping the eighteenth century was linen. When Gibbon summed up the advantages of the civilization in which he lived over the one he was describing – in the *Decline and Fall of the Roman Empire* – he said that 'the plenty of glass and linen has diffused more real comforts among the modern nations of Europe than the senators of Rome could derive from all the refinements of pompous or sensual luxury'. The bleaching of linen was refined through the century. Dowries included great chests of the stuff, and the prestige of linen can be heard again in the words of William Cowper's John Gilpin,

I am a linen-draper bold,
As all the world doth know[1]

Not that the century was a bridal suite. A beau as well as an officer might wear scarlet, coats in the street might be dark blue, deep
russet, bottle-green – or black – and within a musket-shot of palaces
and mansions were reeking, gin-sodden slums, thieves' kitchens,
streets deep in horse manure beside the sometimes open sewers. But
nor, on the other hand, was the light, bright tone of high life merely
a fashionable frivolity. For the eighteenth century believed in light.
It has been called the Age of Reason, and Reason was recurringly
described as Light. The phrase 'the light of reason' had been current
in Neoplatonic thought, but its use multiplies widely from the late
seventeenth century on. The metaphor of light is alive, not dead, in
the names by which this period is known – 'the Enlightenment' in
England, the *siècle des Lumières* in France, *die Aufklärung* in Germany,
where *klar* has the clear-and-bright sense of the English 'lucid' (from
the Latin *lux*, 'light'). We can even hear Light arriving audibly (a
little late in the century) in Handel's oratorio *The Creation*, first performed in 1798: on the word *Licht* in '*es werde Licht!*' ('and there was
Light'), the fading pizzicato of the strings is shattered by the hugely
fortissimo C-major chord from every flute, oboe, bassoon, clarinet,
trumpet, trombone and kettledrum in the orchestra.

The same phrase from Genesis is echoed in the epitaph for Sir
Isaac Newton penned by Alexander Pope, which closes: 'God said
"Let Newton be" and all was light.' Newton shed light not only on
gravity, which held the universe together, but also on light itself when
he used a prism to divide a slender ray of light into a spectrum of the
rainbow's colours. The colour historian Michel Pastoureau sees a
connection between Newton's spectrum and the general brightness
of the eighteenth century: 'The traditional order of colours was overturned . . . there was no longer a place for black', which now 'was
situated outside of any chromatic system, outside the world of colour'.
He calls this change a revolution 'that had consequences in all areas
of social, artistic and intellectual life'. Among the 'consequences' he
includes the disappearance of black from clothing and furnishing
fabrics and from the palettes of painters.[2]

There is some overstatement here, for black did not disappear.
The new, bright look of society cannot have been caused by Newton

since, though he worked on light in the 1660s, his *Opticks* was not published until 1704, when styles had been brightening for 40 years. One could as easily say that Newton was *of* his time in being so interested in light and colour. Nor did Newton ever say (as Leonardo da Vinci had) that black was not a colour. On the contrary, if one reads the *Opticks*, one finds Newton referring to the colour black a good deal, since he used it in his experiments to cut out the ambient light. As he puts it:

> The Sun shining into my darken'd Chamber through a hole
> . . . I placed at the distance of two or three Feet . . . a Sheet
> of Pasteboard, which was black'd all over on both sides . . .
> I made a little hole in the midst of the Paper for that Light
> to pass through and fall on a black Cloth behind it . . .

Or again:

> I took a black oblong stiff Paper . . . distinguished into two
> equal Parts. One of these Parts I painted with a red colour
> and the other with a blue. The Paper was very black, and
> the Colours intense and thickly laid on . . .

Examining the dark places in water-bubbles, he notices that some areas 'reflect so very little Light as to appear intensely black'.[3]

Far from disowning black, Newton is interested in experiments 'which produce blackness', for the reason that blackness causes light to disappear, and he wonders how that can be. He speculates that the 'corpuscles' of light (we might say 'photons') reflected by black objects might be so extraordinarily minute that their own light is trapped within them, where they 'variously refract it to and fro within themselves so long, until it happen to be stifled and lost, by which means they will appear black in all positions of the eye'.[4]

Other scientists were interested in blackness. In the decade when Newton worked especially in dark and blackened rooms – the 1660s – Robert Boyle published his *Experiments and Considerations Touching Colours*. He too had analysed light and 'Refracted . . . Prismatical Colours', but was especially interested in 'The Nature of Blackness and Black Bodies' and in the way in which, as he repeatedly puts it, black will 'Dead the Light'. He had studied reports of a blind man who claimed to be able to tell colours by touch, and who said that touching a black surface was like 'feeling Needles points'. The blind man was not always right, and Boyle noted that to the ordinary touch a black surface might seem perfectly smooth, but he speculated that if one could look closely enough, one might find

> the Surface of a Black Body to be Asperated by an almost Numberless throng of Little Cylinders, Pyramids, Cones, which by their being Thick Set and *Erected*, reflect the Beams of Light from one to another Inwards, and send them too and fro so often, that at length they are Lost before they can come to Rebound out again to the Eye.[5]

It is interesting that his language should anticipate so particularly the language of Newton in describing how light is 'lost' at the sub-atomic level. And though black bodies may not be as Boyle describes, his description of light-corpuscles bouncing between cavities is not a bad account of the way in which iridescence occurs within the microscopic lattices in the black-to-turquoise feathers on the head of a mallard duck. Boyle, like Newton later, noticed that when light falls on black bodies, the dancing 'corpuscles' of light 'Produce . . . such an Agitation, as (when we feel it) we are wont to call Heat'. He reported the claim of a travelling friend that, in the hot parts of the world, one may roast an egg by painting it black and setting it in the midday sun.[6]

Through the following century other scholars and virtuosi studied the effects of prisms, and narrow slits in black cards, within enclosures which they too made black. Their laboratories were a variation on the camera obscura (dark chamber) that artists like Vermeer had used in the seventeenth century, and perhaps were little different from the large camera obscura of Caravaggio's studio. Scientists working on subjects other than light were interested in the reasons why not-black things turned black: Joseph Priestley, investigating gases, noted that plants deprived of air turned black, as did iron filings and olive oil when confined in bad air. He had medical interests also, and reported the way in which, in certain fevers, the tongue became 'covered with a thick black pellicule', while on the teeth of another patient 'a black fur collected'.[7]

It is simply not true – as Michel Pastoureau claims – that black 'departed the colour order'. Dr Johnson quotes Newton in his

Dictionary, defining 'blackness': '1. Black colour . . . "There would emerge one or more very black spots, and, within these, other spots of an intenser blackness." *Newton.*' He cites the old transitive use of 'black' as a verb (as when men 'blacked' their boots), and many of his compound words containing 'black-' have a colour reference (as in 'black-pudding', 'blackberry', 'blacktail', 'blackthorn'). The principal exception is 'blackmail', which at that date meant to pay protection money – 'A certain rate of money, corn, cattle . . . paid by men allied with robbers, to be by them protected.'

Black was still a 'colour' for artists. It is true that eighteenth-century art is often luminous with the different bright colours of the spectrum: Fragonard's girls gambol in a fluff of rose, cream and silver; Hogarth will paint an election dinner with the hard, strong colours of life. But both of these painters had black in their palettes, while in many portraits of the time the sitter stands before a dark-to-black background, often wearing quality black items – as does Gainsborough's Lady Alston, who wears bands of black velvet at neck and wrists and a shawl of fine black lace, clearly painted by the artist with a fascination for both solid and translucent blacks (illus. 66). Often a painting will be partly ordered by a tonal scale between its brightest and its darkest point. In the Gainsborough there are two scales: a scale of brightness, rising through the blue lustre of her dress, her gold satin and white lace, to the white radiance of her chest; and a scale of blacks, strengthening from the background through the blue-black of her lower skirt, and the see-through darks of her black lace, to the almost-black of her hair, and so to the true jet-black of her velvet, where the paintings's darkest blacks stand next to its brightest whites. The scales coordinate and contribute to the sense of a distinct but circumspect persona; though still we return to the black points of her eyes, where dark tone turns to vigilance.

Black, in other words, is active, and not mere shadow, in the palette of Thomas Gainsborough. George Stubbs will paint black horses with a manifest delight in the lustre of their jet coat. To go further afield, Pietro Longhi, in the 1750s, paints the Carnival of Venice in a richly sombre range of whites, browns and solid blacks (illus. 67). His emphasis is not on colour, but on the snow-cold white both of the dresses and of some of the masks, and again on the clearly menacing blacks of mask, hat, cape, mantilla and domino. The round, black masks the women wear, which are smaller than their

66 Thomas Gainsborough, *Gertrude Durnford, the Future Lady Alston*, *c.* 1761, oil on canvas.

faces, seem then both surreal and a sly, pert part of the tantalizing game. And again, if one turns from oil paint to the engravings of the time, one finds Piranesi's massive nightmare-dungeons (also of around 1750) burdened with deeply shadowed arches, gloomy bridges that lead nowhere, and dark looping ropes and hawsers lowering at us in a richness of black printing ink.

To come to dress: the period had, from the start, a use for smart black as well as white. Although Charles II was a 'merrie monarch', raised partly in France, he resolved early in his reign on 'setting a fashion for clothes which he will never alter', aiming 'to teach the nobility thrift'. His 'fashion', introduced in 1666, consisted of a long, close black coat, with an extended black waistcoat or 'vest' beneath it, pinked with white silk. As Samuel Pepys records, the style was quickly copied, but when Charles saw his courtiers en masse, he found the white pinking made them look like magpies, and thereafter used plain black velvet. This smartly plain black coat, with its simple line of buttons from bottom to top, evolved in time into the modern suit.[8]

As portraits, royal and otherwise, show, neither Charles nor most men wore black all the time. But many men, through the eighteenth century, continued to be smart in black, apart from the fact that the

67 Pietro Longhi, *The Ridotto in Venice*, 1750s, oil on canvas.

clergy, lawyers, doctors and many merchants, and also many who were serious in their Protestantism (Huguenots in France, dissenters in England), continued to go about in black. In David's portrait of the French aristocrat-scientist Antoine Lavoisier, Lavoisier wears a black coat, black breeches, black hose and black shoes in the smartest style, at once wealthily aristocratic and dedicated to serious inquiry (illus. 68). He also wears a white wig, shows white materials at the neck and cuff, and writes with a white quill on white paper. His wife and co-scientist Marie-Anne Lavoisier has white skin (well-sheltered from the sun), hair (not a wig) that is powdered white, white lace at the neck, and a beautiful, diaphanous gown of white muslin (worn with a sash of pale blue silk). Strong colour attends them, however – in the over-ample tablecloth of sumptuous red velvet on which the scientific instruments stand. Lavoisier named both oxygen and hydrogen, but this did not save him from the guillotine.

In this portrait white shows strongest, and Lavoisier's black is like an accent, giving the picture intensity. Black may best be thought of, in the eighteenth century, as a strong – the strongest – accent in a light and coloured world. Whatever colour coats might be, the male figure still was punctuated by black. A black tricorn hat sat on most white wigs; black slippers on the white hose on most male legs. The wig might be tied at the back with black ribbon, or gathered in a black silk bag. Or again, one's real hair (not a welcome sight) might be gathered in a bag. In Richardson's *Pamela*, Pamela complains of a Frenchman she meets, 'he wears his own frightful hair, tied up in a great black bag'. Both gentleman and lady might have black 'beauty spots' on their white-powdered faces – small discs of black silk stuck on with gum. In France they were called *mouches*, black flies on the face. In the court of Catherine the Great in Russia some ladies had their teeth lacquered black – for beauty (and doubtless for other reasons).[9]

Women's dress, like men's, might have a black accent, as in the thick black velvet bands worn by Gainsborough's Lady Alston. For the ladies (and some men) the muff had arrived, and could be of the lustrous black fur of the sable. Women might also wear (from the mid-seventeenth century) a dark or black fur mask. Wenceslaus Hollar's etching *Winter*, of 1643, suggests the intrigue, and possibly a sinister edge, in dark-to-black furs (illus. 69). The poem beneath the print reads:

68 Jacques-Louis David, *Monsieur Lavoisier and His Wife*, 1788, oil on canvas.

The cold, not cruelty makes her weare   Winter   For a smoother skinn at night,
In Winter, furrs and Wild beasts haire   Embraceth her with more delight.

69 Wenceslaus Hollar, *Winter*, 1643, etching.

The cold, not cruelty makes her weare
In Winter, furrs and Wild beasts haire
For a smoother skinn at night
Embraceth her with more delight.

Though the lines are dissociative, their effect is to sexualize the mask, while the shadow of cruelty falls both on it and on its wearer. Putting this print together with Hollar's other fur studies, where his eye caresses every hair, one may suspect a fetishism in his attaction to black softnesses – the more so given the routine way in which he draws women, their little mouths inert and mute. The mask can seem as active in looking as the cold-kitten eyes behind it.

Masks were not entirely new, for in Tudor England ladies sometimes wore light vizard-masks to protect them from wind or sun. But it was in the mid-seventeenth century, and especially after Charles II returned to the throne bringing fashions from France, that masks became notably à la mode. Tudor masks had often been white, but the new fashion-masks were almost always black: the word 'mask' may derive from the old French *mascurer*, to blacken. They were worn at the theatre, partly for reasons of discretion. In 1663 Samuel Pepys noticed Lady Falconbridge put on her mask as the playhouse filled, and keep it on throughout the performance. She was Mary, the daughter of Oliver Cromwell, whose body had recently been exhumed in disgrace; she may have preferred to be incognito. Pepys's general comment is that the wearing of masks 'is become a great fashion among the ladies, which hides their whole face'. Leaving the playhouse – it is late afternoon – Pepys and his wife go shopping, partly so she too can buy a mask.[10]

Probably there was nothing sinister in the mask bought for Elizabeth Pepys, simply a pleasure in teasing, such as Pepys observed on another visit to the theatre, with his wife and Sir Charles Sedley.

And one of the ladies . . . did sit with her *mask* on, all the play, and, being exceeding witty as ever I heard woman, did talk most pleasantly with [Sedley]; but was, I believe, a virtuous woman, and of quality. He would fain know who she was, but she would not tell; yet . . . did give him leave to use all means to find out who she was, but pulling off her mask. He was mighty witty, and she also making sport

with him very inoffensively, that a more pleasant 'rencontre'
I never heard.

Clearly the mask gave both parties an exhilarating freedom, justified
by their play of wit, while perhaps what they managed, through the
longueurs of the play, was a satisfying – and safe – sublimation of sex.
Sedley and the lady, flirting through the eyeholes of a mask, are more
innocent than Pepys himself, who earlier that day was at his office,
'where je had Mrs Burrows all sola a my closet, and did there baiser
and toucher ses mamelles' before going to the theatre with his wife.[11]

Both the intrigue of the mask, and its utility as disguise, were
appreciated by the prostitutes who haunted London's theatreland,
and it was said that by the century's end, prostitutes were the principal users of masks. Thus, if the mask had not been too sinister in the
mid-century, it could be so in the 1690s, leering beside a street-
door – 'Good sir, come hither.' Then it no longer hid the character
of its wearer, and was perhaps worn simply to entice, though it
might conceal a syphilitic sore, or a nose with the cartilage eaten away,
such as Fielding described and Hogarth drew. A genre of popular
print evolved, where we see – though the lover does not – that the
maiden's mask conceals a rotting skull.

By the early 1700s, if not before, masks had been both sexual-
ized and dramatized. One might then expect society to drop them,
but the opposite happened. In the 1710s Johann Jacob Heideggar
– a Swiss count and unsuccessful diplomat who had become man-
ager of the Haymarket Theatre – began to organize masked balls
on nights when the theatre had no opera. The 'masquerades' were
vastly popular, and were patronized by the merchant class, the aristocracy and sometimes the monarchy, while the ticket price, of five
shillings or less, allowed in footmen, housemaids and apprentices –
and prostitutes also. The arrangements reflected the Carnivals of
Catholic countries, where social ranks were reversed, and sometimes genders: a duchess might come as a milkmaid, a hairdresser
as a Sultan, a young gentlewoman as a hussar, all of them wearing
masks. Unlike the Carnival, the London masquerades were not confined to the period before Lent, and did not overflow into the streets
or go on for days. They were run for profit and were contained by the
Haymarket Theatre or the Vauxhall or Ranelagh Gardens; or, after
1760, by Carlisle House in Soho, and the assembly rooms known as

the Pantheon, where the opera-singing courtesan Mrs Theresa Cornelys took over as principal impresario.[12]

Behind the masks, the great dressed regularly as the humble, and the humble as the great, though it is hard to say now to what extent their dressing up provided a 'safety valve' that preserved the status quo, and to what extent a subversive impulse worked with real effect. It is a fact that as political tensions increased in Europe, moving towards real revolution in France (in 1789) and to serious fear of revolution in England, the fashion for the masquerade faded, and could be said to have died by the 1790s. Attendance in the 1780s was 'thin', Carlisle House was demolished in 1788, the Pantheon burned down in 1792, and Mrs Cornelys (after a brief period trading in asses' milk) died bankrupt in the Fleet Prison in 1797.

In their heyday, however (from 1710 to 1760), the masquerades were a show of noise, laughter, colour. Wine (canary and champagne) was free, several orchestras played at once, and the Haymarket was lit by 500 candles. Revellers might come as Persian monarchs, orange-girls, Harlequins, Roman soldiers or Circassian maids. There was a touch of Halloween: a corpse came to one ball, a dancing coffin to another, and one or more devils, black from head to cloven foot, brandished their pitchforks at most masquerades. For black was the most common single colour. Many masqueraders came in a domino – a loose, enveloping gown – which could be white or blue, but most often was black. Others came in the black habits of monks, friars and nuns, the black gowns of rabbis and Orthodox priests, or the black clothes of Methodist preachers; or as chimney sweeps with black brooms. Africans were not forgotten, though a 'blackamoor' would be tribal, not a slave; the sexual prestige of Africans was alluded to when, in 1768, a Miss Pelham came in the guise of a blackamore, with legs that were entirely bare but also entirely black.

The single most common black item of costume was the mask itself. It was either a black disc with holes for eyes and mouth or a black rectangle for the top half of the face; it was tied on with strings or sometimes held on a stick like a lorgnette. The century clearly loved to play at showing and hiding both face and eyes. In Francis Hayman's painting of David Garrick and Mrs Pritchard there is a witty reciprocity in the game the man and woman play with each other and with us (illus. 70). He lifts his black tricorn hat to hide

70 Francis Hayman, David Garrick as Ranger and Mrs Pritchard as Clarinda in a scene from Benjamin Hoadly, *The Suspicious Husband* (*c.* 1747), 1752, oil on canvas.

his face, while she holds her black (slightly sinister) mask down from her face. Neither sees the other's face, though we see both; they play with masking and performance within the play *The Suspicious Husband*, even as they perform it.

Instead of black, one might wear the mask of a blood-red devil, or a dead-white half-mask with a grotesque big nose, but this again had a black veil hanging under it, to cover mouth and chin. Dancers played with false voices (masqueraders were said to squeak and hoot), but above all they played – or worked – with their eyes. They had the freedom of disguise, and the resource of libido on the loose. For the mask, one might say, is the supreme mascara and needs small prompting from the eye that it accentuates to launch its innuendo of mystery and excitement.

One might here consider at large the relationship between the human eye and blackness. Eyelashes are often dark, and at its centre the eye has a black pupil, which dilates in dim light or during sexual arousal, when it may darken the whole iris. Perhaps for this reason eye cosmetics (such as kohl) have been predominantly dark and very often black. Literature may associate deeply dark eyes with a chaste, longing love, but the dominant association of 'black eyes', Black-Eyed Susans and black-eyed maidens in fiction is with powerful desire and desirability, even to the point of fearfulness. These associations were already established when Shakespeare's Biron both complained and exalted in the fact that his girl 'had two pitch-balls stuck in her face for eyes'. And when Andrew Marvell paints his beloved, in 'The Gallery', as 'an inhuman murderess', he places 'black eyes' among 'the most tormenting . . . engines' within her 'cruel arts'.[13]

'The Ballad of Black-Eyed Susan' was itself written early in the eighteenth century by a poet much involved with the London theatre and the London streets, John Gay. Susan's eyes are black and shine from weeping – though actually she is both white and black, containing together the lights and darks of India and of Africa. Her departing lover, a naval seaman, sings:

If to fair India's coast we sail,
Thy eyes are seen in diamonds bright:
Thy breath is Afric's spicy gale,
Thy skin as ivory so white:

His ship itself is a fertile woman ('Her sails their swelling bosom spread'). Hereafter black-eyed maids recur in poetry – in the early verse of William Blake, for instance ('to my black-eyed maid I haste away'), and in Byron's *Don Juan* they are numerous. Most notably, Juan's 'Romagnole' has eyes that are 'black and burning as a coal'. Byron's attitude is relaxed – he later says 'an eye's an eye, and whether black or blue, / Is no great matter, so 'tis in request'.[14] In later verse and popular song 'black eyes' may at times be a cliché, and then again reassert their original power. For the arresting potency, the enticing menace of actual 'black eyes' would seem a permanency in human life.

As to the general role of black in masquerades, one could say that black plays with its own solemnities when revellers come as monks, nuns or priests, and that it plays with its dark side when they come as devils, witches or as hooded Deaths. But that sort of play was a dance on a knife-edge, since the masked enticer might lead you away to forced sex, an unwanted pregnancy or the discovery (later) that your genitals burned with the pox. The contemporary novel played on these uncertainties. When the heroine of Fanny Burney's novel *Cecilia* (1782) goes to a masquerade, 'the very first mask who approached her . . . was the devil! He was black from head to foot . . . his face was so completely covered that the sight only of his eyes was visible.' He bows obsequiously, looms close above her and, using his fiery wand as a weapon, menaces or strikes other maskers, who retire, including a Don Quixote who briefly defies him and 'the black bile which floateth within [his] sable exterior'. The devil then begins 'a growling, so dismal and disagreeable' that other onlookers desert Cecilia, while she learns that if everyone is disguised, then you are truly alone. She is increasingly molested and menaced until a chimney sweep of equal blackness, dropping real soot, accosts the devil roughly and allows her to escape. It is no surprise to learn later that the devil, this 'black Lucifer', is the novel's unscrupulous villain Monkton, who is the real scheming devil in Cecilia's story, being equally infatuated with her body and her fortune.[15] Names with 'monk' in them serve well for villains in Protestant novels, like the villain 'Monks' in Dickens's *Oliver Twist*, who gives 'dark and evil looks' and wears a dark cloak, as monks, villains and devils were all known to do. In the direct representation of monks as villains in other Protestant novels – in the Gothic genre – one may see the black of the church becoming little different from the black of goblins and devils.

In later art the masquerade can be morbidly gruesome – in the etchings of Goya, for instance, where masks may seem alive with evil. In Edgar Allan Poe's 'The Masque of the Red Death', of the next century, the unknown mask, dressed in a winding sheet spotted with blood, is Death. But the eighteenth century too saw the shadow behind its play: in contemporary engravings, those attending the masquerade may huddle and squabble, a half-animal rabble, and Death may be among them. In Rowlandson's drawing *The Masquerade* Death is a supple skeleton; he brandishes his dart and a devil's-face mask (illus. 71). His black domino dances with him, curling through the air, while in the foreground Harlequin (in a black mask) and other dancers, dressed like the Devil or like pashas, tumble over each other as they flee. In the further background the dance goes on, with the hectic abandon of Death's own dance. Earlier, in Edward Young's *Night Thoughts* (1742–5), Death had been 'the dreadful masquerader' who 'leads the dance . . . gaily carousing' until he 'drops his mask . . . his black mask of nitre . . . and devours'.[16]

71 Thomas Rowlandson, 'The Masquerade', illustration from William Combe, *The English Dance of Death* (1815–16), hand-coloured etching with aquatint.

In Young we see the dark side of the masquerade joined with the ongoing fashion for melancholy. For eighteenth-century poetry had its own 'black accent', in the gloomy visions of the 'graveyard poets'. Their focus is on transience and death, contemplated in the darkness of night and the tomb, standing alone beneath sad cypress trees. In Young's *Night Thoughts*, 'the black raven' hovers while Night, the 'sable goddess, from her ebon throne' lets her 'black mantle fall'. In Robert Blair's *The Grave*, of 1743, the poet wanders 'the gloomy aisles / Black plaister'd' of some 'hallow'd fane' while 'night's foul bird, / Rook'd in the spire, screams loud' and 'grisly spectres rise'. A 'new-made widow . . . crawls along in doleful black'.[17] The poem's tone is not however morosely depressed, and could even be called exalted, while Young had said 'How populous, how vital is the grave!' At times these pensive, pessimistic poets seem positively to revel in death's accessories, in crypts and vaults, in skulls and winding sheets and coffins, which recur again in the growing fashion for the 'Gothic' novel. For though the eighteenth century knew real depressive illness – such as affected William Cowper and possibly Samuel Johnson – the culture of melancholy has an element of theatre about it. Thomas Young and Robert Blair are latter-day Hamlets, and at times echo, with a sombre delectation, his truly depressive eloquence.

In the last decades of the century it became positively fashionable for young people to be mournful, to dress in black, and to read sad verses in country cemeteries. In doing so they were pioneers in the new black fashion which was to envelop so many departments of life as the eighteenth century moved into the nineteenth. Then it might seem, to someone watching from a distance, as if the black shadows of the sixteenth and seventeenth centuries had, after all, been simply sleeping, and woke again with an appetite to swallow the world.

72 Detail of cast-iron balconette at 7 Adam St, Westminster, London, *c.* 1770s.

NINE

Britain's Black Century

AT THE END of chapter Four of Virginia Woolf's *Orlando*, the heroine watches over London as midnight strikes. She notices

> a small cloud gathered behind the dome of St Paul's. As the strokes sounded . . . she saw it darken and spread with extra - ordinary speed . . . As the ninth, tenth, and eleventh strokes struck, a huge blackness sprawled over the whole of London . . . The Eighteenth century was over; the Nineteenth century had begun.

Much was black in the nineteenth century – frock coats, velvet dresses, hansom cabs, chimney sweeps. Wine came in a black bottle. If ill, injured or concussed, one took a 'black draught' (made from senna, Epsom salts, cardamom and ginger). The air itself could be bitter with soot. Running the different blacks loosely together, one may see the century as the Age of Black in an almost mystical way. Is there a unitary meaning to the century's blackness? But first one must distinguish the different blacks in play. I concentrate on Britain because the new black turn began here, but draw some images from elsewhere because of their clarity and quality.

Black menswear, which had a smart but low profile through the eighteenth century, became more prominent at the turn of the century. The move to black in evening dress (for men) became decisive when it was adopted by Beau Brummell in the 1810s, and mimicked by his then friend the Prince Regent, setting the fashion for all of society. Knee-breeches by now looked dated and were succeeded by black trousers, first in the skin-tight form known as pantaloons, though by 1820 the loose leg (much like modern trousers) had arrived.

Men's daytime wear blackened through the 1820s, the frock coat becoming mainly black in the early 1830s and daytime trousers in the later '30s (in the cool months especially). Also in the 1830s the cravat changed from mainly white to mainly black, while the evening waistcoat gave up colour for black or white in the 1840s. George Routledge added, in his *Manual of Etiquette* (1860), 'And let your hat be always black.' A gentleman's handkerchief might be of black silk. More colours could be worn in the daytime, but many men still chose black. Anthony Trollope remarks in *The Eustace Diamonds* (1871), 'With Mr Dove every visible article of his raiment was black, except his shirt, and he had that peculiar blackness which a man achieves when he wears a dress-coat over a high black waistcoat in the morning.'[1]

In the learned professions, barristers and clergy of 'the old school' still wore black breeches with black hose, but physicians and teachers, and new professionals like engineers, wore the new smart evening style during the day; so did bankers and merchants. The style, with its rules, percolated downwards, so that clerks in the lawyer's chambers or in the merchant's counting house wore black, as servants did in the home. For to flaunt extreme wealth it was now necessary to have two sorts of servant, some in livery and wigs from the eighteenth century and others in the new black. Describing the household of a great financier, Trollope says, 'Of the certainty of the money . . . there could be no doubt . . . There were the servants with the livery coats and powdered heads, and the servants with the black coats and unpowdered heads.'[2] The best coats were of black kerseymere (cashmere) or of superfine black broadcloth, but cheaper black woollens were available, and the use of black as a work-colour spread, until in the 1870s Thomas Hardy noted that farm-workers went to the fields in black suits. At all levels black had brilliance because it was worn with white – a white shirt especially. There were also the white gloves that a gentleman kept in his pocket in the evening, and slipped on were he likely to touch his partner in dancing a waltz or a polka. The top hat was occasionally white, and made of beaver-fur.

As with any colour used widely, black acquired different and even opposite values, which coexisted without confusion because everyone understood them. With differences of material, and in age, cut and costliness, black could signify wealth, a competence or shabby-gentility. Black could be proudly aristocratic, or solidly respectable; sexually exhilarating, or churchy and moralistic. It was however seldom frivolous, and on its serious side it embodied the anxious severity of a class-ridden and Bible-ridden society that was frightened by its own rapid changes and latent unrest and devoted to many forms of control, including self-control. There may be exaggeration in fiction's depiction of sadistic father-figures in black being piously harsh to their wives, children and employees. I have nonetheless argued, in another book (*Men in Black*, 1997), that men's habitual wearing of modest but assertive, serious, Christian, all-black clothes did serve to reinforce a severe male authoritarian-ism in the world, in marriages and in the home.

The world was not all monochrome, and in *Tancred* (1847) Benjamin Disraeli describes 'a character of the class of artists' who wears a bright blue frock-coat, green trousers (frogged and braided), a maroon waistcoat and primrose gloves. Some high-life dandies, like the Count d'Orsay, also dressed so. They were however con-spicuous because the world was different; the outward character of men's black clothes is given in Mrs Catherine Gore's novel *The Banker's Wife* (1843), when the banker Hamlyn walks through his count-ing-house, 'spruce, black, lustrous', with a brow that is serene and a smile that is bland.[3]

Black was not so widespread in women's dress, which was light in tone and often white, the colour-coding of gender being more marked in the nineteenth century than ever before. Stronger colours were available, however – deep reds and blues – even before the arrival of aniline dyes in the 1850s added mauve, magenta and chrome yellow. But a black item was often worn – a lace shawl, a velvet mantle, a black fur jacket, a silk pelisse. The 'best dress' a woman had was very often black. It might be of black velvet: the novelist Dinah Craik admired a 'black velvet gown, substantial, soft, and rich, without any show'. Often the 'best dress' was black silk, but while silk was good, black satin was better. In Charlotte Bronte's *Shirley* a daughter forbids her mother to wear her 'old gown any more' – 'You shall put on your black silk every afternoon . . . And you shall have a black satin dress for Sundays – a real satin, not satinet, or any of the shams.' The mother responds economically, 'My dear, I thought of the black silk serving me as a best dress for many years yet.' For the nineteenth century knew how to make black silks last: Mrs Beeton advised on washing ('if old and rusty, a pint of common spirits should be mixed with each gallon of water') and drying ('in the shade, on a linen-horse . . . they will be improved if laid again on the table, when dry, and sponged with gin or whiskey'). But the daughter will have none of this. 'Nonsense, mamma. My uncle gives me cash to get what I want . . . and I have set my heart on seeing you in a black satin.'[4]

These dresses are not mourning dresses, but nineteenth-century women spent many weeks or months of their lives mourning for relatives at various degrees of remove as well as for sadly many children. Also, as Mrs Beeton said, 'visitors, in paying condoling visits, should be dressed in black'. Though mourning dresses should not be lustrous, and were mostly made in dulled silk crape, they could be elaborate in their crochet insertions, slashed velvet borders and trims of goffered tulle – not to mention the coiffure, perhaps of black velvet coral with black ostrich feathers. Sarah Ellis in *The Women of England: Their Social Duties and Domestic Habits* (1839) mocked the wasteful expense of mourning: 'So extremely becoming and ladylike is the fashionable style of mourning, that, under the plea of paying greater respect to the memory of the dead, it has become an object of ambition to wear it in its greatest excellence.'[5]

These blacks may sound sedate, but black is also worn by Trollope's attractive, dynamic American woman, Mrs Winifred Hurtle, who has killed a man 'somewhere in Oregon'. Her 'silken hair' is 'almost black', and 'her dress was always black, – not a sad weeping widow's garment, but silk or woollen or cotton as the case might be, always new, always nice, always well-fitting, and most especially always simple. She was certainly a most beautiful woman, and she knew it.' In June she wears the light silk weave known as grenadine, 'a light gauzy black dress . . . It was very pretty, and she was prettier'. There is no suggestion that her black style follows from her (self-defensive) skill with firearms, nor is she a widow. Her blacks do relate to her being American, since the fashion for black – both for men and for women – was stronger again in America than in Europe, influenced both by the puritan tradition and by the emerging association of black with democracy.[6]

Then there was the jewellery. Men had jet buttons at their pockets and cuffs, and their shirt-studs might be of black pearl. Women wore black jewellery not only when in mourning (mourning wear was not to glitter), but because – in the 1860s, '70s and '80s especially –

black jewellery was the fashion. The stones might be jet, onyx, vulcanite or black tourmaline, or again black pearl. *Routledge's Manual of Etiquette* noted that 'a natural rarity, such as a black pearl, is a more distingué possession than a large brilliant', and warned against common black beads.[7] A jet pendant or locket would be worn round the neck with a strip of black velvet.

Items about the home would be black. In the lady's dressing room, her powder jar, glove-stretcher, bonnet brush and darning egg might be of ebony. If tea were served in the drawing room, it might be brought in on a tray of papier mâché, japanned black all over. When the well-to-do family rode out, their barouche, chariot, landau or phaeton might again be black-japanned. If open, its hood would be of blackened leather, as would the harness of the horses (which might again be beautifully black). Not everything was always black: there was a fashion called the 'French Style' with deep and florid colours. Still, considering the number of fine blacks in use, we could imagine that the nineteenth century had something like an aesthetic of blackness.

Not all the furniture was ebony, but oak – which was much used – was often stained black. In his *Hints on Household Taste* (1869) Charles Eastlake said that 'unpolished mahogany acquires a good colour with age', but he went on: 'it also looks very well stained black and covered with a thin varnish'. He said of mirror frames that 'if in the commoner kinds of wood they can be ebonized (i.e. stained black)', and many chairs, rocking chairs, tables and sideboards were. Eastlake recommended also bedroom chairs and rush-bottomed nursery chairs 'of which the woodwork is stained black'.[8]

Also, the century's new products often came in black. Cast iron is a blackish grey, lying fresh in the foundry mould, and it was normally 'dressed' with paint that had a high bitumen content to protect it from corrosion – bitumen or pitch being a natural black preservative whose use goes back to Ur and earlier. Bitumen was already the principal ingredient in japan, the black varnish applied to woodwork (named after Japanese lacquer). By adding a small amount of vegetable carbon, the paint for ironwork could be given an eggshell finish, and this fine black paint was known as Berlin black (because it was used for their cast-iron jewellery by the Berlin Royal Ironworks). Berlin black is the recommended 'best finish' for many cast-iron fenders and fire-irons offered in the 1875 catalogue of the

Coalbrookdale Company (a principal producer of wrought and cast iron), as also for fire dogs, door porters and umbrella or stick stands. The surround to a cast-iron fire insert might be of Welsh grey-black slate, often painted to mimic black marble. A fireplace might be one massive piece of cast iron, dressed black, with gothic finials and Solomonic (corkscrew) columns built into it, with small cast-iron angels beside the fire basket supporting an Anglo-Saxon arch, thus completing the consecration of a pious and British hearth. Fine cast iron decorated the house, both inside and outside – as in the 'balconettes' designed by Robert Adam which decorate the house, also designed by him, at 7 Adam Street, Westminster (illus. 72).

Not that black is an easy colour, since it shows up dust and smears. Mrs Beeton gives numerous tips for keeping blacks 'bright'. Among her first duties each day, the housemaid should black-lead the cast-iron grate, and brush it to a polish. If rust has appeared, she should apply Brunswick black (less lustrous than Berlin black), and a recipe is given for this (asphalt, linseed oil and turpentine). Furniture should be polished with a gloss made of wax, black rosin and turpentine. For such work the maid should wear a black apron; for serving tea to guests she should wear a white one. Moving to menservants, Mrs Beeton recommends for boots and shoes good commercial blacking, and if that is not available she again gives a recipe (ivory black and treacle, plus sulphuric acid, olive oil and vinegar). For patent leather footwear, a little milk may be used 'with very good effect'. Visiting the stables, she gives a recipe for blacking harnesses and the leatherwork of carriages (wax mixed with ivory black, thinned with turpentine and scented with 'any essence at hand'). If the leather was not black to start with, she recommends one or two coats of black ink before the polish is applied.[9]

To know more of the century's 'aesthetic' of black, one might turn to the article on ironwork in the *Art Union* journal of 1846.

> The characteristic, and what may be called the 'natural' colour of those [iron] castings, is a brilliant and beautiful jet black produced upon the casting when dressed . . . This [the 'dressing'] is a very delicate operation, and requires great skill in the manipulation, but the results are beautiful.

The author is not uncritical, for those recommending black were aware of its difficulties. 'There is however one defect: all shadow is lost on the black surface, and hence delicate tracery and minute details of form run a very obvious hazard of being overlooked.' The author notes that many products are 'bronzed over', but is unhappy with 'a disguise of material'. His attitude, in sum, is divided: he celebrates forcefully 'a brilliant and beautiful jet black', but also says at one point, almost poignantly, that 'perfect blackness, even accompanied by a high polish, has a sombering effect, from which the wearied eye in vain seeks for the relief it finds by the introduction of colour'.[10]

The author was not alone in his divided attitude to black. In his *Hints on Household Taste* Charles Eastlake recommends the use of black all over the house, but still is troubled by the black clothes that are worn so widely, in which 'occasions of public and private festivity' become indistinguishable from 'occasions of public and private mourning'.[11] Not that a young nineteenth-century couple, wearing their best blacks and surveying a new home at once dark and bright with jet-black accessories, would have been troubled with thoughts of their sombre mournfulness, any more than we have such thoughts about a jet-black BlackBerry, puffer jacket or huge, flat-screen television.

THE PREMIUM ON black was assisted by the fading of the Neo-classical style, with its love of white marble. In architecture taste jumped to the Middle Ages and then advanced backwards, from Gothic (pointed arches) to Romanesque (round arches) to Byzantine (round and florid), all with deep-toned facades often using much brick. China might be deep-coloured, or set its flower patterns against gleaming black. Walls that had been painted a light greenish-grey were covered now with deep-toned wallpapers (assisted by the invention in the 1790s of machines that produced continuous wallpaper, and by the steam-powered printing presses of the 1810s). In the high art of the painting academies, English and French (which both followed, and fed, the general taste), black paint was laid on canvases both to catch Romantic gloom and also from an increasing fascination with Rembrandt.

The return of Rembrandt is an index of the darkening taste, for from the late seventeenth until the late eighteenth century

Rembrandt's art was in dim eclipse. But then in portraiture (Rembrandt's art), from the mid-eighteenth to the late nineteenth centuries, in Reynolds, Lawrence, Romney and Watts, admiration for Rembrandt showed in many dark-to-black backgrounds and in the pleasure in rendering fine black clothes. When thinking of nineteenth-century art, one may think first of protest art, the Pre-Raphaelites in England and the Impressionists later in France, both schools bright with gorgeous colouring. But in both cases the protest was against the dark tones in so many other paintings, and (as they sometimes said) against the quantities of bitumen deployed in innumerable grand battle scenes and deaths of famous generals. John Ruskin, who supported the Pre-Raphaelites so vocally, also said 'you must make black conspicuous . . . it ought to catch the eye'.[12]

For artists, black was not 'outside of any chromatic system', as Michel Pastoureau put it. The popular Royal Academician Edwin Landseer was not committed to chiaroscuro but he loved to render the more-than-silky sheen in the black coats of dogs and horses, in the fine coats of men and in the fine dresses of young women and duchesses. In his painting of Queen Victoria on horseback wearing mourning clothes, the subdued lustre of her silk plays against the more strongly silken lustre in the coat of the beautiful black horse she rides, while John Brown in mourning attendance wears the lustreless black proper to men in his black bonnet, jacket, dark kilt and black socks (illus. 73).

In prints and illustrations there was a positive renaissance of black-and-white art. At the turn of the century Thomas Bewick had revived wood-engraving, which had fallen to the level of street art. He used harder woods than those used for broadsheet ballads, especially box, and he cut into the end-grain rather than the plank. This made finer cutting possible, and printed rich blacks, since ink caught well in the texture of the wood grain. His masterpiece, *A History of British Birds*, came out between 1797 and 1804, with deep blacks and a lively, bold notation for plumage, foliage and water. With time, wood-engraving became the medium of choice for books, journals and news-sheets. The great master of the medium was Gustave Doré, with his genius for dark tones, the deepest blacks and silvery glimmering lights (see illus. 56).

Wood-engravings print like linocuts – or like the letterpress of books – where paper is applied under light pressure to a well-inked

73 Edwin Landseer, *Queen Victoria at Osborne* (*Sorrow*), 1867, oil on canvas.

surface. Most quality prints, however, between the fifteenth and eighteenth centuries, had been made using the intaglio process, where the ink lies in grooves and needs to be picked up by damp paper under high pressure. Dürer and Rembrandt had worked with copper, but in the 1790s engravers began to work on steel, at first in producing banknotes and then for general illustration. The cutting is harder work but finer, and yields its own rich darks. And since acid of the right strength bites into iron as easily as copper, a revival of Rembrandt's art of etching followed. The illustrations for nineteenth-century novels by Dickens, Thackeray and their competitors were etched in steel. The line-work in these plates can be as dense, dark and dramatically black as that of any earlier etcher or engraver, as can be seen in George Cruikshank's gruesome study of a career-executioner readying his tools, 'Mauger Sharpening His Axe', for William Harrison Ainsworth's serial novel *The Tower of London* of 1840 (illus. 74). The artist shares Mauger's relish for well-tempered steel – such as the silver-gleaming plate of new Sheffield steel on which the design itself was etched.

The process of making an etching was as labour-intensive in the nineteenth century as it had been for Rembrandt. The spirit of mechanization did, though, produce some shortcuts for deepening chiaroscuro. *The Stranger at the Grave* is by Hablot Knight Browne,

74 George Cruikshank, 'Mauger Sharpening His Axe', illustration from
William Harrison Ainsworth, *The Tower of London* (1840).

who called himself 'Phiz' when he illustrated Dickens (illus. 75). But
he illustrated Dickens's competitors also, and in this plate for
Ainsworth's novel *Mervyn Clitheroe* (1858) the waxy coat laid on
the metal has been lightly traced with a ruling machine. The fine lines
expose the metal but are then covered, in stages, with stopping-out
varnish. Those lines which are last to be stopped out will be bitten
so deep by the acid that they add a deep tone to the close cross-
hatching, which will again be strengthened by running over the plate

75 Hablot Knight Browne, 'The Stranger at the Grave', illustration for
William Harrison Ainsworth, *Mervyn Clitheroe* (1858), etching.

a 'roulette', a spiked wheel, which directly pits the steel so it holds
more ink. Both effects can be seen in the brighter gravestones, while
the clear spots of moonlight reflected in the lake were made by stopping out the lines before the acid touched the metal. Browne has
worked like any film-maker managing a night scene – balancing
deep darkness with dramatic but low lighting.

   Another intaglio technique, revived and turned to black effect,
was mezzotint. Here the metal is roughened with a fine-toothed
'rocker' until the surface is so rough that it holds much ink and
prints jet-black. If now, with a burnisher, one rubs some places
smooth, they hold less ink and print in greys – or white, if one scours
the metal to flatness.[13] John Martin used this technique for his
visionary illustrations to an edition of Milton's *Paradise Lost* of
1827 (illus. 76). 'The Bridge over Chaos' shows the road that Sin
and Death have built – or rather excavated – to connect our world
with Hell, following the Fall. The tiny crouching form of Sin, and
black Death with his crown, can just be made out in the top right
corner, beside their incestuous parent Satan, who stands with wings
triumphantly spread. Their tiny figures seem hardly equal to this
vast construction work, which resembles the bridges, viaducts and
tunnels which engineers had begun to make in the 1780s and '90s.
But the 'slimie' stuff of Chaos also has an organic look, and might
call to mind the nineteenth century's passion for looking inside the

76 John Martin, 'The Bridge over Chaos', proof of an illustration for
Paradise Lost, 1827, mezzotint.

body (which led to the invention of the endoscope and laryngo-
scope), especially since the tunnel resembles a throat. The succulent
blackness of the mezzotint makes such ambiguous suggestiveness
easy, while the straight black road from earth to Hell looks here
like a ray of Milton's 'darkness visible'.

So for the intaglio print. And in 1796 the Bavarian author Alois
Senefelder invented lithography. Here the artist-printmaker draws
with a greasy crayon or ink on a polished slab of limestone. The image
is fixed with dilute gum arabic. Thereafter, each time one dampens
the plate, then applies an oily printing ink, the ink stays only on the
greasy parts, and prints in black. The process may sound an oily smear,
but it reproduces the most sensitive touch of pen or brush, textured
with the grain of the stone. In the nineteenth century lithography was
used more in France than in England, above all by Honoré Daumier.
An early masterpiece, *Le Ventre législatif* of 1834, shows his genius with
black (illus. 77). The coats, waistcoats, lapels and hats show the different grades of broadcloth, silk and velvet which were then in fashion
– especially in the stout foremost waistcoat – while the black eyes and
eye shadows show other grades, of irony, misgiving, calculation.

By the later nineteenth century the development of photo engraving made possible the line-block, in which a drawing, in Indian ink

on paper, is reproduced exactly. In Aubrey Beardsley's cover for an
1894 issue of *The Yellow Book*, the dramatic, slender woman dressed
in black can seem a touch demonic though she is also young and
pretty – and a literary connoisseur (illus. 78). Her shallow profile
suggests she is of mixed race, and her clear sexual magnetism pro-
vokes a suspicious, delectating stare in the old pot-bellied bookseller
who is so oddly dressed in the white masquerade outfit of a *com-
media dell'arte* Pierrot. With its steep perspective, and obscure menace,
the drawing implies an ambiguous intrigue in the contents of this
'illustrated quarterly'.

The development of photoengraving could occur only after
the invention of photography – the most significant innovation
in the century's nurture of the black-and-white image. That invention effectively occurred in the 1820s, when pewter or copper plates
were coated with light-sensitive compounds such as bitumen of
Judea. The process became commercial with the development of the
daguerreotype in the 1830s, in which copper is coated with iodized
silver. It would be easy to demonstrate, in the deeply dark tones of
early photographs, a 'Caravaggesque' or 'Rembrandtesque' use of
chiaroscuro, in which the shadows on face and background abruptly deepen to black. The photograph *Paula, Berlin* by Alfred Stieglitz

77 Honoré Daumier, 'Le Ventre législatif', published in *L'Association Mensuelle*
(18 January 1834), lithograph.

78 Aubrey Beardsley, cover for *The Yellow Book* (15 April 1894), line-block from drawing in Indian ink.

79 Alfred Stieglitz, *Paula, Berlin*, 1889, photograph.

shows a broader continuity in European image-making (illus. 79).
It could recall those paintings by Jan Vermeer in which a woman, lit
by a bright window to the left, is almost still in thoughtful privacy.
In Vermeer she may be reading a letter, as here she is writing one, while
the shadows round her deepen to black. But Stieglitz's photograph
uses light and shadow in a way no painter would. The slats in the
Venetian blind cast bars of shadow throughout the interior. This
element of abstract pattern plays against other patterns (such as the
finer grids of the wicker chair-back and the birdcage) and against

80 Georges Seurat, *The Artist's Mother*, 1882–3, Conté crayon on paper.

the human clutter of photographs and paper hearts pinned to the wall. This effect has often been used later in film, most patently in the works of Orson Welles, most beautifully in the scene in Fellini's *La dolce vita* in which the character played by Mastroianni meets briefly a young girl in a seaside tavern. He, she, all the tavern, are lightly crossed by thin lines of shadow from the reed sides and roof, which together with the light breeze contribute to the sense of an evanescent interruption within the orgiastic drift of the sweet life. In *Paula, Berlin* too the slats add a living indeterminacy.

If photography was the newest art-black of the century, the oldest black of all continued, in the widespread use by artists of charcoal – charred sticks. The beautiful drawing of his mother by Georges Seurat is not actually in charcoal but in Conté crayon, but the interrupted play of the carbon stick on the roughness of the paper has the same eloquent materiality which the first artist found, when he or she outlined a prized animal on a cave wall with burned firewood (illus. 80). We see a flat, black-rubbed texture and a face sunk deep in time – in human time, through the distance of a life, and in art time too, since this picture made by the oldest means is modern in effect but recalls the art of Holbein.

GIVEN THE STRONG part played by black in nineteenth-century image-making – including the invention in 1840 of the photographic negative – it is no surprise to find that black had a positive character for those who wrote on optics. It is true that black lies outside the spectrum, but in any case there was a growing interest in colours beyond the colours we see. In 1800 Frederick William Herschel discovered invisible light when he held a thermometer with a blackened bulb just beyond the red end of the spectrum, and got a higher reading of heat than he had from the spectral colours. This un-seeable wavelength was named infra-red, and in 1801 Johann Wilhelm Ritter, working in the German city of Jena, discovered ultraviolet light when he placed silver chloride – which turns black in sunlight – beyond the other, violet end of the spectrum, and found that it darkened more intensely there than when placed among the visible colours.

The study of sight and optics extended to black's role in design. When the French chemist Michel Eugène Chevreul became director of the dye-works at the Gobelins Factory, most famous for its tapestries, he needed to understand how the perception of a colour affects the colours next to it. In *The Principles of Harmony and Contrast of Colours and Their Applications to the Arts* (1839), the discussion of fundamentals is rich with incidental advice as to clothes, complexions, carpets. In clothing and pictures alike, he notes, a black will be tinted – but slightly – by the colour that is complimentary to the strong colour next to it (so black, next to red, will look slightly green). Also black looks less black when next to a dark colour – so soldiers who mean to be inconspicuous may wear, with black trousers, a sombre tunic. Addressing the elderly, he observes that black dims the tone of other clothes; and while black clothes make the skin look white, they also make flushed skin look redder, and redder again in a mottled complexion. He is concerned also for 'the dress of women with black or olive skins', noting that 'if the complexion is intense black, or dark olive, or greenish-black, red is preferable to every other colour; if the black is bluish, then orange is particularly suitable. Yellow will best accord with a violet-black.'[14]

The most comprehensive investigation of sight was Hermann von Helmholtz's *Treatise on Physiological Optics* (1856). Helmholtz was emphatic on the positive character of black: 'Black is a real sensation, even if it is produced by entire absence of light. The sensation of black is distinctly different from the lack of all sensation.'[15] Though emphatic, Helmholtz is not here analytical, and it remained for Karl Ewald Hering, in the 1880s, to argue that the receptors in the retina worked according to contrasts, and that the black-white receptors would signal their excitement both when they 'saw' white and when they 'saw' black. This view conforms to the current understanding of the way in which we see darks and blacks.

I have left until now Goethe's *Theory of Colours* (1810), because it stands proudly separate from the broad development of colour theory. Goethe looks a degree perverse, since, in his determination to refute Newton, he refused to accept that the colours of the spectrum are contained in white light. White light, for Goethe, had to be pure, and he harks back to Aristotle in arguing that strong hues – crimson, gold, deep blues and greens – are made by mixing white light with darkness. And it is true, as he says, that yellow is a lighter colour than blue, and that efforts to deepen yellow pigments drive them down towards orange and red. But though he is mistaken on the nature of light – comparing Newton's theory to an abandoned castle 'nodding to its fall' – he is minutely observant on the subject-ive aspect of colour vision, noticing for instance that black or white objects will often seem to show a blue or red edge. Black has a pri-mary value for him, since he argues that deep, rich colour is, as it were, a refraction of darkness – he speaks of 'the dark nature of colour, its full rich quality'.[16]

Goethe's theory was certainly of interest to England's greatest painter (then and so far), J.M.W. Turner, who titled a late painting *Colour and Light (Goethe's Theory) – The Morning after the Deluge – Moses Writing the Book of Genesis.* And the element of mysticism in Goethe's attitude to light and darkness would surely have appealed to Turner, whose representation of dazzling radiance – in *Norham Castle, Sunrise* for instance – can verge on the transcendental. As to black, it is notable that something dark or black often occupies a near-central position in Turner's paintings. Often it is in tension with a radiant setting or rising sun, also near-centre, which is both the brightest and the furthest thing we see, while the dark object is near, and nothing stands between it and us. The most dramatic black central presence is the paddle steamer of death in *Peace – Burial at Sea* of 1842 (illus. 81). The black mast and sails stand tall like a silhouette crucifixion, reflecting the grief and reverence – at once artistic and religious – which Turner felt at the solemn com-mittal to water of the remains of his great contemporary, the painter David Wilkie.

If not a sailboat in silhouette, the dark object may be a crag or a hazardous pile in shallow water. In several paintings, as in *Peace*, it may also be an item of the age's new machinery, both black and luminous in its coal-fuelled steam power. In *The Fighting Temeraire Tugged to Her Last Berth to Be Broken Up* (1838), the small paddle-wheeled tug which makes towards us is all black or brown, with a tall black funnel issuing brown-black smoke (illus. 82). The novelist and art critic William Makepeace Thackeray called the tug 'spiteful', 'diabolical' and a 'little demon' because of its contrast with the majes-tic, whitely luminous warship (whose redundant white sails are tightly furled). The painting is also, though, a portrait of irresistible power, with the tiny modern vessel pulling slowly but with ease the grand, doomed bulk behind it. The tug's black is fiery, and there is clearly some comparison between the black and the white ship

81 J.M.W. Turner, *Peace – Burial at Sea*, 1842, oil on canvas.

and the white beauty of the setting sun, which is attended by a
light hang of red-black clouds, while an obscure, near-black object
to the right rises ominously out of the water. Thackeray's facetious
demonism simplifies a picture that has a big ambiguity, in which
a strong sense of fate or fatality is joined to an enormous peace
and beauty.[17]

There is no such play of past and present in *Keelmen Heaving in
Coals by Moonlight*, a Tyneside scene showing coals from Newcastle
being loaded for London (illus. 83). What is remarkable, rather, is
the way this scene of heavy labour, in a rising cloud of coal-dust, has
struck Turner with its beauty. For the glory of moonlight at its
brightest, made with grades of blue and silver, touches evenly the
placid water and the labouring men, one of whom can be made out
lifting high a shovel-load of coal. The men and boats are black as their

82 J.M.W. Turner, *The Fighting Temeraire Tugged to Her Last Berth to Be Broken Up*, 1838, oil on canvas.

83 J.M.W. Turner, *Keelmen Heaving in Coals by Moonlight*, 1835, oil on canvas.

coal, and the torchlight flares in places, but the regular activity has a calm: as it were, the peace of work, such as Turner too may have felt in the concentrated labour of painting. The whole scene may be quiet, except for the tumbling of coal in the chutes, for what struck Henry Mayhew in the London docks – at the other end of the coal-ships' voyage – was the steady silence in which the coal-whippers lifted coal from the hold, compared with the songs the sailors sang when hauling up sails or turning a winch.[18] The dark objects in the foreground here are the broad black bucket and wooden ladle – utensils presumably of the coal-trade – on the puzzling brown shape in the water near us: emblems, nonetheless, of the Industrial Revolution – which so far I have hardly mentioned, though it had so much to do with the blackening of the century.

TO MOVE, THEN, to the century's 'other black'. For the Industrial Revolution had reached its black fruition through the same run of dates that saw the growth of black fashion in menswear and home furnishings and the invention of new black techniques in art – that is, through the first half of the nineteenth century and especially in the four decades from 1800 to 1840.

The rise of coal, steel and steam had been in several senses black. As to dates, the mechanical revolution had gathered speed in the later eighteenth century. But though steam was harnessed in the 1760s, James Watt's engine was relatively weak, working more by suction as the cylinder cooled than from the thrust of pressured steam. It could however pump water out of mineshafts, enabling coalmines to be dug deeper and with longer galleries, leading to the vast expansion of coal-production – reflected in Turner's *Keelmen* – which fuelled home fires as well as manufactures, spreading coal-smoke and soot over London as well as Birmingham.

Happily for the neat chronology of Virginia Woolf, it was specifically in the years 1800 to 1801 that the early engineers harnessed high-pressure steam. Now superheated steam under explosive pressure, inside cast-iron cylinders bored more finely than cannon had ever been, forced forward a heavily laden piston which turned a cast-iron wheel which drove a locomotive and trucks down a track (1804), or a 'steamer' through the sea (1802–7), or a shaft that ran the length of a workshop, turning belts that drove lines of lathes, drills, steel-shears and presses, or spinning mules or power looms. Thus the multiplying textile mills could leave the pleasant hills where they were driven by waterwheels (the water sometimes pumped by Watt's engine) and move to the centre of the crowding towns, and help to make them jam-packed cities. For there, where labour lived, the steel factories grew, and the foundries which made cast iron, and there the new railways ferried coal easily, and iron ore from the ironstone quarries.

Consequently, in the English Midlands – in Birmingham, Wal - sall, Wolverhampton – the coal and coke were black, their cinders and ashes were grey or black, the smoke was black and the soot was black. The cinders from the furnaces were pounded down on dirt roads to make a surface, so the roads were black. The urban air became laden with flakes of soot, which were known as 'blacks'. Both brick and stone – in factories, churches, new hospitals and homes – developed an acid black crust. It is possible that the area round Birmingham was known as 'the Black Country' before indus- try came, from the outcrop of coal seams which made the soil black, but this name gained massive currency in the 1830s and '40s. Ruskin claimed that because of the soot 'a beaten footpath, on a rainy day, near a manufacturing town' turned to 'the blackest slime'. Carlyle spoke of 'the black air'.[19]

The 'best finish' for cast-iron goods – and for wrought iron too – was Berlin black, and larger products also wore black as a shield. Railway engines had been colourful when first invented – the *Rocket*, at the steam trials in 1829, was white and canary yellow – but loco- motives soon found sooty reasons to be mainly black. The new iron- clad steamships had great black hulls, though they were red below the waterline and often had white superstructures. Black was frequent in machinery because bitumen saved the iron from corrosion, and smaller new machines, less liable to damp, were also painted black, presumably by association. So, when their time came, sewing machines, early adding machines and typewriters were black – often with slender lines of gold for distinction.

And the workers who made the machines were black. Black - smiths were called black from ancient times because of the black 'smithy scales' (ferrosoferric oxide) which form on iron when forged. In the new blast furnaces the foundry workers were black with soot, coke and iron dust. Metalworkers in the workshops, making locks, keys and small machines, were black with iron dust and iron filings. A metalworker in Disraeli's *Sybil* is 'rickety and smoke-dried, and black with his craft'. Dyers had 'blue and black skins'. Coal-miners wore white clothes – for visibility underground – but came home black from head to foot. And not only the men. As Disraeli describes a pithead:

> They come forth . . . wet with toil, and black as the children of the tropics; troops of youth – alas! of both sexes . . . Naked to the waist, an iron chain fastened to a belt of leather runs between their legs clad in canvas trousers, while on hands and feet an English girl, for twelve, sometimes for sixteen hours a-day, hauls and hurries tubs of coals up subterranean roads, dark, precipitous, and plashy: circumstances that seem to have escaped the notice of the Society for the Abolition of Negro Slavery.

The English girl's exact situation can be seen in a wood-engraving published three years before *Sybil* – as an illustration to the official report of the Children's Employment Commission (Mines) which the Government had instituted (illus. 84). The girl is nearly naked because of the heat underground, and it is hard to imagine a clearer picture of a human being reduced to a beast of burden. Later in the narrative, Disraeli says the miners, eating and drinking at a pub, 'looked like a gang of negroes at a revel': the comparison is visual, and perhaps aloof, but the word 'gang' here refers specifically to the gang system used in slave plantations.[20]

It was however a foreign visitor who best described the black side of working life. In *The Condition of the Working Class in England* (1844), Frederick Engels describes the bodily deformities fostered by a (short) working life in the mines; also the diseases, like the 'Black spittle', which come when the lung is saturated with coal-dust, producing a 'thick, black mucous expectoration'. As to the mood of the working men, he quotes Carlyle on cotton spinners – 'black, mutinous discontent devours them' – and notes too the use of face-blacking when workers formed in 'combinations'. He recalls that 'in 1843, the famous "Rebecca" disturbances broke out among the Welsh peasantry; the men dressed in women's clothing, blackened their faces, and fell in armed crowds upon the toll-gates, destroyed them amidst

84 Girl coal-miner, illustration from the reports of the Children's
Employment Commission (Mines), 1842.

great rejoicing and firing of guns'. The illegal practice of blacking
the face, used earlier by thieves and poachers, was now used by those
active in political 'agitation'. Charlotte Bronte, in her industrial novel
Shirley, mentions a confrontation where the leader went on horseback to hide the fact that he had an artificial leg, while 'the rest only
had their faces blackened'.[21]

What made the strongest black impression on Engels was not 'the
blackened brick buildings of Lancashire', or the housing at Long
Millgate 'all black, smoky, crumbling', or the thickly crowded factories of Ashton-under-Lyne 'belching forth black smoke from their
chimneys', but the coal-black stinking water he smelled with freshly
reeling disgust in each industrial town he came to. Bradford 'lies
upon the banks of a small, coal-black, foul-smelling stream'. The
Medlock, running through Manchester, is 'coal black, stagnant and
foul'. In Leeds the river Aire 'flows into the city at one end clear and
transparent, and flows out at the other end thick, black, and foul,
smelling of all possible refuse'. The meaning of 'all possible refuse'
is clarified when he comes to the fitly named river Irk. At the bottom
of Long Millgate, he notes, 'flows, or rather stagnates, the Irk, a narrow, coal-black, foul-smelling stream, full of debris and refuse' with,
on its bank, 'the most disgusting, blackish-green, slime pools [which]
give forth a stench unendurable'. The Irk is foul not just from the
refuse of 'the tanneries, bonemills, and gasworks' upstream, but from
'the contents of all the neighbouring sewers and privies'. Further
from the rivers, the courts within the densely crammed housing are
piled deep with 'debris, refuse, filth and offal', or with ash heaps (a
Victorian euphemism), 'the filth of which cannot be described'. It

was no wonder that disease and sickness thrived, that bodies were malformed and life-expectancy minimal.[22]

The rubbish-and-excrement heaps, the sewage-choked waters, are the vile 'other side' of the century's black coin. To move to London itself, when Henry Mayhew made his survey of London labour and the London poor, he found several degrees of black, to be set against the smart black clothes and households situated less than a mile away. Here it is not the factories, but the ships crowded into the London docks that have 'tall chimneys vomiting clouds of black smoke' – especially the coal-ships (10,000 came each year). These are the ships Turner painted by moonlight. The sails (of those that have them) are black, as are their once-gilded figureheads. The 'coal-whippers' who unload the coal, and whose negligible pay comes partly in alcohol, are bruised black sometimes from fighting (literally) for the work, and have black skin since they work stripped to the waist – the coal-dust sticking to their sweat – and black hair and whiskers ('no matter what the original hue [in which] the coal-dust may be seen to glitter').[23]

The coal-whippers do at least have employment – for the day. But in a poor lodging-house, where the chimney-piece is 'black all the way with the smoke', with roof-beams 'of the same colour', Mayhew finds the blacks of the unemployed. Sometimes the starving men and women wear clothes that long ago had been 'once black': an out-of-work painter tells Mayhew he once had 'a beautiful suit of black'. Or their black is that colour to which other colours of clothes, and skin colours, come in time if they cannot be washed. Of an out-of-work carpet-maker, now a 'vagrant', he says, 'his clothes, which were of fustian and corduroy, tied close to his body with pieces of string, were black and shiny with filth, which looked more like pitch than grease'. Apart from the carpet-maker (thrown out of work, presumably, by the power looms), I cite one among many eloquent, even heart-rending, portraits:

> On the form at the end of the kitchen was one whose squalor and wretchedness produced a feeling approaching to awe. His eyes were sunk deep in his head, his cheeks were drawn in, and his nostrils pinched with evident want, while his dark stubbly beard gave a grimness to his appearance that was almost demoniac; and yet there was a patience in his look that

was almost pitiable. His clothes were black and shiny at every fold with grease, and his coarse shirt was so brown with long wearing, that it was only with close inspection you could see that it had once been a checked one: on his feet he had a pair of lady's side-laced boots, the toes of which had been cut off so that he might get them on. I never beheld so gaunt a picture of famine. To this day the figure of the man haunts me.[24]

The smart black world, then, of silk hats and black, japanned barouches may seem in a different universe from the world of the dirt-and-grease black destitute, and work-blackened families living in soot-blackened terraces by sewage-black waters. As William Blake put it, with appalling simplicity,

Some are born to sweet delight,
Some are born to endless night.[25]

But the two worlds – the two nations, Disraeli called them, and each had its own black – were at most a coal-fuelled rail journey apart. Economically they were connected directly. The best superfine black broadcloth and the many black silks and crapes were woven on power looms (dangerous to the hair of the poorly paid women tending them) driven by steam engines which were fuelled by coal-dust-blackened stokers in their stoke-holes, and dyed black in dye-blackened dye-shops by black-dye-blackened dyers. In the home the cast-iron clawfoot bath (dressed black on the outside, enamelled white on the inside), together with the cast-iron kitchen range and the cast-iron fireplace in the sitting room, had perhaps travelled for only half a day from the flame-topped blast furnaces where they were cast. That iron fireplace, and the chimney above, were kept clean by a soot-blackened sweep, and especially by his soot-crusted boy, who climbed with a brush to the top of the flue – 'a little ugly, black, ragged figure, with bleared eyes and grinning white teeth', as Charles Kingsley describes Tom in *The Water-Babies* (1862–3).[26] In the winter that hearth had a hearty fire, burning coals ferried daily from the pits upcountry where they had been mined by malnourished minors. Round that fireplace the family sat, listening perhaps to a Dickens novel read aloud, while in another room the 'boots' – the bootboy – carefully applied blacking to the family's footwear. The blacking itself came from close at hand, from warehouses like Warren's in London, where, during the 1820s, it was mixed, bottled and labelled by the underpaid child labour of, among others, that same Charles Dickens who later provided both tears and laughter for heartwarming family readings.

Dickens preferred for his blacking days to be forgotten in his later success, when he posed for several portraits in the smartest of black coats – though he would also shock the black taste by dressing sometimes in a 'flash' style. The son of a poor naval clerk who was confined for a time to the debtors' prison, and of a mother who had probably been in service and who said whenever she saw him 'Hello, Charley, lend us a pound', Dickens had more direct experience of the 'two nations' than most of the authors who sought to describe them; which makes more poignant the odd twist he gives to an idea that rightly had some currency then – the idea, the perception, that parts of England had become a hell on earth.

Hell in the past had been both terrifying and picturesque, with black demons forking sinners into undying fires. Early depictions – by Bosch, Bruegel and others – draw both on the sight of cities on fire, and also perhaps on the older style of industry as it looked in the later Middle Ages, in the arsenals of the emergent nation states, where in fire, smoke and smithy-scales bombards were forged (the ancestor of the cannon) and white-hot iron was hammered on many anvils into blades. The nineteenth century did not believe in this black and fiery hell, but it did recall the old pictures of it in describing the new landscape. When William Cobbett sees the blast furnaces of Sheffield he is both appalled and awed, but more awed than appalled:

> It was dark before we reached Sheffield; so that we saw the iron furnaces in all the horrible splendour of their everlasting blaze . . . This Sheffield, and the land all about it, is one bed of iron and coal. They call it Black Sheffield, and black enough it is; but from this one town and its environs go nine-tenths of the knives that are used in the whole world.[27]

It is the fires of hell that are everlasting, and the foundry/hell equation is more explicit in Dickens. In *The Old Curiosity Shop* Nell sees a foundry, where

in this gloomy place, moving like demons among the flame
and smoke, dimly and fitfully seen, flushed and tormented by
the burning fires, and wielding great weapons, a faulty blow
from any one of which must have crushed some workman's
skull, a number of men laboured like giants.

The scene is all black and red, with the works surrounded by an
'interminable perspective of brick towers, never ceasing in their black
vomit'. The industrial city of Coketown, in Dickens's *Hard Times*,
is 'a town of unnatural red and black like the painted face of a savage'.
The scene is again black and red when Nell sees the factories at night
– 'when the smoke was changed to fire; when . . . places, that had
been dark vaults all day, now shone red-hot, with figures moving to
and fro within their blazing jaws'. The giant jaws here must recall the
image of Hellmouth.[28]

Like Cobbett, Dickens sees the new factories with a horrified exhilaration, and it is possible too that the spectacle of the blast furnaces
fed the imagination of those who wished to depict hell itself. In John
Martin's painting of Satan's new-built palace of Pandemonium,
hell's rivers of fire resemble molten iron, poured flaming into a
succession of moulds (illus. 85). The demon palace itself has some
resemblance to Charles Barry's design for the Houses of Parliament
– done over in the Babylonian style – especially since it stands on
a brink like the Thames embankment, complete with Victorian-
looking street lighting. The resemblance must be coincidental, since
Barry's design was produced only in 1836, and construction took many
years, while the painting belongs to 1841; but Martin does at times
show a remarkable gift of anticipation.

What is most notable, however, in Dickens's depiction of the
industrial hell, is that for him the working men are the demons, while
the machines they tend suffer like the damned. Passing other workshops, Nell had noticed that 'strange engines spun and writhed
like tortured creatures; clanking their iron chains, shrieking in their
rapid whirl . . . as though in torment unendurable'. And in *Hard
Times*, Dickens recurs to the image of 'the piston of the steam-
engine [working] monotonously up and down, like the head of an
elephant in a state of melancholy madness'.[29] Of this odd reversal,
where men who often suffered from dangerous machinery become
demons who torment machines into madness, we might say that, like

85 John Martin, *Pandemonium*, 1841, oil on canvas.

Disraeli's comparison of coal-miners to Africans, it shows the great divide, or gulf, between the author and the workers who move his sympathy (even if Dickens had, briefly, known the working life). Part of the distance we could perhaps call 'cultural', for, with all their toil, pain and deprivation, the communities of third-generation factory workers might well have seemed brutalized and worse to the educated world in which Dickens now moved. Disraeli had been appalled not only by the working conditions of young girls in the mines, but also by the violence of these girls' language ('oaths that men might shudder at, issue from lips born to breathe words of sweetness'). Nor could an author, in the nineteenth century, allow a character to speak violent, obscene, blasphemous slang (though this had been possible, two centuries earlier, for Shakespeare and – even more – Ben Jonson).

Apart from the gulf that might be called cultural, there were the politics. Nell's night vision of the industrial town includes a description of other men, who had been thrown out of work by the machines, being 'maddened' by the 'frightful cries' of their leaders, and urged on to 'errands of terror and destruction' – that is, machine-breaking. Though Dickens had radical sympathies, he also shared the public alarm at the destruction that might ensue both when the unemployed banded together, and also when the employed joined

together in 'combinations'. His novel *Hard Times* is filled with indig-
nant sympathy for the 'good' working man, Stephen Blackpool, and
with suspicious hostility for the local trade union, which Blackpool
refuses to join. Like others in the nineteenth century, Dickens feared
England could easily suffer a revolution, such as had occurred in
France and elsewhere, and he also believed, as Engels came to believe,
that in England the revolution could begin in the factories.

Actually Dickens's picture of revolution is, in a sense, not greatly
different from his picture of industry, since he believed that revolution
also would be a hell on earth. The revolutionaries would mainly be
innocents, goaded into action by intolerable wrongs, but the revolutionary process would turn them into demons. The novel he wrote
immediately after *The Old Curiosity Shop* was *Barnaby Rudge*, in which
his description of the eighteenth century's Gordon Riots becomes a
picture of revolution in England. 'The more the fire crackled and raged,
the wilder and more cruel the men grew; as though moving in that
element they became fiends, and changed their earthly nature for the
qualities that give delight in hell.' The imagery of hell, fiends and
blackness recurs through the novel: the rioters, 'a legion of devils',
advance 'like an army of devils' with 'demon heads and savage eyes'
to ply 'demon labours', while one among them is 'a Lucifer among
the devils'. When, later in life, Dickens came to describe the French
Revolution itself, he recurred (with a less gross emphasis) to the
imagery of hell, saying of a revolutionary crowd gathering round the
guillotine, 'there could not be fewer than five hundred people, and
they were dancing like five thousand demons . . . No fight could have
been half so terrible as this dance . . . a something, once innocent,
delivered over to all devilry'.[30]

It should be said that in Dickens's later fiction his attitude to
industry becomes more complex and objective. The foundry in *Bleak
House* is a place of wonder, with

> a great perplexity of iron . . . mountains of it broken up, and
> rusty in its age; distant furnaces of it glowing and bubbling
> in its youth; bright fireworks of it showering about under
> the blows of the steam-hammer; red-hot iron, white-hot iron,
> cold-black iron; an iron taste, an iron smell, and a Babel of
> iron sounds.

His comparisons now are less with hell than with Babel and Babylon. In the ironmaster's office 'there is iron-dust on everything; and the smoke is seen through the windows rolling heavily out of the tall chimneys to mingle with the smoke from a vaporous Babylon of other chimneys'. But though the office and the view are dark-to-black, the tone here is light, since Dickens likes this ironmaster, who has on his table 'pieces of iron, purposely broken to be tested'. The iron-master is not an ogre, though Dickens also depicted monstrous bosses, like Mr Bounderby in *Hard Times*. The protagonist of the late novel *Little Dorrit* becomes, and enjoys being, the accountant of an engineering works. His 'little counting-house' is

> at the end of a long low workshop, filled with benches . . . and straps and wheels; which, when they were in gear with the steam-engine, went tearing round as though they had a suicidal mission to grind the business to dust and tear the factory to pieces.

The apparent frantic destructiveness is accommodated, however, and industrial relations in *this* factory are harmonious – even though those working at the benches are 'swarthy' (black) with iron-filings. For this is dancing iron ('The patient figures at work were swarthy with the filings of iron and steel that danced on every bench and bubbled up through every chink in the planking'). The picture still has strong blacks and a deep and ominous chiaroscuro. The rays of light striking down from a trapdoor through the dusty dimness of the workshop remind Clennam (the accountant) of the rays from angry clouds which, in old biblical pictures, were 'the witnesses of Abel's murder'.[31]

If Dickens's attitude to the factory itself is more positive in *Little Dorrit*, this is partly because his thought, by this stage, has moved from dark workshops to the darkness of black-suited finance. The good factory fails, and both machinists and accountant are thrown out of work, when the novel's great, ignoble symbolic financier, 'Mr Merdle' (Dickens liked to betray his knowledge of French), is exposed in his fraudulence, and kills himself.

❖ ❖ ❖

TRYING TO SEE the nineteenth century whole, one may wonder what *is* the relation between the smart blacks the century loved to wear, and the factory blacks, and sad blacks, of its mechanical inno-vations. It is easy to draw specious connections, and it is sometimes said that the nineteenth century wore black because black was good protective colouring in the new coal- and soot-black world. The difficulty here is that while this principle may work for railway loco-motives, it does not work for clothes, since black cloth shows up the dirt. But also men wore white – in their shirts – and women wore a great deal of white, both in the smoky cities and also when waiting in railway stations, which they would not have done if their main goal in dressing had been protection from the falling soot. So if black clothes were thought helpful in some smoky places, still one cannot say the black fashion was determined by the smoke.

Those working manually in factories and mines would unavoid-ably be blackened by their work. But if those administering industry wore black – the mechanical inventors, the ironmasters and mill-owners – this was for other reasons also, which relate in part to the black of the Christian church. Thomas Newcomen, who invented the first working steam engine, was a Baptist lay preacher. James Watt, who made crucial improvements to steam power, was the son of Presbyterians, both of whom were ardent Covenanters. William Murdoch, who was employed by Watt, and himself invented the oscillating steam engine – and also designed a steam-powered gun – was again raised in the Kirk. Ranging further afield in time and place, Henry Merrell (1816–1883), who developed steam power in Georgia in the 1840s and later in Arkansas (in the 1850s), and who was also a major in the Confederate army, was an ardent evangelical in the Second Great Awakening and an influential elder in the Presbyterian Church of Arkansas. This association – of mechanical invention with severe strains of Protestantism – has much to do with the emphasis on mathematics and the natural sciences (as against Greek and Latin) in Presbyterian schools and in the dissenting academies (which were noted also for their well-equipped laboratories). The history is intri-cate, and must take account of various migrant communities (such as Scottish Presbyterians in Pennsylvania), but in sum, the reason why many of those who were most active in the Industrial Revolution wear black in their portraits – in the eighteenth century as well as the nineteenth – is neither because black was smart, nor because they worked with black materials, but in fact because black was regularly worn in their Christian denomination.

Not all inventors and industrialists belonged to dissenting congregations, however, and insofar as there was a relation between the stylish blacks of the metropolis and the diverse blacks of the industrial towns, that connection must have been both broad and indirect. Some space in one's thinking must be left for indeterminate and fugitive influences; and the visual tone of a society may reflect, obliquely, large material changes which weigh upon the consciousness. One thing that people will do with oppression is to turn it into style, and this has happened often in the history of the colour black. The severity of life in Inquisition-ridden, absolutist sixteenth-century Spain had turned to elegance in the tight black doublet with high tubular collar and tiny starched ruff, which compelled the Spanish gentry to be literally, rigidly, smartly stiff-necked. And in twentieth-century street culture the dashing use of black in punk, Goth and other styles is related by commentators, such as the theorist of subcultures Dick Hebdige, to the expression of anxiety and frustration.

For the nineteenth century too some indirect influences may be traced. Certainly one could say that, following the American, French and Industrial revolutions, the new tone of society would not be set by the old aristocracy. And when Beau Brummell and the Prince Regent adopted black for eveningwear in the 1810s, their change of style may have been both intuitive and tactical: for chic attaches to success and power, which then increasingly lay with the new industrial money, spent frugally but not without ostentation by the new, often Calvinist 'captains of industry'. The new money itself was managed by experts in finance and accounting, who wore – humbly or opulently – the black of clerical work, in the process giving more employment and wealth to black-clad lawyers. Bankers, and those lending capital at interest, already wore black. But none of these black prosperities could have increased as they did without the crucial rise of that vital new profession, the engineer. And engineers wore black, in imitation of the learned professions, as we see in daguerreotypes of Brunel standing in black beside black iron.

There were other connections. For the colour black was also, and independently, associated with democracy, especially after the French Revolution in 1789. This may seem an odd connection, since black silks and velvets had earlier marked aristocracies and, in some nations, the monarchy. The plain black cloth worn by the priesthood, however, had been humble, not aristocratic – the colour most suited to sinful mankind. Speaking of Venice in the sixteenth century, Goethe had said, in his *Theory of Colours*, that 'black was intended to remind the Venetian noblemen of republican equality'.[32] Much the same could be said of the sober black style of the Dutch Republic in the seventeenth century, and the same is also true of American black, which was puritan in origin but came to be seen as democratic and republican after the Revolutionary War. And in each of these republics black was worn as much, or almost as much, by women as by men.

Those leading the French Revolution did not mean to dress in black: they had fashions drawn up for universal clothing based on the tricolore, all red, white and blue. The tricolore styles did not take, however, and instead fashion moved to what was called 'Engish black', which came to be seen in France as distinctly republican. Baudelaire said of the black fashion in menswear that 'a uniform livery of grief is a proof of equality', and again that 'the black frock-coat' had its 'political beauty, which is the expression of universal equality'. 'English black' itself had some association with the restraint of an emphatically constitutional – and bourgeois – monarchy. 'Whence comes it, this universal big black Democracy?' Thomas Carlyle asked in his *Latter-day Pamphlets* of 1850.[33]

Though not a republic – and afflicted with a landowning aristocracy – England illustrates the degree of democratic value which black had acquired. There was a widespread complaint that the general wearing of black made it harder to distinguish the ranks and roles of people. Charles Eastlake, whom I quoted before on the black and funereal style of dress, went on,

> Nor is this all, for many a host who entertains his friends at dinner has a butler behind his chair who is dressed precisely like himself. To add to this confusion, the clergyman who rises to say grace might, so far as his apparel goes, be mistaken for either.

In Charles Reade's novel *Hard Cash* (1863), a lady asks who has called while she was out, and is told by a young relative, 'There was a young gentleman all in black. I think he was a clergyman – or a butler.'[34]

Black had a levelling role. It is hard, though, to see English society, with its limited franchise and unlimited anxiety about social standing, as being precisely democratic. And behind the democratic

association of black – and perhaps lying deeper – was again its associ -
ation with the Christian Church. When Eastlake complains that the
clergyman is dressed like the host and the butler, what he registers is
that hosts and butlers had come to dress in the colour of the clergy –
as had employers and employees in general. If black was democratic,
even more it was Christian. England in the nineteenth century was
marked by religious revivalism, among Catholics, High Churchmen,
Methodists and non-conformists generally, all of whom had distinct
black styles for their priesthoods and for their laity. It may be that
one reason why England differed from so many European countries
in its failure to have a revolution in the nineteenth century was because
the Christian faith helped placate dissent. Even more than the newly
confessional Catholicism, Calvinistic Protestantism encouraged each
individual to be his own vigilant moral policeman who must seek,
before all things, to be diligent in his duty.

For the Christian Church, at this time, was no friend to social
change. This has, of course, often been said, of the Church of England
especially, with reference made to the 21 bishops who voted against
the Reform Bill in 1831. How far English Protestantism might go
in supporting an unequal status quo could be illustrated by the letter sent by the bishop of London – a century earlier, it is true – to
slave-owning families in the colonies who were reluctant to allow their
slaves to be converted, for fear that they might become unruly if
they learned all men were equal in the eyes of God. They need not
worry, the bishop explained, for

> Christianity . . . does not make the least Alteration in . . . the
> Duties which belong to Civil Relations . . . The Freedom which
> Christianity gives, is a Freedom from the Bondage of Sin and
> Satan . . . but as to their *outward* Condition, whatever that
> was before, whether bond or free, their being baptiz'd, and
> becoming Christians, makes no manner of Change in it . . .
> And so far is Christianity from discharging Men from the
> Duties of the Station and Condition in which it found them,
> that it lays them under stronger Obligations to perform those
> Duties with the greatest Diligence and Fidelity.[35]

A Church and faith which had argued – as another bishop, George
Berkeley, put it – that 'Slaves would only become better Slaves by

being Christians' was more likely to reinforce than to upset a social order that was, in a more ordinary way, unequal.[36] Nor, in the nineteenth century, were the dissenting churches necessarily less conservative. Jabez Bunting, the president of the Methodist Conference, supported 'subordination and industry in the lower orders' and is famous for saying 'Methodism is as much opposed to democracy as it is to sin.' He is famous also for supporting the transportation of the Tolpuddle Martyrs in 1834, even though their leader, George Loveless, was himself a Methodist preacher.[37]

As a Methodist George Loveless wore black, as we can see in the engravings and daguerreotypes of him. For now he may represent the black worn by the very many good Christians in the nineteenth century who were at odds with church leaders, and who actively sought to improve British social arrangements.

In the meantime many suffered in Christian patience and humility. The divided attitudes of the time are apparent in the fate of Stephen Blackpool, the 'good' working man in Dickens's *Hard Times*, who refuses to join a trade union. Blackpool suffers a form of martyrdom when 'sent to Coventry' by his fellow workers, and a subterranean crucifixion when he falls down a mineshaft and lies alone, severely injured, for many hours in the dark. He dies – movingly, Dickens always does death well – a saint of diligent, obedient, Christian selflessness, which shows in his refusal to complain too much:

> The bearers being now ready to carry him away, and the surgeon being anxious for his removal, those who had torches or lanterns, prepared to go in front of the litter. Before it was raised, and while they were arranging how to go, he said to Rachael, looking upward at the star: 'Often as I coom to myseln, and found it shinin' on me down there in my trouble, I thowt it were the star as guided to Our Saviour's home. I awmust think it be the very star!' They lifted him up, and he was overjoyed to find that they were about to take him in the direction whither the star seemed to him to lead. 'Rachael, beloved lass! Don't let go my hand. We may walk toogether t'night, my dear!' 'I will hold thy hand, and keep beside thee, Stephen, all the way.' 'Bless thee! Will soombody be pleased to coover my face!' They carried him very gently along the fields, and down the lanes, and over the wide landscape; Rachael

always holding the hand in hers. Very few whispers broke the mournful silence. It was soon a funeral procession. The star had shown him where to find the God of the poor; and through humility, and sorrow, and forgiveness, he had gone to his Redeemer's rest.[38]

FOR BEHIND THE industrial association, and the democratic association, and the Christian association, was the oldest association: of the colour black with death. The sense of it was often voiced, and often with dismay. Alfred de Musset said in 1836 'that vestment of black which the men of our time wear is a terrible symbol . . . Human reason . . . bears in itself sorrow'. Balzac said, 'we are all dressed in black, like so many people in mourning'. Charles Eastlake had wondered why men wore, at festivities, the dress of death; as had Henry Mayhew, who also observed that 'a gentleman . . . attired for the gayest evening party, would . . . be equally presentable at the most sorrowful funeral.'[39]

One must ask, finally, whether the century's festive blacks were in part an oblique reflection of a familiarity with death. Death was certainly a growing fact, since mortality increased directly with the expansion of the unsanitary cities, and – in spite of medical advances – refused to decline in the middle decades of the century. Death truly was a leveller, since the successive epidemics of cholera and typhoid killed the rich with the poor, and in 1861 killed Prince Albert. Death was also a large fact in the art, and fiction, of the time. Dickens was celebrated at once for his comedy and for the power of his deathbed scenes, while Thackeray famously ended a chapter in the middle of *Vanity Fair* with a picture of his heroine Amelia 'praying for George, who was lying on his face, dead, with a bullet through his heart'.[40]

In painting, too, death was popular, and was the centrepiece of the popular genre of history painting. In the public art galleries – themselves an innovation of the nineteenth century – crowds flocked to emote at deaths that were naval (Nelson, by West, 1806, by Devis, 1807, by Maclise, 1859–64), military-imperial (Gordon, by Joy, 1885), literary (Chatterton, by Wallis, 1856), historical-factual (Lady Jane Grey, by Delaroche, 1833), historical-exotic (Sardanapalus, by Delacroix, 1827) and classical (Caesar, by Camuccini, 1798, and by Gérôme, 1867) – to name a delegation. Spectators were moved to tears by depictions of the deaths of the unknown sick, the unknown poor, and unknown children. The living were painted contemplating the dead (Cromwell gazing at Charles I in his coffin, by Delaroche, 1831), fathers were painted (or engraved) beside their dead daughters (Tintoretto by Cogniet, *c.* 1857, and by O'Neill, 1873, King Lear by Barry, 1786–8, by Romney, 1775–7, by Pecht, 1876).

In many paintings, the quality black of the century's smart style joins with the descending shadows of death. In *The Execution of Lady Jane Grey* (1833) by Paul Delaroche, the grieving lady by the wall wears a rich black velvet dress which merges with the jet-black shadow on the wall, while the executioner seems half a dandy, smartly sporting black with red – the colours of death and bloodshed (illus. 86). The enormous black cloak worn by the elderly man who comforts Jane – Baron Chandos – is not a mourning gown, but a grand velvet robe of state. Lady Jane herself wears white satin, as fine ladies did in the nineteenth century (as also in the sixteenth), so the tragedy of her cruel death is represented at once in the absolute good and bad of white and black, and in the smart two-colour contrast of nineteenth-century civility.

Again, in Millais's painting of the Princes in the Tower of 1878, the doomed children are dressed in sumptuous jet-black velvet (illus. 87). Because they are tragic victims Millais has made them beautiful, with a fair, northern European beauty. They seem beautiful boys except that they could equally be beautiful girls – or a couple, and then it would be anyone's guess as to how one reads the genders. The black clothes they wear look like mourning black, worn because, with a painter's poetry, they are in anticipatory mourning for themselves. But it is also smart black – the smartest, with a lustrous beauty which is at once medieval-princely and upper-class Victorian. And still, for all its luxurious stylishness, their black is also tragic. For youthful mortality was high in the nineteenth century as in the fifteenth, whether one died in an urban epidemic or of some disease in the colony where one's parents had been stationed.

Although the nineteenth century was indeed familiar with death, however, it does not seem that – away from actual interments – death was found disheartening, but rather the reverse. In literary studies, reading great tragedies, one is accustomed to think of vicarious dying as an enlarging and heartening experience. And away from formal tragedy this may again be true. It does seem that life draws strength

86 Paul Delaroche, *The Execution of Lady Jane Grey*, 1833, oil on canvas.

from a close approach to death, quite apart from the consolations of religion. And if the nineteenth century had a culture of death, which is reflected at a distance in its fine black style, that culture evidently worked with a positive effect. As to the history of the colour black, it is a fact that widespread fashions for wearing black, together with an extravagant culture of death, have arisen not when nations suffered defeat, but when they were at their high point of international power. This is true of Burgundy in the fifteenth century, Spain and also Venice in the fifteenth and sixteenth centuries, Holland in the seven - teenth century, and England not only in the sixteenth and seventeenth centuries, but again and above all in the nineteenth century. It is not that nations never look sombre when things go badly; nor are all empires dark at their high point. Both France and Austro-Hungary were lighter in tone (and both often dressed their soldiers in white). But still it is true that black fashions and the cult of death have accompanied extremes of wealth and power. There are obvious con - nections one could make – for instance with the cost in lives that buys international power. But perhaps one should allow an element

87 John Everett Millais, *The Two Princes Edward and Richard in the Tower,
1483*, 1878, oil on canvas.

of mystery to the connection there may be, both between death and the enhancement of life, and between death, power, the colour black and triumphal festive socialization.

That connection is visible in the culture of the funeral when nations are at their greatest. For the funeral of Nelson in January 1806, the black coffin was mounted on a royal barge beneath a black canopy crowned with black ostrich feathers, and progressed with 60 ships, many decorated or draped with black, from Greenwich to Whitehall. The next day the coffin was mounted on a funeral 'car' shaped like his ship the *Victory*, all black and draped with black, again with a black canopy crowned with black feathers. All London watched the procession from Whitehall to Saint Paul's, where the funeral service lasted four hours. Horatio Nelson was then laid to rest, and rests still, in the crypt of St Paul's, in a massive sarcophagus of black marble (which had originally been made for Cardinal Wolsey).

Grand as Nelson's funeral was, it cannot compare, as a communal event, with the funeral of the Duke of Wellington in 1852. Arthur Wellesley, the Iron Duke, a victor of Waterloo and ex-prime minister, died of a seizure at the age of 83 at Walmer Castle in Kent. Suitable to his military prowess, 'his medical attendants . . . were surprised at the great development of strength and muscle exhibited by his body even at the period of his death'. As was usual with the better class of death, the body was laid in a lead casket, which was placed in a coffin 'of the finest polished mahogany'. This in turn was covered 'after the fashion of royalty' with crimson velvet, with the handles and decorations richly gilt; a massive pall of black velvet was rested upon it, but pulled back for visitors.[41]

For the formal lying in state, the coffin was transported to the Hall at Chelsea Hospital. There the black drapes were shaped into a gigantic tent, within which the coffin rested on a black velvet bier on a cloth-of-gold carpet. Round the bier were ten pedestals, on which Wellington's military honours were displayed on black cushions. Queen Victoria was the first visitor, with her consort and several of the royal children. They were followed the next day by the principal members of the aristocracy, the principal members of the government and foreign ambassadors. There was not a large public attendance.

Queen Victoria proposed a state funeral, and on Thursday 19 November the body was conveyed to St Paul's in a procession which took two hours to pass. It was led by six battalions of infantry, the artillery with nine guns, the Chelsea Pensioners, Wellington's standard and his servants, Wellington's physicians in a mourning coach and Prince Albert in a royal carriage. Then came the heralds, Wellington's baton as Field Marshal on a black velvet cushion in a mourning coach, his coronet on a black velvet cushion in a separate mourning coach and the pallbearers, consisting of eight generals in two mourning coaches ('mourning coaches' being invariably black).

There followed the enormous funeral 'car', advancing slowly to dead marches by the military bands, the beat of muffled drums and the periodic firing of cannon (illus. 88). There had been a touch of fancifulness in Nelson's car, shaped like the *Victory* with a prow and figurehead, and something even light in spirit in its slender columns and swags, appropriate both to the Regency and to Nelson's reputation as a lover as well as an admiral. There was nothing light in Wellington's 'car', which was compared to a juggernaut, the towering vehicle with wheels like millstones used to transport Indian gods. It was drawn by twelve horses, three abreast in four rows – 'the largest and finest black horses that could be procured' – themselves covered to the ground with black velvet housings set with black plumes. Their appearance and slow advance, each led by a groom in full black mourning, was described as 'elephantine' – as it may have been, since the car weighed eighteen tons. It was made of iron and bronze, and stood 17 feet high – that is, 3 feet higher than a double-decker bus, and 2 feet wider. It was 12 feet long, the length of many railway engines, and in engravings it can resemble a giant locomotive, with its three bronze wheels, on either side, evenly spaced beneath a metal rim (also, like a locomotive, it carried a nameplate, 'Waterloo'). The upper structure was muffled by a vast pall of black velvet (powdered with silver and with a silver fringe), on which, at a height, rested the red and gold coffin, beneath a canopy trailing black streamers. In the engraving by Thomas Ellis the car itself is dwarfed by the magnificent funeral drapes laid over Temple Bar, beneath which it is soon to pass.

The car was followed by Wellington's relatives, his horse, led by his groom, officers and men from every regiment in the Service, and the carriage of the Queen (without the Queen). But I pause on the car, because it was this gigantic, snail-paced, black-draped vehicle that drew most comment. It was emphatically military, bristling on all sides with massed lances, halberds, battle-axes, banners, breastplates,

88 Thomas Ellis, *Funeral Car of the Late Field Marshal Duke of Wellington –*
Passing through Temple Bar, on its way to St Pauls Cathedral, where the remains of
the Great Duke was entomb'd Novr 18th 1852, 1852, engraving.

helmets, cannon-barrels and cannonballs, though what most struck
contemporaries was the apparent absence from it of any religious
sign or emblem. This was not utterly the case, for the bier carried the
legend 'Blessed are the dead that die in the Lord', but the very small
Christian presence in the procession is striking.

And the procession was the great communal event, in contrast
to the lyings in state. Not many visitors came when the body lay in
Walmer Castle, and the rest at Chelsea Hospital was poorly attended
when opened to the public. This is hardly surprising, given Welling -
ton's recent reputation as an ineloquent prime minister who resisted
reform with poor success. But the funeral procession was watched,
it was said, by a million and a half people. Every window overlooking
the route was filled, as were the roofs above. Along with its many
blacks, the procession had an element of festive colour, with the
reds and blues and golds and whites of the military uniforms and
banners. Nor was the public emotion that of grief, since – as was said
at the time – grief will be qualified for a leader who dies peacefully in

his eighties. But public emotion there was, described by an onlooker as 'sentiments sublimer far than sorrow'. The emotion had in part to do with the commemoration of campaigns in many parts of the world where the victories, like the casualties, were national as well as being Wellington's. In some sense, the funeral procession was a triumph in the Roman Imperial sense – the victory procession of a supreme victor – though in the nineteenth century such a victor could process with such sombre magnificence only after he had died, making the victory procession a death procession, gravely and grandly black, and only the more triumphal for being so. Sublimity, Burke said, combines the great and the terrible, and in almost excluding Christian symbolism the Wellington funeral discovered perhaps a continuity with the triumphalism of other empires that had crumbled to dust many centuries before. There is something barbaric in the blatancy of its pageant of power and death.

When connected with the military, black has of course its menace, together with its mournfulness. To pass briefly from a vast construction to a relatively small one, there is in the Victoria & Albert Museum a silver and crystal table centrepiece (illus. 89). It was presented by the officers of the combined forces to Queen Victoria on her Golden Jubilee in 1887. On either side of this towering table-architecture, two figures stand who are, oddly, lacquered black. A black Britannia with flowing black drapes holds high the fearsome trident of British naval might. We used to hymn her praises, though here we might think her a demon queen. On the other side of the table piece, with his back to us in the photograph, stands – or rather swaggers – a black-lacquered St George. He wears black, baroquely furling armour and, beyond our view, brandishes a black and lethal scimitar. At the centre of the royal banquet both death and national grandeur, in both male and female form, show one deadly mask-face: it is the face of world power both on the land and on the sea.

As to hymns for the dead, both Nelson's funeral and Wellington's included the 'Dead March' from Handel's *Saul,* but that piece too has a Christian accent. If one sought a music more apt to the spectacle it occurs to me one might find it in the 'Dead March for Siegfried' in Wagner's *Götterdämmerung,* which for all its gravity is savagely barbaric and pagan; Wagner being another artist who wore black with panache, favouring black silk and velvet and a black velvet cap. If this suggestion is extravagant, still it seems to me that one may find

89 Black-lacquered figures of St George and Britannia, at either side of the crystal and silver centrepiece presented by the officers of the combined forces to Queen Victoria on her Golden Jubilee, 1887.

in Wagner the music that fits best the nineteenth century's passion for black, since so often it is a death-music – inspiring neither depression nor grief, but rather exaltation. And in *Tristan*, Wagner makes music for the intimate union of love with death. The conjunction of love and death was a recurring theme in the century, in opera, drama, fiction, painting. Often the private love and death are linked to a public cause, as in the paintings by John Everett Millais in which we are invited to think that one of the parting lovers will die the next day (in the St Bartholomew's Day massacre in *A Huguenot, on St Bartholomew's*

Day Refusing to Shield Himself from Danger by Wearing the Roman Catholic Badge and on the field of battle in *The Black Brunswicker*). The theme was not new – one thinks of Romeo and Juliet, whose near-simultaneous deaths buy peace between the warring clans, or Richard Lovelace's 'I could not love thee, dear, so much, Loved I not honor more' – but in the nineteenth century the love-death-and-honour theme swelled.[42] The idea of sacrifice, for love but not for the love of God (though maybe for the love of the nation), was dear to the century. One might relate this sense to the rigid, erect dignity with which the nineteenth century *stands* in so many portraits – single, family and communal – and in so many daguerreotypes and early photographs; the men, and not seldom the women, in black, and with their dark or black goods about them. The stance, and the black, have in part to do with piety but also often with pride, and often with power – exerted or served – together with a sense of the price to be paid for living in what was then called the great age of the world, though mainly it was the great age of Europe.

90 The annual banquet of the National Boot and Shoe Manufacturers'
Association, New York, 1906.

TEN

Our Colour?

IF ONE USED those large terms which take history by the handful, one would say that the high nineteenth century shaded – or rather brightened – into the belle époque. Lighter woodwork came in, gilded plaster returned, women's dresses and their bustles had sharp, aniline colours – lime, rose, mauve. Even the original Ford Model T was originally (from 1908 to 1914) red, green, blue or grey: it was only in 1914 that it became, as Henry Ford famously said, 'any colour . . . so long as it is black'.[1] The other, now-forgotten vehicles of those years – the steam-lorries and steam-trams – could be red, green or blue. The fronts of buildings might excresce, corrugate and curve in waves; Barcelona facades by Gaudí may grow like fungus-trees up from the ground, topped by iridescent tiles which hump like the scales of a restless dragon. Paris Metro stations curled slender, cast-iron tendrils. It was the period of Art Nouveau on both sides of the Channel (of Jugendstil in Germany and Secession in Austro-Hungary). In paint-ing the strong colours of the 1890s – best known now in Cézanne, Van Gogh and Gauguin – were followed by the saturated reds and yellows of the Fauves. The most famous Fauve is Henri Matisse, and in his paintings of the early 1900s it is clear that modernism has arrived, with its freedom, its flatness – its colour.

As the new century advanced, the brightness of the Modern style grew only clearer. The pioneering architect Le Corbusier (Charles-Édouard Jeanneret) worked principally in white. As a young traveller he had celebrated colour more broadly: 'colour . . . exists for the caress and for the intoxication of the eye'. But as his priorities clari-fied through the 1920s he insisted with emphasis that 'there is only one colour, white'; white, he said, 'cleans, cleanses, and *is* cleanness and hygiene . . . It is the eye of truth.' Visiting America, he was dismayed to see how dark the quintessential modern building, the skyscraper, was: appallingly, parts of the Empire State Building carried black marble cladding. Nor was Le Corbusier the first modern architect to celebrate white. In 1901 Charles Rennie Mackintosh had designed, for a competition, a 'house for an art-lover' with a flat roof, all-white walls and large expanses of windowless space. More generally in early modernist taste the love of white was balanced by the love of colour: the painter Fernand Léger thought white alone 'an obstacle, a dead end'. Le Corbusier too said, 'if you want to highlight the delicious brilliance of white, you must surround it with vibrant suggestions of colour'.[2]

Seeing this change, from the nineteenth into the twentieth century, one might recall the similar change that had occurred between the seventeenth and the eighteenth century, when tones also lightened, moving towards the whites and brights of the classical age – to darken again in the period spanning the late eighteenth and early nineteenth centuries. It seems that different periods have, as it were, a tonal index which changes in slow cycles – the change being visible, to varying extents, in dress, in painting and in the look of buildings, inside and out. The tonal swing, through centuries, might be said to have a wavelength of about a hundred years. Such a broad tonal movement is I think first apparent in the fifteenth century, when dress tones deepen and black is increasingly popular – though this first dark wave is slower to gather, and could perhaps be said to peak in the late sixteenth century, finding its signature in the black art of Caravaggio. Styles are diverse throughout this period, however, and it is only in the seventeenth century that a clear tonal trend is fully discernible. Thereafter one can more consistently point to light tones in the mid-eighteenth century, dark tones in the mid-nineteenth century, light tones in the mid-twentieth century, moving in our time to darker tones again. Of course tones and colours vary greatly at all times everywhere, but still a tonal preponderance is visible. As I have I hope emphasized from chapter to chapter, the factors that affect society's visual tone are diverse and unpredictable; they include the relative rise and fall of nations and empires, changes in religious revelation, wars and epidemics, changing technologies, economic booms and busts and the evolution or revolution of social hierarchies. But the very diversity of the causal factors, and the changing complexities of connection between them, make it the more remarkable that there should be any pattern so consistent as the slow swing of a pendulum between dark and light.

What is further clear is that tonal change does not relate in a simple way to perceived goods and bads. Light tones may sometimes have a benign dimension, and dark tones can reflect anxiety and oppression. But one could also say that the sense of well-being was strong in those who set the dark tones in sixteenth-century Spain and in nineteenth-century England. And, on the other side, in the Black Death which raged in the mid-fourteenth century, one-third of the population died in great pain, but the 'culture' kept its bright look, with parti-coloured clothes (green on one side, red on the other).

Again in the First World War, in the influenza epidemic which followed it, and then in the Second World War, the mortality – and mortality among the young – was horrendous. But though widespread mourning had some effect on dress styles, the broader visual tone stayed light. And now that dark tones are increasingly in fashion, with a growing use of black in many departments, we find – happily – that this change does not need to be correlated with an overt vast disaster, like the atomic war which used to be feared. This is not to suggest that there is no connection between the look of a period and large-scale prosperity or anxiety, grief and death, but that such connections have an indirect, complex and elusive logic. There does seem to be present within this logic a visual or even aesthetic principle which works with some autonomy. One should not perhaps characterize this 'principle' precisely, when its fundamental value may be abstract. In general vision dark and light matter almost equally to us, and broad tendencies in style towards either dark or light may have a neutral or equivalent value simply *as* communal movement. Broad change is evidence of cultural life and, with its slow, large rhythm, may reflect an element of integrity within divided societies.

To return to the first half of the twentieth century: if visual values brightened, it was not that black had vanished. Rather, black concentrated, and came to occupy a narrow but central position. Amid the bright canvases of 1915, Malevich painted his *Black Square*. And if you visited Le Corbusier, you would find him wearing a smart black suit. His style was consistent with his theory. He believed black had the value in clothing which white had in architecture: it was pure and resistant to decoration. He imagined his large white spaces to be peopled by slender, clear figures in black, and in his own drawing of Vitruvian Man, his 'Modulor' human is a black silhouette.

In the general wear of men, nevertheless, black retreated steadily. Checks and oatmeal tweeds bulged, the blazer and the straw hat came, and patterned sleeveless knitwear. By the 1930s a man's smart suit could be almost any colour but black. In the 1920s dark tones had been privileged – deeply dark greys, browns, navies – but in the '30s and '40s lighter greys were smart both in business and in society. There were exceptions. The longstanding connection of black with finance, associated with money's gravity and the need for trust, meant that, in the City of London, a uniform of black jacket, black bowler and dark pinstripes continued into the second half of the century. Black had also been popular with national varieties of the Fascist movement: it was worn with calculated and terrifying effect by Himmler's ss in Germany, and on a smaller scale by the British Union of Fascists. In Italy the black shirt had first been worn by the volunteer *arditti* in the Great War, the elite shock troops who included D'Annunzio. Disaffected after the war, they attached to the Fascist movement, and came to set the style of Mussolini's elite bodyguard of Musketeers, of the Italian Fascist Movement generally and of Mussolini himself, as we see him still in photographs, in the urgency of his oratory (illus. 91).

Fascist black also passed, however – as more locally, in London, the 'blackout' ended. By mid-century one could say – for the first time since the end of the fourteenth century – that black had disappeared from the general daily dress of men. But not from their dress in the evening. When men's black began its territorial expansion, at the start of the nineteenth century, it arrived first in eveningwear. And it is in eveningwear, still, that black has been the last to leave. Indeed, it has not left, for the smart jet-black three- or two-piece known as the tuxedo or dinner-jacket suit is with us still. It is not worn often, and one could say that its claim to be the last word has become theoretical. Yet it survives.

Because it has proved such a long-lived classic, the dinner jacket deserves a further word. For what shows, if one consults the fashion illustrations decade by decade, is how little the style has changed. The first dinner jackets, in the 1890s, are all smooth curves, and look as if they were cut out of circles of cloth. They have shawl lapels, and the front edge of the jacket makes a perfect smooth curve running

91 Benito Mussolini speaking in Rome, *c.* 1932.

round to the back. The main changes to this streamlined shape consisted of adding corners. Almost at once the peaked collar arrived, to
compete with the shawl – a friendly competition that continues still.
And around 1900 the jacket became more square-cut, though its
corners still were bevelled. Evidently some squareness was needed, in
a shape that may have seemed too casual or too feminine. Thereafter
its fundamental form has stayed, together with its black-and-white
colour scheme (including a black bow tie). Collars have changed, lapels
have daggered outwards or gone notched, occasionally other colours
have visited (briefly). The material too has lightened from the weighty

92 Fred Astaire and Joan Leslie dancing in *The Sky's the Limit*, 1943.

wool of the past. The result still is that a dinner suit offered for sale in 1904 looks virtually identical, as to jacket and trousers, to one that might be sold today. The members of the American National Boot and Shoe Manufacturers' Association, gathered for their annual banquet in 1906, show some difference from contemporary style in their shirt collars and waistcoats, but their black suits could be ours (illus. 90).

This constancy is so unusual in the history of fashion that one asks, is the dinner jacket some sort of ultimate garment, with nowhere else to go? Certainly it demonstrates the finality of black, and insofar as it has sometimes been midnight blue, this has been because midnight blue gives a better black in electric light. Not that one should omit the importance for the dinner jacket of black's opposite, white. For if black is one kind of ultimate colour, black-with-white looks to be, by this point in history, the ultimate colour contrast. Will games of chess or piano keys – or the pages in a book like this – ever leave black-and-white for red and green?

The latter decades of the twentieth century – now into the twenty-first – have seen a return of black to menswear, alike in the leather jacket and in top-of-the-range designer suits. And still the dinner jacket is not dead. In the 1970s and '80s it came to look like a classic book which few people read, and now again it is in demand. Men have long been drawn or driven into uniforms – as soldiers or servants, as senators or executives – and the dinner jacket perhaps is the ultimate uniform, shorn of all duty but impersonal smartness. Often it was the uniform of inherited money, but James Bond has helped to change that – somewhat. As the first black president of the United States, Barack Obama could be said to be historic change personified – though he also wears a tuxedo, and wears it well. But perhaps the classic icon still is Fred Astaire, near the mid-point of the tuxedo's century. He danced in tails so the coat-tails flew, but he sometimes danced in tuxedos too (illus. 92). In his black-and-white outfit his movements are as clear as a matchstick man dancing, while his lithe swoops show there need be nothing stiff in the way tuxedos move.

If, however, black has returned to menswear, one could not say now that the black style is led by men. On the contrary, men's black seems simply the men's department in a general movement of fashion which, if anything, is led by women's styles. For it was to women's clothes especially that the colour black moved when it took leave of men's.

IN THE PAST women had sometimes worn black for its smartness rather than from grief. There are those Roman statues where the limbs are of white marble and the swirling gown of black; we do not know whether black marble, here, signifies a gown which we would call black. And in the court of Burgundy in the fifteenth century, where black styles flourished, both old and young women sometimes wore luxurious black gowns when apparently not in mourning. The velvets have disappeared, but their pictures survive in Books of Hours and the leaves of triptyches. And when Rubens visited Italy in the early seventeenth century, he painted one of his hosts in a tall black hat (see illus. 33), and his host's wife (Veronica Spinola Doria) in a tight-waisted jet-black velvet dress which fills a third of the picture space, setting off her bright, cold, young face.

In the twentieth century, while black steadily withdrew in menswear, in women's fashions it did not withdraw. Rather, black came to centre stage. In 1922 the fashion house Premet brought out, with success, 'a plain, boyish-looking little slip of a frock, black satin with white collar and cuffs'; and in 1923 Madeleine Vionnet designed a sleeveless black dress with a black dragon outlined on it in red. Then in 1926 Coco Chanel designed a light black dress with long sleeves but a knee-length skirt, with no dragon and no white collar, though there was a small zigzag at the cuff (illus. 93). Even now its simplicity is striking, and its slender black arms have still an impact – for in exposing the calf but hiding the forearm Chanel vivacious-ly controverted the trend of two centuries. The design was publicized by a drawing in *Vogue* in October 1926, though how much the design was made up and worn is now hard to know. The photograph shown is not of the original, but of a reconstruction made in 1990, and so far I have found no photograph of the dress, or its wearers, from the 1920s. This is perhaps odd, since *Vogue* called it 'the frock that all the world will wear' and I have toyed with the thought that a fash-ion may have been launched by a Little Black Dress That Never Was. *Vogue* says, however, that it was 'imported by Saks', the Fifth Avenue store, so mostly likely it was made and traded, but caught on much more slowly than *Vogue* had predicted. Other Chanel outfits that are little and black survive from the 1920s, for instance in the collection of the Fashion Institute in the Metropolitan Museum of Art, and other designers took up the style. Later, sleeve length varied or the sleeves disappeared, and the skirt extended or rose, but the concept of a dress that was jet-black, light and easy to move in became – though not immediately – the archetype of women's fashion.[3]

Most of the century's leading designers, often known for their bril-liance with colour, still gave pride of place to black. The black of Cristóbal Balenciaga 'hits you like a blow', *Harper's Bazaar* put it in 1938, and Christian Dior said he could write a book about black. If

93 A photograph of a model wearing Coco Chanel's 'little black dress', designed in 1926, 1990.

the black style faltered it was quickly revived, by Yves St Laurent in the 1970s, by Vivienne Westwood in the 1980s – drawing now on the street black of punk. The style was fed also by the age-old tradition of Japanese black: Rei Kawakubo announced in 1983, 'I work in three shades of black', and Yohji Yamamoto noted at the launch of his evening line, 'Noir', that the 'samurai spirit is black'. The stage was set for Gianni Versace to call his deep-rent safety-pin dress, worn by Elizabeth Hurley at the premiere of *Four Weddings and a Funeral* in 1994, 'just a boring old punk classic'.[4]

Instantly dramatic, the black dress made its mark in the performing arts. Edith Piaf and Juliette Greco sang in black, and Martha Graham danced in a form-fitting black dress. The black dress co-starred in films: it was worn by Marlene Dietrich, with a mantle of spiky black feathers, in *Shanghai Express* (1932); by Rita Hayworth, with a leg-length slit to the skirt, in *Gilda* (1946); and by Ava Gardner, with one striking diagonal shoulder-strap, in *The Killers* (also 1946). Best-known now, perhaps, is Audrey Hepburn in the opening shots of *Breakfast at Tiffany's* (1961), loitering by the jewellery shop windows in a high, long, slender, bare-armed dress designed by Hubert de Givenchy and worn with similarly slender, long black gloves. This is a highly elegant version of the 'slim cool black dress' which her character, Holly Golightly, had worn – with black sandals – in the original novella by Truman Capote. If black's popularity dipped in the 1960s, with the fashion for whites and 'neon brights', still Twiggy showed Biba's 'deep black tragedy' minidress, Jean Shrimpton wore black with a tall black hat and Diana Rigg in *The Avengers* sent bad men flying while wearing a black leather catsuit. And the geometric, black-and-white, Op art shift dress is iconic from that period, popularized by designers such as Mary Quant, John Bates and André Courrèges.

Away from the catwalk, the screen and the microphone, black was worn to parties and in the street, when working at the till or when presenting to the boardroom. There was ultra-smart black, but also fun and casual black. Especially there was professional black, worn by women lawyers and women executives, and it is in the professional arenas that black has been smartly worn by women where in the past it was worn by men. In history black had often been the colour of insurgents, of groups making their way from a disadvantaged starting point. Black was worn so in the 'dark ages' by the Church, as its clerks moved into government; by merchants and by Jewish

communities rising in the sixteenth century; by engineers and industrialists rising in the nineteenth century. And black, with its gravity,
its discretion, its determination, has an advantage for a group that is
quietly overhauling a profligate ruling elite. Both the conspicuous
and the inconspicuous blacks that women have worn in the twentieth
century are indices of independence, of importance, of emergence
from the shadows cast by men.

A key moment came in 1966, when Yves St Laurent launched Le
Smoking, a tuxedo for women, of velvet or wool. There had been
experiments in this direction in the early 1930s: in 1930 Marlene
Dietrich wore a top hat, tails and trousers in Joseph von Sternberg's
film *Morocco*, and in 1933 the New York firm Zuckerman and Kraus
began to manufacture women's tuxedos for eveningwear. Trousers
were still a stride too far, however, and smart evening fashion re-
verted to the sheath dress, worn with a tailored jacket such as in designs
by Elsa Schiaparelli of 1936. In August 1966, however, the world, the
women's movement and also men, were ready. At first with shock-
ing impact but quickly with success and verve, Le Smoking arrived.
It was worn with a white shirt with frills or simply with ruffled cuffs,
and the cummerbund was optional. In September a lower-priced,
younger version sold furiously, and in December the *Washington Post*
announced in a headline: 'Le Rage in Paris Is Le Smoking Jacket'.
Other designers followed and in 1972 Chanel produced their own
smoking, with a white organdy blouse and black sequined trousers.

Le Smoking, and the accompanying daytime trousered fashions,
were daring, empowering and glamorous together. In general, women's
black fashions have been more mobile than men's and have moved
easily between authority, responsibility and fun. Men's biker jackets
may have had their style, but there has been no male equivalent for
the little black dress. And if women's black fashions relate in part to
empowerment, another aspect is the growing association, in Western
culture especially, of the colour black with sex. For black clothing
was not in the past identified greatly with sexual excitement. Pining
lovers wore black in the late Middle Ages, but from grief, not desire.
And when women posed as Venus in the sixteenth century, in paintings intended for the cabinets of gentlemen, their few brief garments
or 'zones' were rose or white, not black. Pornographic copperplates
of the eighteenth century show ingenious copulations in impatient
half-undress, but their frisson derives from a birch brandished above

bare buttocks, or from a papal crown worn while whoring, rather than from any play with black accessories. There are strong blacks in Japanese erotic prints of the same century, but their blacks – in hair, sash, a lacquered cabinet – reflect the smart blacks of Japanese culture, and are not in themselves erotic. It is true that during Carnival black was used ambiguously, and the seventeenth century had sexy black fur masks. Otherwise, to see the development of erotic black dress, one must wait for the black stockings, black corsets and black neckbands that were worn (not at the same time) by otherwise naked models in nineteenth-century erotic photographs.

In discussing pornographic black I am moving to the blacks men place on women, as against the blacks women choose to wear. As to the nineteenth century, it is hardly surprising if pornographic black expanded in an age that became famous both for black goods and for repression. But while black was not uncommon in nineteenth-century erotica, one could not say it was common. It is in the twentieth century that black has become *the* erotic colour, extending beyond the use of mascara, together with black bras and panties, to arm-length gloves, thigh-length boots and high spike-heels – shading, by even gradations, towards the fetish extreme of whole-face hoods and whole-body straitjackets in glittering pvc.

Erotic black relates to the danger-loving side of sexuality – perhaps ultimately to the dream, mixed in with a death wish, of a meltdown of being in the cauldron of coitus. And if men, especially, relish erotic black on women, this may relate to the inclination of men to demonize women, in a mix of fear and excited temptation. The femme fatale, even more than the prostitute, was shown wearing black in nineteenth-century paintings. There is an element of this dangerous black demonism in the black-clad, sexually attractive girl who seems oddly interested in antiquarian books on Aubrey Beardsley's cover for *The Yellow Book* (see illus. 78).

It may be that behind the demonic-sexy 'femme fatale' there lurks the older black form of demonized woman – the witch in black. But actually, though witches date back to the sixteenth century and earlier, their black outfit does not go back so far. To digress for a moment: the black cats of witches date back to the Middle Ages, and their steeple-crowned hats to the seventeenth century, when both men and women wore high black felt hats. But in pictures of witches from before the nineteenth century, only a minority wear pointed black hats, and extremely few a black gown; it is the devils with whom they carouse and mate who are black from head to foot. The witches themselves, though arriving on broomsticks, are often withered, naked hags. Nor would they have worn black, since that would make them widows, when witches were understood to be elderly ill-willed single women.[5]

In the nineteenth century the black hat, but not the black gown, becomes the regular wear. In 'The Witches' Frolic' in *The Ingoldsby Legends* of 1837 we are told of three witches,

> On each one's head was a steeple-crown'd hat,
> On each one's knee was a coal-black cat;
> Each had a kirtle of Lincoln green –
> It was, I trow, a fearsome scene.

Even so, in an accompanying illustration by George Cruikshank, only some of the witches wear black, pointed hats, while the others wear some sort of cowl. Their dresses are made of old, patterned cloth.

As with erotic black, one must wait until the twentieth century to meet, in full force, the all-black witch. She arrives with a clap of sound and smoke, in her trailing gown, played by Margaret Hamilton in the film version of *The Wizard of Oz* (1939, illus. 94). In the still shown here, she and her black shadow seem the equal of each other – our shadow being our doppelgänger, which in art and film is often black, for in imagination the shadow we cast is our dark side made visible. Both she and her shadow are, however, inventions of the film, for in the original story by L. Frank Baum (1900) she was scarcely described, except for having one all-powerful eye; and in the original illustrations by W. W. Denslow she wore a light-coloured hat, jacket and ruff over a black skirt covered with frogs and snakes. Since then a horde of pointed, black-clad witches have ranged through the realms of visual imagery – most charmingly in the illustrations to Jill Murphy's *Worst Witch* books, of 1974 and after. If this digression on witches has seemed a detour, still it leads back to the twentieth century. The witch in black is our witch – a highly popular version of our knowledge that formidable women may dress in black.

Witches may also be glamorous in black. In the Reverend Barham's *Ingoldsby Legends*, just quoted, two witches were hags, but the third 'was young, and passing fair, With laughing eyes and with coal-black

94 Margaret Hamilton as the Wicked Witch of the West in
The Wizard of Oz (1939).

hair'. In film and television series, witches may be hideous or they
may be sexily attractive. Demonized stereotypes are hardly stable.
Nor should one forget the ancient association of black with fear of the
feminine. The Furies of the ancient Greeks wore black. Both the
classical and the Nordic worlds had black goddesses of night, and
Hel, the Nordic goddess of the dead, was half white as a corpse and
half black as the decomposition in death.

I have travelled far from the little black dress. But the black
dress too was aware of the dark side. Chanel's rival, Elsa Schiaparelli,

commended her clients for their taste in 'severe suits'. The black of Balenciaga was 'a night without stars'. Yohji Yamamoto said of his blacks and his almost-black indigoes that 'the samurai must be able to throw his body into nothingness, the colour and image of which is black.' Rolf Snoeren of the Dutch design firm Viktor & Rolf said, at the launch of their 'Black Hole' ready-to-wear collection in 2001: 'We were inspired by black holes, which absorb all light and energy.'[6]

The dark vibration is not, however, the main point of long or little black dresses. Their black has a particular visual value, because black is the colour which accentuates shape. A black dress is an eye-dress. The texture of the wool crêpe or silk-jersey knitwear, or the detail of laser-cut, fine black leather, may be hard to make out, but a black dress often will happily accentuate the mobile body and limbs of the wearer. Much as they are mocked, modern catwalk creations can be halfway to abstract art, while being at the same time both theatre and dance, with a value as a kind of visual poetry to which their dark side values are secondary.

More quietly, there are the famous photos by Bert Stern of Marilyn Monroe, in black, pensive and clasping herself for support. Their soft black brings out an insecurity, screen goddess though she also was.

IN THE SECOND half of the twentieth century the black dress led, but has not been alone in, the slow return to black of both men and women, not only in haute couture but also in the street. Rockers in the 1960s wore studded black leather, Mods neat black suits. In the following decades punks had gelled crests which often were jet-black; Goths favoured the vampire look, with dead-white faces and all else black. Some of these styles might recall the cult of the masquerade in the eighteenth century, with its passion for disguises that played with fear. One could say the demon and corpse style then, and the vampire, zombie and fetish styles now, are Gothic-lite and superficial. Or one could say they escape the social straitjacket, and enhance sex appeal with daring games. Heroin chic again was white and black. Apart from such eye-catching, ominous styles, one may count today, on any Western city street, the variety of black tops, black trousers, black snoods, that give style to young and old in the twenty-first century. My granddaughter, aged ten, wears emo black. More worryingly, far-right and fascist black has begun again to flaunt itself, in the black banners and outfits, and swastika and Iron Cross designs of neo-Nazism, and also in the streamlined, swastika-like logo and black t-shirts, leathers and suits of the Golden Dawn party in Greece.

Colour thrives in our world, but still black, with its ambiguous inflections, is king – as it is again in most fields of commercial design. For two or more decades now, IKEA has offered (along with white and scarlet goods) black armchairs, beds, bookshelves and bathmats. There is the all-black kitchen complete with black mixer-tap, high black stools and black clothes-pegs – all carefully appraised by customers who wear often black leather jackets, black baseball caps, black boots and carry black handbags or purses. Website advice on decorating the ultimate Bachelor Pad may note 'the furniture is all black', 'there's a wall that is entirely black' and 'the black floors are a really nice detail'. With 'a large, black bed . . . the whole apartment seems very manly' and 'nothing complements a bachelor pad more than a nice big, black leather couch.'[7] Hi-tech goods come often in black, from flat-screen televisions to laptops and BlackBerries. Black is economic for the manufacturer, since it is easy to mix carbon black (some form of soot) with molten plastic. In these designer goods we do not need to say that black plays with the dark side or alludes to death, mourning or the Christian Church. Rather black has become – more completely than before – the signature colour of smartness and style. Still it is serious: it says we are neither harlequins nor lightweights. And still black depends on contrast – on a companion item that is white or red or any colour – but the black has pride of place.

In architecture too, in the second half of the twentieth century, the obsession with white abated. Le Corbusier might exclaim if he saw a contemporary kidney-shaped building covered entirely with plates of black glass; handrails and doorframes, when we go inside, may be of blackened aluminium. And when our buildings are black it is because we want black, for our synthetic black materials have a poor resistance to weather (as also does black marble – black granite is good). And unlike the dark skyscrapers, contemporary black architecture has caprice, with nothing of the mortuary. In 1989 Philippe Starck designed an all-black office block for the Japanese brewer Asahi (illus. 95). It stands beside the river in Tokyo, looking exactly like a gigantic, square, black-lacquered Japanese beer cup, its convex sides widening upwards. It is capped by a preposterous bronze shape like a carrot, which may represent beer froth blowing away. With less caprice, in 1999, part of the Royal Library of Denmark was rehoused in the Black Diamond Building in Copenhagen, designed by Schmidt Hammer Lassen (illus. 96). Like Starck's building it stands beside water so that, in spite of its apparent crushing weight – like the bottom, and heaviest, section of a pyramid – it seems to float or hover. And its huge but drastically simple bulk, on one side like the rampart of a fort, on the other like an overhanging cliff, recalls ancient structures. At the same time the two plain, skewed rectangles clad in black marble place it in the world of art after Malevich – the world of flat, abstract art one might say – though these black shapes resemble gigantic jet-black crystals, hence its name. In sum, it looks both like a bunker for future wars in the galaxy and like parts of the lower course of a ziggurat – which Herodotus said could be black. The glazed space between the crystals, with its glimpse of high bridges and people at leisure in a white interior, has its own light-reflectiveness, answering to the water.

WITH SUCH POPULARITY in design, it is hardly surprising that black returned in visual art. Nor had black disappeared in the jouissance of modernism. In 1915 Kazimir Malevich painted his *Black Square*; when first exhibited, it was hung in the upper corner of the room, as is the practice in Russia with icons. I do not show it here because reproductions are so easy to see. Instead I show another of his works, where again his black rectangle has, as it were, an implacable visual force (illus. 97). The word 'colour' itself seems to have a different meaning when applied to the white background, which is light; to the blue triangle, where the colour is plain and close to the eye (though blue is often said to recede); and to the black oblong, which is enigmatic and at once opaque and unfathomable. There is both an affinity and a tension between the simple geometrical forms. One is reminded perhaps of the related roles which blue and black have had in Western imagery, with both being tied to spirituality so that the Virgin, from the Middle Ages on, has worn now black, now blue.

Matisse, a virtuoso colourist, used black richly and with clear sensuality – even, for example, when making a linocut of a basket of begonias (illus. 98). And Picasso moved to black-and-white for his masterpiece, *Guernica*. The painting is a surreal nightmare, as if one switched on the light in one's cellar and found a bullfight taking place, with a writhing horse hideously gored. But then everything is

95 Philippe Starck,
Asahi Beer Hall, Tokyo,
1989.

96 Schmidt Hammer
Lassen, The Royal
Library in Copenhagen,
1999.

97 Kazimir Malevich, *Suprematist Painting: Black Rectangle, Blue Triangle*, 1915, oil on canvas.

recessed by the drastic flat geometry, with textured areas reminis-cent of newsprint, as though the artist chose to speak through mock news-photos (our language of sensation), saying: 'Forget colour – something terrible is taking place here.'

The use of black by the early modernists is however occasional. The case is different when we reach the mid-century. In 1949 Barnett Newman painted the large abstract *Abraham*, which he later claimed was 'the first all-black painting' in history. Actually *Abraham* is not 'all-black', since the thick black stripe which runs from top to bottom has a panel on either side of it of black mixed with green. The canvas is narrow, and at 6 feet 10 inches is just a little taller than a tall man would be. It is deeply dark and solemn, and, as commentators suggest, it may reflect Newman's tragic feeling for his father – Abraham Newman – who had been ruined in the Great Depression and had died two years earlier. Newman himself spoke of the 'tragic honesty of the first black painting', and felt he had approached a dangerous, even terrifying, limit:

> Well, I was in the state of terror because what would hap-
> pen – I never had black on black . . . Well, I finally made it
> black. And that moment was almost, I don't know, it
> would be wrong to say that it was violent.

Such a combination of terror and awe was associated, in earlier times, with the sublime.[8]

Perhaps because, as he said, 'the terror of it was intense', Newman did not again paint an all-black (or nearly all-black) painting. And it was because he believed that *Abraham* was an ultimate moment in art that Newman became obsessive, in later years, in claiming *Abraham* as 'the first and still the only black painting in history'.[9] He

98 Henri Matisse, *Basket of Begonias I*, 1938, linocut.

was concerned when he heard, belatedly, of the *Black on Black* paintings which the Russian artist Aleksandr Rodchenko had made in
1918, and decided that Rodchenko's dark tones were brown.

Abraham did not remain the 'only' black painting. In 1951 Robert
Rauschenberg produced an untitled abstract known as 'Glossy Black
Painting'. This was evidently not felt to be a serious challenge; nor
did Rauschenberg stay with black. Newman was, however, infuri-
ated, and attempted to sue for plagiarism when Ad Reinhardt began
to produce black paintings in the early 1950s. Reinhardt certainly
knew Newman's work, since he had helped to hang Newman's first
exhibition – which included a black painting – at the Betty Parsons
gallery in 1950. Newman's criticism was a double one, since he accused
Reinhardt both of derivativeness and of dilution – of producing blacks
that were less than black: 'There is a difference between a black with
pigment that is black and an arrangement of pinkish, bluish "blacks"
which ends up in grays.'[10]

It is true that Reinhardt's black paintings depend on the subtlest
visual vibrations, as one tells the off-blacks from the blacks, discover-
ing barely perceptible rectangles and residues of colour at a near-zero
level of light. Reinhardt liked to quote the Japanese artist Hokusai,
who said, 'there is a black which is old and a black which is fresh . . .
black in sunlight and black in shadow'. And Reinhardt did produce
a darker black than Newman's in the sense that he went to great
lengths to remove sheen from his paint. He diluted the oil medium
with vast quantities of thinner, then overpainted many layers on a
canvas which rested flat on the table. The resulting paint surface
was certainly matt, and extremely fragile. Reinhardt called his black
paintings 'useless, unmarketable . . . inexplicable' icons, but he also
called them 'ultimate paintings', 'timeless, spaceless, changeless . . .
aware of no thing but art'. At the same time, he kept to the human
scale. He said his later, square black paintings should be 'five feet
wide, five feet high, as high as a man, as wide as a man's outstretched
arms'. He was interested in both Christian and Zen Buddhist mysticism, and in transcendence achieved through subtraction and
negation. His lightless paintings are free of anguish: perhaps they do
offer a visual Nirvana.[11]

Nor was it only in New York that black reconquered canvas in
the mid-twentieth century. In Paris, from the late 1940s on, Pierre
Soulages used scarcely any other colour (his first works had been in

99 Robert Motherwell, *Samurai No. 4*, 1974, acrylic on board.

dark walnut stain). His broad, black lines have thrust and attack; his constructions have a firm, upright stance. He himself distinguished 'three ways of black': the deep 'black ground' which sets off the lighter areas; the black surround which sets off small areas of strong colour; and 'textural black', where the paint surface is disturbed with an effect of energy.[12] There is no surprise that the Senegal poet Léo - pold Senghor found in Soulages a kind of white *Négritude*, and welcomed Soulages' marriage of *Négritude* with 'la modernité'. Senghor organized a major exhibition of Soulages' work in Dakar in 1974. The

connection between modernist black and Africa is repeated, back in
New York, in Robert Motherwell's series of screenprints for the
Africa Suite in the 1970s, where again the black forms – more curved
and capricious than those of Soulages – seem a clear unloosing of
pent-up visual energies. The same is true (mostly) of his *Samurai*
series, as if his art were inspired by the connection he saw – or sought
– between his explosive innovations and the impulse of ancient con-
tinents (illus. 99). His forms spring, they move, they seem filled with
life, though the samurai also sparks with danger and has the four-
square firmness of Japanese kanji.

To return to Soulages, jet-blackness swallows ever more of his canvases through the 1960s and '70s, until in 1979 he adopted the style
he called *Outrenoir* (Ultrablack). His canvases now became black all
over, with pale lines discernible where the paint has been combed.
Outrenoir followed, however, the innovations of other artists. In 1960
Frank Stella had begun his own Black Paintings, in which bands
of black house-paint – horizontal, vertical or diagonal – were separated by pinstripes of unpainted canvas. A similar style was practised,
in the mid-1970s, by a less-known French painter, Jean Degottex. In
his parallel black strips, in acrylic, not house-paint, there is a subtle

100 The Rothko Chapel, Houston, Texas, 1965–6.

279

play with the saturation of the paint which perhaps offers more to the dwelling eye than may be found in Stella's hard stripes.[13]

With these near approaches to the truly all-black painting, we perhaps do come to the final step – along one path – which art may take. Black panels have been painted for two or three millennia: they often made the background, in Roman villas, to a small group of figures or plants. Again in the Renaissance, Leonardo da Vinci would set a calm young woman, or the Saviour of the World, against jet-black. Since his time, and that of Caravaggio and Rembrandt, jet-black has sometimes occupied most of the picture-space. It perhaps was inevitable that, in the course of time, the all-black field would advance and come to *be* the painting.

Such an event may mark an epoch of art. To the questions it raises there is no one answer, for the 'black paintings' of different painters are, in effect, different answers. But perhaps the most signal event was the decision of Mark Rothko, in the mid-1960s, to devote himself entirely to blacks, deep browns and deep black-mauves in preparing the canvases for his Chapel in Houston, Texas (illus. 100). Though not uniformly black, they are known as his 'black paintings'. Their effect is well described by James Elkins: 'The paintings are like traps: harmless looking from a distance . . . But if you step too close to a Rothko, you may find yourself *inside it*.' Elkins recalls the exhilaration of Rothko's earlier, luminous canvases, paintings which 'sweep forward, curling around you, filling the very air you breathe with color'. But Elkins finds the effect of the 'black' paintings more negative, and at the end of his first day in the chapel, Elkins records that he

> had given up because it was finally just too hard to take in so much darkness (whole walls of it), and too exhausting to play the game Rothko played, toying with a world of pure featureless black. It had felt a little dangerous, like playing at drowning.[14]

A black question mark hangs, perhaps, over the black paintings of the twentieth century. Already they recede from us, being so closely tied to a particular elite, and so dependent on the spectator's readiness to read in large-order significances. Nor were the Chapel pictures all painted by Rothko, whose second marriage was soon to fail, and who was depressed, seriously ill and exhausted: assistants worked under his direction, producing what he also called 'something you don't want to look at'. Elkins records that he did not weep in the Chapel, though many visitors do, and though he had expected that he might: he was then writing his book *Painting and Tears*.

What does emerge, from many testimonies, is that the Chapel paintings are indeed black, not merely in their large-scale use of dark pigments, but also in the sense that covers dark experience – heartbreak, despair, misery, sterility. Rothko himself said his work addressed 'basic human emotions . . . tragedy, ecstasy, doom, and so on', far though such language is from the favoured idiom for the New York school, from Clement Greenberg's celebration of the truly flat 'picture plane' and from the explicit concern of Reinhardt and Stella that their work should represent 'no thing but art'.[15]

The Chapel is not often discussed as a place for religious contemplation, though Rothko had intended it to be Roman Catholic. Not that the paintings show religious affirmation. Rather they seem the record of an abandonment for which the true remedy would need to be spiritual, though hope of such a remedy has died. Elkins calls the paintings 'suffocating'.[16] It may be that the actual masterpiece in Houston is the Chapel as a whole – this temple of lost faith, lost love, lost potency, and of life and its colours in the last stage of being lost – as the proof of an honesty in plumbing dispossession. The Chapel is not just a bench, on which one may sit in Zen tranquillity or have a comforting cry. It is a house of no escape: a place where desolation must be acknowledged, and in that sense a station on a pilgrimage. It was at that station that Rothko died, though we may not need to die there.

AN ELEMENT IN Rothko's depression – and in the disappointment of other notable black painters – was the sense that they had led art to a final high place, and art had not stayed there. On the contrary, already in the 1960s, the successors had landed. The flat plane of the abstract painting was replaced by paintings flat as an advertising hoarding: a giant Campbell's Soup tin, stacked ranks of Coca-Cola bottles. Pop art had arrived. Andy Warhol guyed but relished supermarket modernity and made a screenprint of the same dollar bill replicated into a grey-green wall. True to his caprice, Warhol said (or is said to have said), 'black is my favourite colour and white

101 Ansel Adams, *Moonrise, Hernandez, New Mexico*, 1941, photograph.

is my favourite colour'. He was liable to wear black and dye his hair
white, and in his later *Disaster* series of screenprints his use of black
is analogous to strong chiaroscuro. Hideously crashed cars, replicated
in multiple from black-and-white photos, cross a green, pink or
orange ground.

Pop art was not, however, strongly given to black. Roy Lichten-
stein used hard comic-book colours, while in England Peter Blake,
nostalgic for old fairground placards, liked the effect of lurid poster
colours faded by English weather. Then, in the later 1960s, Op art
came. Black was back, but in a partnership of equal weight with white.
In paintings by Bridget Riley, Victor Vasarely and Richard Anuszkie -
wicz, a black-and-white chequerboard may zigzag and swirl as if seen
through water, or contract and spin in herringbone spirals. Op art
confirms again the undying beauty of the black-with-white combin -
ation. Not that Op art was confined to monochrome: Bridget Riley
sometimes gave her slanted grids a dreamcoat beauty of oranges,
blues and greens.

The century's major use of black-and-white must however be in
the photograph: a form born in monochrome, in which for many

decades colour was impracticable. Though colour film began to be marketed in 1935–6, by Kodak and by Agfa, the complications of the process meant that black-and-white continued to dominate until 1960. The major historic photographers are mostly known for their work in monochrome – Eugène Atget, Henri Cartier-Bresson, Walker Evans, Ansel Adams – and often we find their tones have been managed to make a powerful use of jet-black. Ansel Adams will make blue skies black. In *Moonrise, Hernandez, New Mexico*, well over half the picture-space is solid black (illus. 101). That sky cannot have been pitch-black, but we read the black here as an endless night-space of crystal-clear air. Against it we relish the wind-streamed white of the distant cloud, stretched out like silk. Near the fore-ground the tiny crosses shine against the blacks of vegetation; beyond the town there are other black strips of heath and forest. The picture, which has an 'abstract' beauty, places human homeliness against the cold, magnificent beauty of the inhuman cosmos.

Long after the arrival of colour photography, black-and-white continues in notable strength. The recent use of flash with mono-chrome has found a new way of making the real surreal. In Mårten Lange's *Anomalies* of 2009, the steep contrast of the flash makes the sky outside black as interstellar space (illus. 102). But for a favourite example of photographer's black in the age of colour I shall cite a picture by the distinguished Greek photographer Aris Georgiou. I have it on my wall, in a large print from the photographer's hand, titled *Montpellier, 1976* (illus. 103). I am teased by the strangeness of the building, and by the oddly slanted wall with the low door beside it, which again is odd with the narrow, scalloped windows along its top. The picture draws me with a double pull, both upstairs to a window dissolving in light and downstairs towards the not-shut door, which half opens on a bright-lit space. What people belong here? I am drawn to the door as by a half-open book, and approaching the stairs seems like starting a story. This could be a still from a black-and-white film, because chiaroscuro easily says to us, 'narrative'. For me this picture has intrigue, which is made by its lights and deep, enclosing blacks.

It is a real question what is gained and what lost in moving between colour and black-and-white. Michel Pastoureau criticizes contem-porary culture for its readiness to believe that a picture may say more in black-and-white than in colour. And in his short book *Chromo-phobia* (2001) David Batchelor traces humanity's love–hate relationship

with colour back to biblical times. The love of colour has been condemned for its association with sensuousness, with crimson sinfulness,
with aesthetic amoralism, with homosexuality. The artist Bridget Riley
has written an eloquent essay on the kind of beauty achieved in
Western oil painting, where the transparency of the paint allows innumerable hues to cooperate in elaborate chords of colour. In the course
of her discussion Riley distinguishes two kinds of black: the black
of chiaroscuro, where Caravaggio and his successors used black in
their shadows to dim and cancel colour; and the black of the colourists
– of Rubens, Velázquez, Delacroix – whose black acts positively *as* a
colour in its play with the reds and blues and golds.[17]

The question remains: what is the fundamental difference between
the monochrome and the coloured image? At a recent exhibition of
Robert Mapplethorpe's photographs, with their many lustrous blacks
beside and within bodies, I have walked back and forth between the
colour and the monochrome versions of his large, dramatic photos

102 Mårten Lange, photograph from *Anomalies*, 2009.

103 Aris Georgiou, *Montpellier, 1976*, photograph.

of orchids. I find the comparison hard to focus clearly because the difference between the modes seems in some way radical. If pressed, I might say that the monochrome image seems to want to tell me something, while the colour seems there to be enjoyed. Perhaps I misdescribe the difference, but still I wonder if that difference could relate to the different ways in which our sight has evolved.

Our vision of black-and-white involves both the 'cone' and the 'rod' cells in the retina; and, as noted earlier, both forms of cell emit an electrical signal on seeing light and whiteness and then again on seeing black and darkness. There is no question why they should signal light, since light lets us know where we are in the world. But why should they flag up dark and blackness? It seems it was important, at the beginning of evolution, for organisms to know where the dark places were – since they might offer safety or hide a predator. Our tonal vision has much to do with danger and safety – as it still does on a dark night or when one is watching a thriller (which will use exaggerated chiaroscuro). These features may have helped monochrome vision to be associated with statement and story, with hope and fear. A young contemporary painter of black (and white) canvases, Wilhelm Sasnal, has said, 'black is the colour when you're thinking of a means for telling stories and constructing narratives'.[18]

At this early stage of vision, colour discrimination was limited. And most mammals, through their long history, have seen only two colours, yellow and violet; a dog sees the world in warm yellows, cold purples. It is three-colour vision that gives us the rainbow – crimson, gold, turquoise, aquamarine. It evolved in our ancestor the monkey – separately in America and in Eurasia – seemingly so our forefathers could see which fruit were ripe, turning to yellow and red amid green leaves. Since then our colour sense has acquired great subtlety, which we exercise immediately when we see a beautiful dress, or an oil painting by Titian. But still we call colours 'delicious': they gives us a pleasure like the pleasure of taste. We might say colour feeds the soul, not the stomach. But still colour feeds, while black-and-white signifies.

I simplify, of course. Colours can have meanings, and black-and-white has beauty. But still the priorities of colour and monochrome vision are different. I may be swayed to this reading by the dominance of black-and-white in our communication media and by the long history of black ink on white paper (or vellum, or papyrus). But that history, on the other hand, may – must – be influenced by the character of monochrome vision. News photos will have a strong chiaroscuro, since they are importantly informative, while our colour vision waits for the fashion or the sports pages.

Reverting to the essay by Bridget Riley, one might say that actually there are not two, but three, blacks: there is black the strong colour, which dances with other colours; and black the shadow, which smothers colour; and also black the semantic colour, the colour of outlines, of letters and words, the colour that divides and also connects. In colour separations for colour printing, the black plate is called the 'key'.

The question of monochrome versus polychrome images arises again in film. On celluloid, the switch between colour and black-and-white has been worked many times since Eisenstein abruptly jumped into colour stock for a late reel in Part II of *Ivan the Terrible* (1958). Often the switch seems simple and arbitrary, as when 'the present' is shot in colour, and 'the past' in black-and-white. But some film-makers have played this transition with a memorable sensitivity.

Tarkovsky's *Nostalgia*, of 1983, ends with two long takes. In the first, a Russian who has been self-exiled in Italy for many years pays homage to a friend who has recently died. He visits a spa which his friend had liked and decides to carry a lighted candle from one end of the drained pool to the other. The scene is in subdued brown-greys, while the candle flame flickers with a pure, bright yellow. Very slowly the camera approaches the man, who retraces his steps when the candle twice blows out, and a kind of marriage develops between spectator, camera and protagonist. At last the candle is set on the stone, then we hear a gasp and – in a brief shot – see an onlooker hurry over. We wonder, has the protagonist collapsed – or died?

Then, in monochrome, we see the same man sitting at the edge of a pool beside a resting Alsatian dog. As the camera tracks back we see their reflections in the water and then, behind them, a small dacha or country home set against dark woodland. But by now we are puzzled by the reflection in the water of tall chimneys of shadow, which prove, as the camera continues to withdraw, to be the reflections of the arches in a ruined church. We have visited this church, which is in Italy, earlier in the film, but now – a clear impossibility – the protagonist, his dog, the pool, house and woodland are all contained within the ruins. The camera has halted, it begins to snow, and we see the snow settle on house-roof and hillside. The snow pauses, then resumes, while the soundtrack continues its remote, quiet noise of whistlings, dog-howls, a woman's song. So the film ends, with a slow-revealed metaphor for – what? The consecration of a lost, remembered world – of a death, a life, with (or without) a faith also lost . . .

One asks then what difference is made by the presence, or the absence, of colour. Would the change be significant if the first take was in monochrome and the second in colour? The candle shot would not lose its incremental suspense if shot in black-and-white – though the yellow of the candle flame is a precious touch of colour. It would be odd, though, if the candle had been in monochrome, to switch to colour for the world in a church, which might then seem too softly nostalgic, when its primary reference is to a yearning for lost things in the shadow of death. The question is a delicate one, but one might claim – contrary perhaps to the implications of Bridget Riley and David Batchelor – that there is no loss in art, suggestiveness, or in beauty either, in *Nostalgia*'s closing move from colour to black-and-white: in which the man's pullover, the windows, the tree-trunks and foliage, all have the emphasis of black.

BLACK, IN THE aesthetic domain, has kept its seriousness. It has, however, lost much of its association with religious faith, and also with evil that is in some way supernatural. One might ask where the black of the Devil has gone – the colour of witchcraft and sinister magic. The answer seems to be into fiction: fiction, that is, that cannot be called realist. Dramatic and threatening blacks thrive in popular fantasy literature today, and have done so since the early nineteenth century, when it became regular practice for fictitious events to be visualized continuously. In the tales of Poe, of the later 1830s and the '40s, the word 'black' had been an excitant, especially when the writer aimed to give water a macabre character. In Stevenson's *Treasure Island* (1881–3) the action had begun in Black Hill Cove with the menacing arrival of the mystery seaman Black Dog, together with Blind Pugh, who dispensed the death-giving 'BLACK SPOT'. In the *Strange Case of Dr Jekyll and Mr Hyde* (1886) the word was used more freely and figuratively. The action began on 'a black winter morning', Dr Jekyll laboured under a 'blackness of distress', and during his transformation Jekkyll/Hyde's face 'became suddenly black and the features seemed to melt and alter'. In Bram Stoker's *Dracula* (1897), the Count, on his first appearance, was 'clad in black from head to foot, without a single speck of colour about him anywhere'.[19]

There was a salient use of black in the twentieth century, in J.R.R. Tolkien's *The Lord of the Rings* of 1954–5. On Middle Earth

the bad wear black mainly, it seems, to show they *are* bad. Black
Riders sniff in the hobbits' tracks, or tower over others in enveloping
black hoods; they are a sort of living dead and among themselves
they speak 'the Black Speech', which sounds, to judge from its 'k's, hard
'g's and 'zgh' noises, repulsively catarrhal. They come from the evil
land of Mordor, which has a Black Gate while its armies wear black
livery. The name 'Mordor' is said to mean, in Tolkien's invented language, 'Black Land'. It would have the same meaning in the Romance
languages, picking up on 'moor', 'blackamoor' and 'Mauretania', also
calling to mind the Latin *mors* (death) and *mordere* (to bite, harm,
sting), as well as assonating with 'murder'. The primordial dark power
Morgoth wears black armour and carries a vast, plain, dead-black
shield. Mordor's own Dark Lord, Sauron, is also known as the Black
Hand and is hideous and terrifying in his form, which we hear, at the
Council of Elrond, 'was black and yet burned like fire'. I have wondered
whether one reason why the film company restricted him to a blazing
eye was because in Tolkien he is black-skinned and could give offence
racially (no one seems troubled, in the world of film fantasy, by a lord
of many rings with no fingers to put them on).

I am sorry if I seem to mock this work, because I was infatuated
when I discovered it, as a twelve-year-old, in the mid-1950s. It may
have contributed to my interest in black, and I have noticed the use
of Tolkienian fantasy-evil-black in its innumerable derivatives. Tolkien
also demonstrates that our new, fearful blacks are rooted in the 'real'
blacks of the Devil, hell and demons. For Tolkien was a medievalist
who had studied Greek and Latin at school and university. His evil land
of Mordor, which is all darkness, fire and blackness, with iron gates
and iron towers, draws both on the medieval Christian hell – a black,
blazing landscape peopled by monsters and black devils – and also
on the preceding classical Hades, which again had black fires and red
fires – and rivers of fire – and giant gates and towers of iron, plus its
own dark lord, 'the Black One', Hades or Pluto, who sat on a throne
attended by hooded Deaths. One difference in the picture is that
Hades had beside him his permanently young, beautiful bride Queen
Persephone, the spirit of spring – but she could not survive into the
Christian Hell and should not be looked for in Middle Earth. Sauron,
unlike Hades – and unlike Satan – is single and sexless.

While evil black recurs in post-Tolkien prose fantasies by Stephen
Donaldson and others, it is most apparent in film: where the fact that

in the real world black is stylish means that both sides may wear black. An evil lord will likely wear black but so may his young, dragon-riding opponents. Or, in a high-tech fantasy such as *The Matrix*, the hostile living programs may wear black glasses with black business-suits, while the youthful resistance figures wear shiny, ankle-length black coats (over black or purple-black outfits). Keanu Reeves as 'Neo' looks at times like a young Jesuit in his button-up black cassock, but he flies like Superman – though black like Batman – when living inside the supercomputer's software.

Batman, through his many incarnations since the comic book of 1939, is the ultimate superhero in black. His original catsuit was grey, worn with a blue hooded cape, trunks and boots, but from the start – from the dramatic first drawing – the front part of his mask was often shaded jet-black, as were the scalloped folds of his cape. Often Batman's accessories were more black than blue, and since 1990, in both comic books and films, his cape, hood and mask have been black while his trunks and boots are often scarcely distinguishable from his deep-charcoal body armour. From the earliest depictions, and more so recently, his appearance hints at the demonic. The bat-mask has slit eyes, a dagger nose and pointed ears like horns; the black cape spreads wide like a demon's pterodactyl wings. Batman offers the special thrill of resembling the Devil in the cause of good while being still, in secret, a millionaire with a conscience. His faithful butler Alfred wears the black-and-white of service, while one of his enemies, the Penguin, is the bad sort of millionaire and wears a black top hat with (in the comic books as in the film) a black tail-coat. Batman is a masked crusader – like the Lone Ranger, and even more like Zorro, who also wore black – but is nearer than either both to the supernatural world and to Wall Street. His black is associated at once with good and with bad money, counted by the million. His leading woman opponent is a cat – a black cat.

Batman shows that if demonic black has passed from true fear into fantasy, it can with a further twist become the style of sympathetic figures – as in those genres of confused fantasizing where we take sides with one or more youthful vampires, witches, werewolves or demons, now seen as a hard-done-by alien race, tending like goths to white faces and black gear, which often glistens like pvc. Zombies, on the other hand, the living dead, wear miscellaneous old clothes – which are liable however to look dark-to-black, since zombies are short on laundering. In these genres fear and style meet, playing half-forbidden games with fetish-black and the sexualization of black synthetics.

There are other dimensions also. The very constancy of young-vampire movies suggests they are the fantasy-deformation of a persistent social sore. The wound in question could be said to be drug use, since the vampire is the ultimate addictive personality, substance-determined, with impaired affect. In his or her trendy death-black outfit the youthful blood-addict both glamorizes and demonizes the half-life of dependency. Werewolves and zombies, too, may be seen as 'altered state' versions of people. But nor are drugs the whole story, for what vampires and zombies have in common is that they are in different ways dead. In other words, fantasy black and evil black are related also to black's ancient role as the colour of death. There may be a shrewd anxiety management going on in this profitable field of production in which, together with other excitements, the fear of death, the fascination with death and the eroticization of death are combined in mass youth entertainment.

THE ASSOCIATION IN fantasy of black with evil is the light side of the profound link that has always been felt between blackness and the most terrible events – also the most terrible acts – which human beings may suffer or do. The Black Death was not called black only because it caused necrosis of the extremities, but because it was – or because it was thought to be – the most evil epidemic of all time. More lightly, 'black' is applied to weekdays on which financial disasters occur, as in 'Black Monday' or 'Black Wednesday'. But especially the word 'black' is used of those events where the motive is evil. Confronted with genocide, with sadistic killing or mutilation, we spontaneously call up the colour-word 'black' because the evil is extreme, like a total loss of light – as though forgiveness, here, would itself be a crime. The use of 'black' in such a context is entirely metaphorical, though the imagery of light and dark has been intertwined for so long with our sense of good and bad that 'black', said of wickedness, feels like the grammatical superlative of 'bad' ('blacker' and 'blackest' are no stronger).

To decide which human acts have been the blackest of all is hardly a pleasant task – and inevitably, and fortunately, the instances that most of us bring to mind will be remote from us, newsreel things, things we have heard reported. I think of a black-and-white shot of countless white, naked, horribly emaciated bodies piled across each other in a pit for burial in a Nazi camp; a photograph of a girl in Sierra Leone holding up her bandaged stumps because 'fighters' have cut her hands off to score a racial-political point; and Fred West – for weeks – torturing young girls trapped in his cellar, while they knew all the time that he would kill them in the end. In England one would think of the Moors Murders also, but every country has (if one looks back) overflowing files of black acts. The use of 'black' for atrocities can be a cliché, but it is not for no reason that 'clichés' are repeated. Some 'clichés' rightly endure forever, and the use of 'black' for utter wickedness is one such.

And then there is that odd rider to black evil, which can come sometimes in the 'black joke'. Black jokes can be loathsome, but they can also be extraordinary in the juxtapositions they make. The most extreme item of black humour I know occurred when Mel Brooks, director of the brilliantly successful movie *The Producers* (1968), which turns on the spoof-musical 'Springtime for Hitler', said wryly in an interview, 'Hitler was bad for lots of Jews – but he's been good to me.' Of course only a Jewish film-maker could say that, but everyone can see the outrageous excess of it. It is almost sublime in its unmention - ability. Actually it does not devalue the hideousness of systematized genocide, but it does perform a mental-linguistic somersault in which an incongruous surprise of vivacity joins with the utterly terrible.

What human beings do with worst things over time may be both astonishing and oddly playful – even soothing. The Black Death itself became a nursery rhyme:

Ring-a-ring o'roses
A pocketful o'posies
A-tishoo a-tishoo
We all fall down.

The ring of roses was the small, circular rash of sores which was one plague-symptom; the posies were the sweet-smelling herbs used in the hope they could disinfect. So countless numbers died in a horror of gangrene and suppurating buboes; and the children join hands to dance in a ring, and laugh as they tumble over.

IN THE BROADER literary field a black emphasis is again apparent. It is beyond the scope of this book to give a fair whole account of black writing in the sense of African, African American or Afro-European fiction, poetry, drama, song; also the time of an insistence on pure *Négritude* has passed. In both the critical and the fictional prose of Chinua Achebe, Toni Morrison and many others, an injustice – a blindness – has been redressed so that it is no longer true to say, as Achebe did of Conrad's work, that 'the very humanity of black people is called in question'.[20]

In fiction at large, the fashion for black things (unrelated to race) is represented surreally in the 'Midnite-Confidential Club' in Salman Rushdie's *Midnight's Children*. The Club exists in pitch darkness, the floor is covered with 'a lush black carpet – midnight-black, black as lies, crow-black, anger-black' and the girl-attendants are blind because the whole purpose of the Club is for the well-to-do of Bombay to manage sexual encounters which society would forbid. In another passage in the novel, the colour contrast in the hair of India's President Indira Gandhi – who had a pronounced 'skunk stripe' – is extended with a Halloween surrealism of black and green. In the novel she is known only as 'the Widow', but the reference is clear: 'the walls are green the sky is black . . . the Widow is green but her hair is black . . . it is green on the left and on the right black . . . the Widow's arm is long as death its skin is green . . . the fingernails are black . . . see the children run . . . children green their blood is black'.[21]

In the theatre an all-black visual field is nearly all one sees in Samuel Beckett's *Not I*, except for one spotlit jabbering mouth. To achieve this effect, the actress – Jessica Tandy in New York in 1972, Billie Whitelaw in London in 1973 – had to be clamped in place dressed in black, with a black hood which left only the mouth uncovered. The mouth is lit for the duration of her hectic, almost Pentecostal gabble, which seems to be an outburst of protest following a life of sterile isolation. Her speech can hardly be a release, since she repeatedly denies that she is speaking of herself. In an earlier play by Jean Genet, *The Screens* (*Les Paravents*) of 1961, there is a character called The Mouth who has been represented in production as a figure swathed and hooded in black so that only his mouth could be seen.

And in poetry there is Ted Hughes's *Crow* (1972). In the first poem, 'Two Legends', the word 'black' begins over half of the poem's 24 lines. Heart, liver, lungs and blood, bowels and nerves are black. They make 'an egg of blackness' which hatches a crow, 'a black rainbow Bent in emptiness . . . But flying'. Crow, the protagon - ist, is a carrion crow, eating the dead, 'grinning into the black'; also a malicious-humorous trickster-spirit; and also a man 'in the silent room . . . smoking . . . between the dusk windows and the fire's embers'. The poems were produced following the suicides of Hughes's wife Sylvia Plath in 1963 and of his lover Assia Wevill in 1969 and, however these matters may be connected, the poems clearly have a burden of painful, dark experience. They have violence and pain, and reiterated blackness, but the blackness of Crow himself is alive, not dead. Crow may be 'blacker / Than any blindness' ('Crowcolour'), but the black beauty in nature is his companion ('black is the wet otter's head, lifted'). Crow is also a tragic-heroic fool: he was once white and decided the sun was too white, so he flew up and attacked it. The sun, however, brightened steadily, and he returned burned black. Still he proclaimed, 'Up there . . . Where white is black and black is white, I won' ('Crow's Fall'). Crow is described as 'flying the black flag of himself' ('Crow Blacker than Ever'), but he is also a father who loses his children: when he enters the 'stupor' of Nature an oak tree grows out of his ear, and his 'black children' sit in a row in its upper boughs, until

They flew off.

Crow
Never again moved.

('Magical Dangers')

The blackness of *Crow* is made of pain, but is also hot, beating, the black inside of being – an irreducible principle of continuation, with a steadiness in facing the inescapable. *Crow* was criticized for its extremes when it first appeared – extremes from which Hughes retreated in his later, more pastoral writings – but in retrospect it may seem one of poetry's closest encounters with what is blackest in life (and in death too) but which still, though black, *is* life.[22]

BEYOND THE BLACKS of our culture is the black of the cosmos – the black of space. Our sky, it is true, is filled with stars; but if we could

travel to the edge of our galaxy, we would see what we don't see in the night sky above us: true emptiness, starlessness, the ultimate black – made deeper by the odd dot, here and there, of other galaxies. I don't know if such emptiness could freeze the soul. It may be too that the universe will end in freezing black emptiness everywhere. But that is not our problem – nor is it a certainty. Nor do we understand how anything – let alone a universe – should have come into being out of nothing, whether in a big bang like a giant firework, or in some other way. We are surrounded by uncertainty, which includes the uncertainty as to whether the emptiness is truly empty – or whether it harbours invisible matter, what has been called 'dark matter', which may exist in unimaginably huge quantities. It seems too that there are – within our galaxy – those places where the stuff of many stars has collapsed inwards, imploding into a 'singularity' whose gravity is so colossal that not even light can escape. 'Black holes', we say, though they are the opposite of empty.

Around us is such vast emptiness – but perhaps also such vast black energy – of almost unimaginable scale. Whether that knowledge affects our fashions is doubtful, though our taste for black may in some way connect with the finality of death and with the absence – from all of space – of benign powers to help us.

Whether black will have in the future the stature it has now, and has had in the past, we do not know. For the present we live in a poly - chrome world – a world of bright pinks, lime greens, sharp blues – a world of more colours than the human race has seen before, in which, nonetheless, the colour in greatest use is black.

I shall close by noting that the day of black paintings is far from over. Recent postmodernist painting has often been polychromatic, to the extent that one could think art had turned its back on black. But in 2006 in Paris the Foundation Maeght held an exhibition, 'Le Noir est une couleur', which was followed in 2007 by the exhibition 'Black Paintings' at the Haus der Kunst in Munich. Also in 2007 was the exhibition 'Dark Matter' at the White Cube Gallery in London. And in 2008 the Kestner Gesellschaft in Hanover, Germany, had its 'Back to Black' exhibition. There have been other black exhibitions since. Between them these exhibitions have represented works by Matisse, Bonnard, Braque, Rouault; also by Reinhardt, Rothko, Rauschenberg, Stella; and by an international generation of younger artists, keen to work in black.

104 Peter Peri, *Modernity will not seduce me*, 2009,
spray paint and marker pen on canvas.

Of the latter, Ned Vena is closest to Stella in his liking for parallel pinstripes, though he works in sprayed rubber over vinyl stencils.
Rafał Bujnowski has broken with the rectangular canvas, and makes
paintings with five, six or seven sides. From the front they look like
black three-dimensional solids. Emanuel Seitz paints abstracts in
which, set in deep jet-black, there are shapes of deep lilac, deep
turquoise, sea-deep blue. The language in which he speaks is dynamic, like his colours:

> Already the dark sky dazzles above the black horizon . . .
> [eyes] lose themselves in deep blackness . . . The imagination
> dashes through the darkness.[23]

Among the new black-on-black paintings I find a special intrigue in the work of Peter Peri (illus. 104). His blacks are crossed by fine hairlines of silver, in which traces of colour may show (pink, yellow, green, blue), and there is also a play of contrasting textures between the black spaces which the fine lines delimit, so that one may be unsure whether thin lines cross black space or whether black solids hover before us. His *Modernity will not seduce me* makes pattern a paradox, like an Escher drawing in the flat, where the shapes which are squared but on the slant seem also to overlap impossibly. The eye may be enticed inside its black maze. In the book that accompanied the 'Back to Black' exhibition in Hanover he quotes from Edmund Burke's *Philosophical Enquiry into the Origin of Our Ideas of the Sublime and Beautiful* (1757),

> Black bodies . . . are but as so many vacant spaces . . . When the eye lights on one of these vacuities . . . it suddenly falls into a relaxation; out of which it suddenly recovers by a convulsive spring.[24]

For darkness is fecund. Out of darkness something springs.

The story of black is far from ended. But I must stop, and having reached contemporary practice, I shall make not one but two ends. Dark as all blacks is a painting by Victor Man, in greys deepening

105 Victor Man, *The Deposition*, 2008, oil on linen.

106 Zbigniew Rogalski, 'Untitled 2004', from the series *Together*, 2004, oil on canvas.

down to black (illus. 105). It is much like a monochrome photo viewed through smoked glass, in which we just make out what may be a family gathered in a waiting room. It looks to be a dysfunctional family, its members set apart though their postures cross. They are gathered round a box not unlike a coffin which rests on a pram, and an obscure serpentine shape is coiled in the shadows over the box. Victor Man quotes Paul Celan, 'Black milk of daybreak we drink you at night', though the words this picture brought to my own mind were those of the prince, late in Henry James's *Golden Bowl*, 'Everything is terrible, cara, in the heart of man.' Not that the painting covers 'everything', but a sense of death and the terrible hangs upon it while its title, *Deposition*, implies that its darkness may be religious also.[25]

And for my best approach to an end which, though black, is happy, I call to mind a painting by Zbigniew Rogalski (illus. 106). His words are a little cryptic: he says 'black paint is the most specific means of describing the essence. It's like print in a book – best when it comes in black.'[26] In his *Together* series there is a painting, 'Untitled

2004', much of which is solid black. Against the dark we make out
– bright-lit in places – a young couple riding from us on a moped.
The girl's outstretched hand clasps a large white cut-out paper shape,
which represents the moped's exhaust, and curls round and down
to the exhaust pipe. A caprice, then, with comedy in the cartoon-
ish bubble shapes of the cut-out cloud. And a nice representation of
a young couple heading on together through the solid midnight
black of world, space, the universe.

A Note on Chessboards, Death and Whiteness

Perhaps the reason that the combination of black with white works so well visually – in the appearance of clothes, tiles, books, the pieces on a chessboard – is because the contrast is between a high strength and an extremely low strength of the same, broad band of light. When bright we call it white, since that is how we name the combined colours of the spectrum, and when dim we call it grey, or charcoal – or black. This combination of kinship with contrast may also explain the ease with which darks and lights, and blacks and whites, may change places.

Take death. It is sometimes said that the colour of death is black in the West, while in the East it is white. And it is true that for centuries in the West, mourning clothes were black, even jet-black, while from India eastwards, mourning clothes have very often been white – in both cases having a stronger association with mourning when the colour is worn by women. A young woman in London would have had the same hesitation in wearing an all-black dress to a wedding that, in Delhi, she would have if she wore a white sari (before, that is, the interaction of Bollywood with Hollywood gave Western-white a romantic association). In Africa also, the colour white has the odour of death. An Africanist friend, Professor Patrick Chabal, has told me that when he asked his African students to describe how they would feel if they woke up one morning and found they were white, they mostly said this would be a catastrophe, because the colour white belongs to death.

Colour values are not so simple, however, as instances like these suggest, and actually, in West, South and East, death is black and also white. Mourners in Africa may be marked both with white and black, and also with black ashes. Historically, in China or Japan, if an attacking warrior flew a black flag, it meant that battle must be to the death. And in the West, though mourning dress has generally been black, both bereaved children and bereaved young unmarried women have often worn white in mourning – as have the queens of France.

In the West, black death has many whites. The shroud or winding sheet was white (often of cotton), and perhaps this is why the risen ghost was imagined as white. And while the mourners at a funeral wore black, the officiating priest would wear a white surplice. Death especially, as a figure, was thought of as white, because he was imagined as a skeleton. In Bruegel's *Triumph of Death*, which has a strong black centre, there are many stark whites: white corpses, white shrouds, a horde of white skeletons, while one Death rides an emaciated, 'pale' horse, which here is white (see illus. 31).

In fact the picture of Death we make today, when we imagine Death as a towering, sometimes empty, black, hooded cloak, is – like the Black Witch – a figure most popular in the twentieth century. There were hooded Deaths in the past, and when Scrooge meets Death in Charles Dickens's *A Christmas Carol* (1843), he takes the form of a 'solemn Phantom, draped and hooded . . . shrouded in a deep black garment'.[1] But though black, hooded Deaths can be found in earlier periods, the predominant visualization – in, for instance, the innumerable 'Dance of Death' engravings – is of a naked, vivacious skeleton. If not fully a skeleton, Death is still aged, pale and emaciated, as in the engravings of Dürer. Or, Death's cloak may be light, not dark. In the *Dance of Death* series (1848) by the German artist Alfred Rethel, Death – a skeleton – wears a hooded cloak, or alternatively the robes of a pilgrim, but his cloak is light in tone and certainly not jet-black. In a Goya etching of 1808–14, in the series *Disasters of War*, Death may be seen draped and hooded in white, looming over cowering soldiers.

If practice changed in the twentieth century, giving the black-hooded phantom pride of place, this may be partly because, when making a film, it is easier to drape an actor in black than to animate white bones convincingly. This black Death often appears as one of the cast in films by Woody Allen. But the great representation of a black-hooded Death had been in Ingmar Bergman's *The Seventh Seal* (1957) where, within his black cloak, Death had a dead-white face and was bald as a skull, though also grimly playful, as Death should be when leading his Dance. Such Death's clothing is perhaps the final, demonized form of the *cappa negra* worn by Christian priests, which then became sinister in Protestant art and literature. This 'mortified' form of Church dress has become iconic in fantasy literature and film, so that Tolkien's Black Riders, whether on horses or on giant pterodactyls, look at once like Death and like black monks, while the evil emperor of the *Star Wars* film series is not grand at all, but again looks like a black monk, or like Death, his damaged skin white in arrested putrescence. His associate, Darth Vader, is also a Death, as his name half hints: he is a more original concept however, exploiting the combined sinister effect of gas masks, skull-masks, Prussian helmets, black capes, hi-tech control panels and old, black-lacquered armour.

A corollary of these contrasts is that, within a single culture, a different colour may predominate in different arts. In literature, one may find white deaths. In D. H. Lawrence's *Women in Love* Gerald Crich dies a snow-death between white peaks and glaciers, while in *Moby-Dick* Herman Melville has a wonderful chapter on the nightmare deathliness which the colour white can have (chapter 42). He speaks of 'the white gliding ghostliness' not of white whales but of the white shark. Even so, and though I cannot quantify, I am certain that in literary usage death is associated with blackness much more than with whiteness. The frequent use of 'black' in eighteenth-century graveyard poetry, mentioned earlier, illustrates this. The black waters of Edgar Alan Poe are death in liquid form, and as the Fay dies lingeringly in 'The Island of the Fay' we are repeatedly told that her shadow 'fell from her, and was swallowed up in the dark water, making its blackness more black'. In Thomas Mann's *The Magic Mountain* (1924) Hans Castorp, admiring the military, speaks of death existentially:

> I think the world, and life generally, is such as to make it appropriate for us all to wear black . . . and for our intercourse with each other to be subdued and ceremonial, and mindful of death.

In visual art, on the other hand, both death and the accessories of death are often painted in the lustreless but glaring whiteness of shroud and bleached bones, while the recently dead themselves are regularly shown as white. In paintings of cemeteries, tombs of white limestone glimmer beneath cypress trees.[2]

Death, through *The Seventh Seal*, plays a game of chess with
the Knight, played by a gaunt but relatively young Max von Sydow.
If we compare cultures, we find various entities may choose now one
and now the other side of the board. Priesthoods in the ancient
world, from Rome to the Druid groves, wore mainly white, as Mormon
elders do now in their temples, and Condomblé priests across Brazil.
On the other hand, both Shi'a Islam and Judaism in recent centuries
have made a large use of black in their dress, as do some divisions of
Buddhism, for instance in Japan, departing from the traditional
saffron-to-red. In Christianity the widespread use of black is complemented by many uses of white, as in vestments such as the surplice
and accessories like the chorister's gown. In many representations,
historically and today, Jesus wears white, as the Pope often does today
on earth (sometimes beneath the red mantum of governance) and as
the winged multitudes are said to in Heaven.

Returning to earth, both white and black have been the symbolic
colours of an incumbent social class, like the Russian aristocratic
'Whites', who called the tsar the 'White Tsar'.[3] In chapter Two, on
classical black, some comparison was made between the roles of
senatorial and imperial purple in ancient Rome, and of patrician and
royal black in later Europe. But, equally, if one is speaking of the dress
of governing classes, one could contrast Europe's nineteenth-century
black, in a fine frock-coat of best black woollen broadcloth, with the
Roman patrician toga of fine, white wool. It is true that while both men
and women wore white in Rome, in the nineteenth century, in
Western Europe especially, women often wore white while men very
often wore black. But gender coding, too, may be reversed, and men
and women in Saudi Arabia use the opposite colours: the men wear
white, and women black. In the nineteenth-century's Colonial era
men used both colours: well-to-do American and European men
wore black in their home countries, and white in their torrid dominions. White became, as it were, the black of the Tropics. In recent
centuries in developed cities, the colour of professionalism has been
black, but in laboratories, hospitals and kitchens, the white of hygiene
and health. On stage, sad Pierrot wore white, and melancholy Hamlet
black. In far-right politics, neo-Nazis took black as their colour, the
Klu Klux Klan white. More frivolously, the 'dandy' of nineteenth-
century Europe wore black – a colour stylish still – but there have
also been white dandies. For his public appearances the novelist and

satirist Tom Wolfe wears a white two- or three-piece suit, now with a dark and now with a white tie: there is an elusive, smart irony somewhere in the radiance. And in contemporary Brazil the *malandro* ('bad boy', hustler, spiv) struts the backstreets in a white suit, shirt and trilby hat, worn often with a red tie and sometimes with a shirt striped red and white.

Examples could be multiplied, which would show at once both the arbitrariness and the consistencies in the practices that fix and communicate values among cultures. The consistencies include the pre-eminence of the black/white contrast if a person wants to signal meanings using colours, as in voting systems which use black and white counters. I must stop short, however, of implying that black and white are simply interchangeable. Their uses and meanings may overlap, but their associations cluster around opposing centres. Thus we may speak of a deathly whiteness, but we do not speak of a 'white despair', nor – though both brides and bridegrooms have sometimes worn black – would we wish to speak of 'wedding black'. Bedouin men, who wear black in the desert, wear white at their weddings – as the British know from T. E. Lawrence, Lawrence of Arabia, who chose for his daily wear the white, silk wedding robe he was given by Emir Faisal.[4]

Wedding white touches on a dimension of white that is antithetical to the dominant senses of black, for wedding white was once worn by everyone, as the colour of jubilation, and was only later confined to brides (while from the Middle East eastwards, brides often wear festive red). White, like black, is not only a colour. We in the West get serious when we wear black – about love, life, faith, ego, money, war – and in dressing in white we may consider ourselves clean, and confer on ourselves happiness too, and virtue, even sanctity. For white is the colour of blinding light. When Jesus was transfigured, his raiment was 'white as the light' (Matthew 17:2), 'shining, exceeding white as snow' (Mark 9:3), 'white and glistening' (Luke 9:29). And the angel who rolled back the stone from the tomb had a countenance 'like lightning and his raiment white as snow' (Matthew 28:3). For when white is transcendent, it is wool, snow and lightning, a blinding, electric flash that lingers. But black too has its charge, and in Christian cosmology God dwells both in dazzling light and in the heart of a sacred darkness.

REFERENCES

Introduction: How Black Is Black?

1 'Black is not a colour', *A Treatise on Painting*, trans. J. F. Rigaud
  (London, 1802), chap. 235, p. 132. Leonardo also said that black,
  'like a broken vessel, is not able to contain anything' (chap. 222). But
  though he noted that 'black and white are not reckoned among colours',
  and called black 'the representative of darkness', he stated that he would
  'not omit mentioning them, because there is nothing in painting more
  useful and necessary; since painting is but an effect produced by lights
  and shadows' (chap. 226).
2 Matisse had much to say on black. His assertion that '*le noir c'est une
  force: je mets mon lest en noir pour simplifier la construction*' is quoted
  in the first number of *Derrière le miroir*, December 1946. For further
  remarks by Matisse on black (for instance at the opening of the
  exhibition 'Black is a Colour' at the Galerie Maeght, Paris, in December
  1946. see Jack D. Flam, *Matisse on Art* (Berkeley, CA, 1995), p. 165ff;
  also Annie Mollard-Desfour, *Le Noir* (Paris, 2005), p. 20, n. 7 (which
  includes '*Pissarro me disait . . . "Manet . . . fait de la lumière avec du noir"*').
  For the Renoir, see A. Vollard, *Renoir: An Intimate Record*, trans. H. L.
  Van Doren and R. T. Weaver [1925] (London, 1990), chap. 12, p. 52.
  On Tintoretto see for instance Eric Potter, ed., *Painters on Painting*
  (New York, 1971), pp. 53–4. On Aristotle and Goethe, see pp. 45,
  227 below. On Beethoven and the black chord, see Michael C. Tusa,
  'Beethoven's "C-Minor Mood": Some Thoughts on the Structural
  Implications of Key Choice', in *Beethoven Forum*, 2, ed. Christoph
  Reynolds (Lincoln, NE, 1993), p. 2, n. 3.
3 Michel Pastoureau, *Black: The History of a Color* (Princeton, NJ, 2009),
  p. 194; Ludwig Wittgenstein, *Remarks on Colour*, ed. G.E.M. Anscombe
  (Berkeley, CA, 1978), p. 37e, section 156, p. 46e, section 215.
4 Thomas Young, *A Course of Lectures on Natural Philosophy and the
  Mechanical Arts* (London, 1807), p. 345.
5 Hermann von Helmholtz, *Helmholtz's Treatise on Physiological Optics*,
  trans. J.P.C. Southall (Menasha, WI, 1924), vol. II, p. 131. The first
  sentence is sometimes quoted without the article, 'Black is real sensation',
  but the German reads '*Das Schwarz ist eine wirkliche Empfindung*'.
6 Hodgkin is quoted in W. D. Wright, 'The Nature of Blackness in Art

and Visual Perception', *Leonardo*, XIV (1981), pp. 236–7. I am grateful
to Dr David Tolhurst for an explanation of the biochemistry of sight.

7 'I conclude, then, that the organ of colour and its impressions were but
partially developed among the Greeks of the heroic age': William Ewart
Gladstone, *Studies in Homer and the Homeric Age*, vol. III (Oxford, 1858),
p. 488; on 'flauus' and other elusive classical colour-words see Mark
Bradley, *Colour and Meaning in Ancient Rome* (Cambridge, 2009),
pp. 1–12; on colour and historical etymology see R. W. Casson, 'Colour
Shift. Evolution of English Color Terms from Brightness to Hue',
in *Colour Categories in Thought and Language*, ed. C. L. Hardin and
L. Maffi (Cambridge, 1997), pp. 224–39.

8 Brent Berlin and Paul Kay, *Basic Colour Terms: Their Universality and
Evolution* (Berkeley, CA, 1969); for an extended appraisal of many aspects
of *Basic Colour Terms* see Hardin and Maffi, eds, *Colour Categories in
Thought and Language.*

9 See Rudolf Steiner in *Colour* (Forest Row, East Sussex, 1992), p. 25.
On the cultural associations of black see Victor Turner, *The Forest of
Symbols: Aspects of Ndembu Ritual* (Ithaca, NY, 1967), especially chap. 3,
'Color Classification in Ndembu Ritual', pp. 59ff; C. Lévi-Strauss,
The Raw and the Cooked, trans. J. Weightman and D. Weightman
(London, 1970); Umberto Eco, 'How Culture Conditions the Colours
We See', in *On Signs*, ed. M. Blonsky (Baltimore, MD, 1985), pp. 157–75.

10 See Jeremy Coote, '"Marvels of Everyday Vision": The Anthropology of
Aesthetics and the Cattle Keeping Nilotes', in *Anthropology and Aesthetics*,
ed. J. Coote and A. Shelton (Oxford, 1992), pp. 245–73; John Ryle is
quoted on p. 251.

ONE: The Oldest Colour

1 *The Elder Eddas of Saemund Sigfusson and the Younger Eddas of Snorre
Sturleson*, trans. I. A. Blackwell (Copenhagen, 1906), p. 260.

2 Andrew Marvell, 'The First Anniversary of the Government under O.C.'
(1654), ll. 341–2.

3 To go from petals to stems, it would have been in plants' interest if their
stems and leaves could have been black, since they would then absorb –
and use – more light in their photosynthetic processes. And plants' leaves
could have been black since, in the waterborne stage of their evolution,
they made use of various photosynthetic bacteria and the different
pigments that derived from them (known as bacteriochlorophylls and
carotenoids). As matters turned out, however, the plant lineage which
made it onto dry land was committed to chlorophyll, which had evolved
with a red-blue absorption to avoid competition with other bacteriochlorophylls. And once established on land, it would have been too demanding
evolutionarily to start again in another colour. I am indebted to Dr Julian
Hibbard for these points about plants and their pigments.

4 On all-black birds, black male birds and piebald creatures, see Charles
Darwin, *The Descent of Man, and Selection in Relation to Sex* [1871]
(Princeton, NJ, 1981), Part II, chap. XVI, pp. 226–7. On the Gouldian

finch see Jennifer J. Templeton, D. James Mountjoy, Sarah R. Pryke and Simon C. Griffith, 'In the Eye of the Beholder: Visual Mate Choice Lateralization in a Polymorphic Songbird', *Biology Letters* (3 October 2012), available at http://rsbl.royalsocietypublishing.org. On the inherited avoidance of warning colours, see Leena Lindström, Rauno V. Alatalo and Johanna Mappes, 'Reaction of Hand-reared and Wild-caught Predators towards Warningly Colored, Gregarious, and Conspicuous Prey', *Behavioural Ecology*, x/3 (1999), pp. 317–22.

5 'H' (possibly Dr Harley), 'Mr Ruskin's Illness Described by Himself', *British Medical Journal* (27 January 1900), p. 225.

6 See G. Bass, 'A Bronze Age Shipwreck at Ulu Burun (Kas)', *American Journal of Archaeology*, xc/3 (July 1986), pp. 269–96.

7 Pliny the Elder, *Natural History*, Book xvi, 40.

8 Herodotus, *Histories*, i, 98–9.

9 Ibid., i, 179.

10 The Book of the Dead, trans. E. A. Wallis Budge, chap. 175, 'The Chapter of Not Dying a Second Time'.

11 Plutarch, *Moralia*, v, 26, 'On Isis and Osiris', trans. F. C. Babbitt (London, 1936).

12 On Hindu beliefs see Wendy Doniger, *The Hindus: An Alternative History* (New York, 2009). I have also drawn especially on H. Krishna Sastri, *South Indian Images of Gods and Goddesses* (Madras, 1916), and on Alain Daniélou, *Mythes et dieux de l'Inde: Le Polythéisme hindou* (Paris, 1994) – see, for instance, 'La Couleur sombre', pp. 242ff; also on conversations with Eric Auzoux, Anita Desai and Simeran Gell.

13 In another myth Shiva is married to the goddess Parvati, who is also called Kali (Black) because of her dark skin, but is later granted a golden body and sloughs off her dark outer sheath, which then becomes the goddess Kali. The goddess Draupadi, also called Krishna (Dark Woman), is associated with Kali, and like Kali is worshipped notably by lower castes, in South India especially. Kali too is said to live, in banishment, in the southern Vindhua mountains. Draupadi is born of fire, so there does seem a correlation in Indian myth between things burned black by fire and southern skin burned black by hard, humble outdoor work, though dark or black skin, and fire, may also be divine. See Wendy Doniger, *The Hindus: An Alternative History* (New York, 2009), pp. 57–8, 301, 396–8.

14 Quoted from A. K. Ramanujan, ed., *Speaking of Shiva* (London, 1973).

two: Classical Black

1 All the early black items mentioned here are displayed and described in the National Archaeological Museum of Athens. As to colour perception and colour theory in Greece and Rome, both the classical and the recent literature are summarized by John Gage in *Colour and Culture: Practice and Meaning from Antiquity to Abstraction* (London, 1993), pp. 11–38, and reviewed more fully by Mark Bradley in *Colour and Meaning in Ancient Rome* (Cambridge, 2009); see especially 'Modern Literature', pp. 12–30.

2 Vincent J. Bruno, *Form and Colour in Greek Painting* (London, 1977), p. 85.

3 For instance, when Strife stations herself beside Odysseus' 'black ship' at the start of *Iliad*, XI, 5. Here as elsewhere 'black' is *melaini*, from the *melas* root. In different accounts emphasis is placed on the black keel, black prow and black hull of the ships. The association of maritime black with death is widespread and has continued, not only in the grand nautical funerals of heroic admirals like Nelson (see p. 250), but in the more local practice of, for instance, blackening the figurehead when the ship's master died. In Greece some beautiful examples of this from more recent centuries may be seen in the maritime museum in the small port town of Galaxithi where, if the figurehead is female her black form may still have red lips, whites to her eyes and a gold crown.

4 Plutarch, *Life of Theseus*, XXII; see also Apollodorus, *Epitome of the Library*, E.I.7–10.

5 On quince and frog colours see Liza Cleland, 'The Semiosis of Description', in *The Clothed Body in the Ancient World*, ed. L. Cleland, M. Harlow and L. Llewellyn-Jones (Cambridge, 2005), pp. 90–93; the funeral procession, Aeschylus, *The Libation Bearers*, trans. R. C. Trevelyan (Liverpool, 1922), ll. 11–12.

6 Pausanius, *Description of Greece*, trans. W.H.S. Jones (London, 1918), VIII.34.3; Virgil, *Aeneid*, trans. C. Day-Lewis (New York, 1953), IV.469ff.

7 The darks and blacks of the classical Underworld, in Greek perception, are described in Homer's *Iliad*, XV, 187ff, and *Odyssey*, X, 495ff; Hesiod's *Theogony*, 736ff, and in the Orphic Hymn 18 to Hades.

8 Plato, *Timaeus*, 44d–47e; Aristotle, *On Sense and Sensible Objects*, section I, part 2.

9 Democritus, *On Colours*; Plato, *Laws*, Book 4, *Timaeus*, 81e–86a; Aristotle, *On Sense and Sensible Objects*, section I, part 7.

10 Pliny the Elder, *Natural History*, Books XXXII–XXXV.

11 Petronius, *Satyricon*, chap. 83.

12 On Turner, see Elbert Hubbard, *Little Journeys to the Homes of the Great* (East Aurora, NY, 1886), pp. 47–8.

13 Lucian of Samosata, *De Calumnia*, 5. Botticelli was encouraged to the subject by his friend Leon Battista Alberti, who had celebrated Apelles' painting in Book III of his *Della Pitura* of 1435, on the basis of his own paraphrase of Lucian. See also Rudolph Altrocchi, 'The Calumny of Apelles in the Literature of the Quattrocento', *PMLA*, XXXVI/3 (September 1921), pp. 454–91.

14 Michel Pastoureau, *Black: The History of a Color* (Princeton, NJ, 2009), pp. 35, 39.

15 Vitruvius, *Ten Books on Architecture*, trans. M. H. Morgan (Cambridge, MA, 1914), Book VII, chap. 10, section 4. On the use of black grounds in Roman frescoes, on the use of black to unify composition, and on the effect of black in creating an inviolable surface, see Roger Ling, *Roman Painting* (Cambridge, 1991), especially pp. 41–2, 66–7.

16 Vitruvius, *Ten Books*, Book VII, chap. 4, section 5.

17 See Mark Bradley, *Colour and Meaning in Ancient Rome* (Cambridge, 2009),

chap. 7, 'Purple', pp. 189–211: on 'black' purples, pp. 192–3, 195–6; Augustus on his rooftop, pp. 200–11.

18 Ovid, *Art of Love*, III, ll. 189–90.

19 Judith Lynn Sebesta, '*Tunica Ralla, Tunica Spissa*: The Colours and Textiles of Roman Costume', in *The World of Roman Costume*, ed. Judith Lynn Sebesta and Larissa Bonfante (Madison, WI, 1994), pp. 65–76.

20 Cassius Dio, *Roman History*, trans. Earnest Cary and Herbert B. Foster (London, 1924), LXVII.7.2ff. In 1668 a black dinner was mounted by Jesuits at Versailles for Louis XIV, and another, with an elaborate all-black menu, is imagined by Huysmans in *À Rebours*: see André Félibien, *Relation de la Feste de Versailles* (Paris, 1668); Joris-Karl Huysmans, *À Rebours* (Paris, 1884), chap. 1. Huysmans' menu, served on a black tablecloth on black-edged plates, includes black olives, caviar, bread, blood puddings, plum puddings, chocolate, coffee and stout.

21 For the features of the Underworld mentioned in context see Statius, *Thebaid*, IV, 520ff, VIII, 21ff; Valerius Flaccus, *Argonautica*, III, 380ff; Ovid, *Metamorphoses*, V, 354ff, and *Fasti*, IV, 417ff; also Virgil, *Georgics*, IV, 471ff.

22 Cacus, *Aeneid*, VIII, ll. 198–9; Dido, *Aeneid*, VI, l. 384; cf. Milton, *Paradise Lost*, 'from those flames / No light, but rather darkness visible', I, ll. 62–3.

23 'Dusky Venus', *Amores*, II, ll. 40–41; Ovid's own black hair, *Tristia*, IX, 8, 2; Aroe into jackdaw, *Metamorphoses*, VII, l. 466; Actaeon and his hounds, *Metamorphoses*, III, ll. 206–352.

24 Phoebus and the Python, I, ll. 438–72; the House of Sleep, XI, ll. 573–649.

25 The mutilation of Philomela, *Metamorphoses*, VI, ll. 549–70.

26 In a placatory play, the name was changed to 'Pontos Euxeinos', 'Hospitable Sea', a phrase which could be used with more or less irony as desired.

THREE: The Black of God

1 Strabo, *Geography*, trans. H. L. Jones (London, 1924), on Lusitania, III, 3, 7; on Iberian wool, III, 2, 6; on the Cassiterides, III, 5, 11

2 Tacitus, *Annals*, trans. A. J. Church and W. J. Brodribb (London, 1923), XIV, 30.

3 Laodicean wool, *Geography*, XII, 8, 16.

4 Jordanes, *The Origins and Deeds of the Goths*, trans. Charles C. Mierow (London, 1915), XXIV, 123; the embassy of Priscus is described by Jordanes in XXXIV, 178ff.

5 Julius Caesar, *The Gallic Wars*, trans. W. A. McDevitte and W. S. Bohn (New York, 1869), V, 14; Pliny the Elder, *Natural History*, trans. John Bostock (London, 1855), Book XXII, 2, 1.

6 See Gillian Carr, 'Woad, Tattooing and Identity in Later Iron Age and Early Roman Britain', *Oxford Journal of Archaeology*, XXIV/3 (2005), pp. 273–92.

7 Lucian of Samosata, *Heracles*, trans. Austin Morris Harmon (Cambridge, MA, 1979).

8 Homer, *Odyssey*, XI, ll. 593–640.

9 See James B. Pritchard, ed., *The Ancient Near East* (Princeton, NJ, 1958), vol. I, pp. 227–30.

10 See for instance Behramgore Tehmuras Anklesaria, *Zand-Akasih Iranian or Greater Bundahishn* (Bombay, 1956), available at www.avesta.org.

11 Biblical quotations are from the Authorized or King James Version. Orestes' curse on the man who defiles a virgin's bed is in lines 71–5 of *The Libation Bearers*, where one presumes the clinging black blood is primarily a metaphor for wrongdoing, since it would be odd to call the virgin's blood black.

12 St Augustine, *Enerratio in psalmos*, 91, 11; St Jerome, *On Jeremiah*, 13, 23; Charles Spurgeon, Sermon 266, 'The Blind Beggar', delivered on 7 August 1859, available at www.spurgeon.org.

13 The Acts of Bartholomew are available at www.newadvent.org; for St Antony's black boy see Athanasius of Alexandria, 'Life of St Antony', in *Nicene and Post-Nicene Fathers*, ed. Philip Schaff and Henry Wace, Series II, vol. IV (Grand Rapids, MI, 1892), p. 197; on St Macarius see H. C. Lea, *Materials towards a History of Witchcraft* (Philadelphia, 1939), p. 67; on Abbot John, *The Conferences of St John Cassian*, Conference 1, chap. 21; on Abbot Apollos, Conference 2, chap. 13; on breaking stones, Conference 9, chap. 6, texts available at www.newadvent.org; on medieval representations of black and African devilry see Geraldine Heng, 'Jews, Saracens, "Black Men", Tartars: England in a World of Racial Difference', in *A Companion to Medieval English Literature and Culture*, ed. Peter Brown (Oxford, 2007), pp. 247–69.

14 *Homily on the Song of Songs*, 1, 6, quoted by Frank M. Snowden Jr in 'Bernal's "Blacks" and the Afrocentrists', in *Black Athena Revisited*, ed. Mary R. Lefkowitz and Guy MacLean Rogers (Chapel Hill, NC, 1996), p. 126.

15 Sermon 28 on the Song of Songs available at www.pathsoflove.com.

16 On monastic dress see G. S. Tyack, *Historic Dress of the Clergy* (London, 1897); Janet Mayo, *A History of Ecclesiastical Dress* (London, 1984).

17 See Giles Constable, ed., *The Letters of Peter the Venerable* (Cambridge, MA, 1967), especially letters 28 (p. 57) and 111 (p. 289).

18 St Jerome's *Life of St Hilarion* (written in 390 CE) is available at www.newadvent.org.

19 On the Dominicans and the Inquisition see Bernard Hamilton, *The Medieval Inquisition* (London, 1981), especially pp. 36–9, 60–63.

20 Pseudo-Dionysius, *The Complete Works*, trans. C. Luibheid (New York, 1987), p. 135; *The Cloud of Unknowing* is quoted from the original by Denys Turner in *The Darkness of God* (Cambridge, 1995), p. 195; 'Stanzas of the Soul' and commentary, trans. Kieran Kavanaugh OCD and Otilio Rodriguez OCD, in *The Collected Works of St John of the Cross* (Washington, DC, 1991).

FOUR: Black in Society: Arabia, Europe

1 See David Nicolle and Angus McBride, *Armies of the Muslim Conquest* (Oxford, 1993), p. 5.

2 On Muhammad and blackness see especially the references to Muhammad in Mumtaz Ali Tajddin, 'Black Clothes', in *Encyclopaedia of Ismailism* at http://ismaili.net. The story of Muhammad's childhood was told to me by Professor Tarif Khalidi of the American University in Beirut, who mentioned also the variant in which two angels in the form of cranes cleanse the chest of the young Muhammad.

3 See Amiram Shkolnik, C. Richard Taylor, Virginia Finch and Arieh Borut, 'Why Do Bedouins Wear Black Robes in Hot Deserts?', *Nature*, 283 (24 January 1980), pp. 373–5; Daniel Da Cruz, 'The Black Tent', *Saudi Aramco World*, XVII/3 (May–June 1966), pp. 26–7. On short-wave penetration of animal hair see J. C. Hutchinson and G. D. Brown, 'Penetrance of Cattle Coats by Radiation', *Journal of Applied Physiology*, XXVI/4 (April 1969), pp. 454–64.

4 William Muir's *The Caliphate: Its Rise, Decline and Fall from Original Sources* (Edinburgh, 1924) is available online at www.answering-islam.org, and a broad account of the caliphate can be found at *A General History of the Middle East*, chap. 10, 'The Arab Golden Age', at http://xenohistorian.faithweb.com.

5 See especially Patricia L. Baker, 'Court Dress: Abbasid', in Josef W. Meri, *Medieval Islamic Civilization* (London, 2006), vol. I, pp. 178–9; on the high black cap see, for instance, the entry on 'Kalansuwa', in M. T. Houtsma, T. W. Arnold, R. Basset and R. Hartmann, *Encyclopaedia of Islam* (London, 1913–36), vol. IV, pp. 677–8. The caliph was not the first monarch in history to wear black prominently. In China both Confucius and the Daoists called black the king of colours, and the Emperor Qin Shi Huang, who unified China in 211 BCE, was appealing to ancient values when he chose the colour black for himself and his dynasty. As with later European monarchs, the choice of black was taken to express humility, austerity and dedication.

6 On the 'green' interlude, see 'Ma'mun, Abu'l-'Abbas 'Abd-Allāh, the Seventh Abbasid Caliph', in *Encyclopaedia Iranica*, at www.iranicaonline.org.

7 Quoted in Paul Wheatley, *The Places where Men Pray Together: Cities in Islamic Lands* (Chicago, IL, 2000), p. 282.

8 Quoted in Israr Ahmas Khan, *Authentication of Hadith: Redefining the Criteria* (London, 2010), p. 20.

9 A detailed and fully referenced account of the development of secular black fashion in Europe via Burgundy and Spain through Italy, England and the Netherlands is given in my book *Men in Black* (London, 1995), especially pp. 51–113.

10 The Sultan is the more moved because his own, Islamic prayers for the cure of his child had been in vain. See J. Perryman, ed., *The King of Tars: Edited from the Auchinleck Manuscript, Advocates 19.2.1*, Middle English Texts 12 (Heidelberg, 1980), ll. 928–9 (his hide) and 1,226 (blue and black). In a comparable episode in the fourteenth-century *Cursor Mundi*, King David meets four Saracens who are 'black and blue as lead', but instantly switch to white on kissing rods blessed by Moses. For further references and contextual discussion see Geraldine Heng, 'Jews, Saracens,

"Black Men", Tartars: England in a World of Racial Difference', in *A Companion to Medieval English Literature and Culture*, ed. Peter Brown (Oxford, 2007), pp. 247–69.

11 On the black painting of armour, see Claude Blair, *European Armour, circa 1066 to circa 1700* (London, 1958), p. 172. On the Black Prince, and the 'shadowy' reference to his 'armure noire', see another John Harvey, *The Black Prince and His Age* (London, 1967), p. 15; also Barbara Emerson, *The Black Prince* (London, 1976), pp. 1–2. Hubert Cole suggests the Prince fought under 'sable banners' (though there is no certain evidence of this) in Emerson, *The Black Prince*, pp. 9–11.

12 See J. R. Boyle, *Ecclesiastical Vestments: Their Origin and Significance* (London, 1896); Herbert Norris, *Church Vestments: Their Origin and Development* (London, 1949).

13 See Hilde De Ridder-Symoens, ed., *A History of the University in Europe*, vol. 1: *Universities in the Middle Ages* (Cambridge, 1992); W. N. Hargreaves-Mawdsley, *A History of Academical Dress in Europe until the End of the Eighteenth Century* (Oxford, 1963).

14 See W. N. Hargreaves-Mawdsley, *A History of Legal Dress in Europe* (Oxford, 1963).

15 For further direction on sumptuary legislation see Aileen Ribeiro, *Dress and Morality* (London, 2003), pp. 43–7, 55–8, 63–9, 74.

16 See, for instance, Albert Racinet, *The Historical Encyclopedia of Costume*, ed. Aileen Ribeiro (London, 1992), p. 155: Racinet's still-classic *Le Costume Historique* of 1888 is available in various editions and selections.

17 Recent studies of Rubens's English diplomacy are Gregory Martin, *Rubens in London: Art and Diplomacy* (London, 2011) and Mark Lamster, *The Secret Diplomatic Career of the Painter Peter Paul Rubens* (New York, 2010). For an earlier study, see C. V. Wedgwood, *The Political Career of Peter Paul Rubens* (London, 1975). The subject is discussed in most biographies of Rubens: see, for instance, Christopher White, *Peter Paul Rubens: Man and Artist* (New Haven, CT, 1987), pp. 215–31; Marie-Anne Lescourret, *Rubens: A Double Life* (London, 1993), 'The Embassies', pp. 141–86. Rubens's letters are edited by Ruth S. Magurn, *The Letters of Peter Paul Rubens* (Cambridge, MA, 1955).

FIVE: Two Artists in Black

1 The standard modern life has been Helen Langdon's *Caravaggio: A Life* (London, 1998), but I have worked principally from Andrew Graham-Dixon's biography, *Caravaggio: A Life Sacred and Profane* (London, 2010), which takes account of later archival finds and contains much fascinating further new material. See Andrew Graham-Dixon on Caravaggio's studio, pp. 184–6; his looks, p. 163; the drawing of him by Ottavio Leoni, fig. 1; the black chest, p. 271; his dog Corvo, p. 399; black cloaks, pp. 70, 99, 162–4, 257, 294, 356; possible pimping, pp. 297–8; attack on waiter, pp. 275–81; house-scorning, p. 287; attack from behind, pp. 293–4; transcript of cross-examination, pp. 260–64; the *Madonna of Loreto*, pp. 288–93;

Carlo Borromeo, pp. 22–44; killing of Ranuccio da Terni, pp. 313–22; in Malta, pp. 358–92; injury and death, pp. 415–34; penalty for sodomy, p. 416. On Caravaggio's lighting and colouring see also John Gage, *Colour and Culture: Practice and Meaning from Antiquity to Abstraction* (London, 1993), pp. 156, 160. On Caravaggio's hostility to bright colours, and his statement that they were 'the poison of tones', see G. P. Bellori's *Le Vite de' pittori, scultori ed architetti moderni* [1672], ed. E. Borea (Turin, 1976), p. 229.

2 John Ruskin, *The Elements of Drawing* (London, 1857), p. 232: Letter VIII, 'Of Colour and Composition', Section C, c.

3 See Graham-Dixon, *Caravaggio*, pp. 354–5, and Christopher White, *Peter Paul Rubens: Man and Artist* (New Haven, CT, 1987), p. 167.

4 On the quality control of cloth, and the portrait of 'The Sampling Officials of the Drapers' Guild', see Simon Schama, *Rembrandt's Eyes* (London, 1999), pp. 646–7.

5 The meanings of the blackness which water can have are memorably discussed by Gaston Bacherlard in *Water and Dreams: An Essay on the Imagination of Matter*, trans. Edith R. Farrell (Dallas, TX, 1999). On black water in Poe see chapter Ten, ref. 17, below.

6 On Jeremias de Decker see Schama, *Rembrandt's Eyes*, pp. 643–5.

7 In the two versions for instance of the self-portrait of himself as a young man painted in 1628 and 1629 (both known simply as *Self-portrait*).

SIX: Black Choler

1 The classic history of humoral medicine, black bile and melancholy in medical theory and artistic practice is that by Raymond Klibansky, Erwin Panofsky and Fritz Saxl, *Saturn and Melancholy: Studies in the History of Natural Philosophy, Religion and Art* (London, 1964). I engage principally with this study because it culminates, as my argument does, in the discussion of Dürer's *Melencolia I*; for a more recent discussion of humoral medical theory, in a global context, see Shigehisa Kuriyama, *The Expressiveness of the Body and the Divergence of Greek and Chinese Medicine* (New York, 1999). The fourfold division of the cosmos – and the four colours – were extended to other domains, such as alchemy, where, during the magnum opus in which gold is created, the philosopher's stone is successively black, white, yellow and red.

2 For Galen and Avicenna, see *Saturn and Melancholy*, pp. 55–95.

3 Quoted, with translation by Fritz Saxl, in *Saturn and Melancholy*, pp. 111ff.

4 My quotations from *The Anatomy of Melancholy* are from the 1922 edition, ed. Holbrook Jackson, currently in print in facsimile in a single volume, with introduction by William H. Gass (New York, 2001). Roman numerals refer to the original Volumes of this edition, which correspond to the First, Second and Third 'Partitions' of Burton's text: both volume and page numbers are reproduced in the facsimile. Definition of melancholy, vol. I, p. 170; on living death, I, pp. 389–402. Otherwise the phrases cited, with others that are relevant, will be found at I, pp. 169, 172, 200, 209, 218, 219, 222, 224, 240, 260, 262, 302, 377, 383, 384, 406, 413, 419,

420; II, pp. 33, 250; III, pp. 84–5, 150, 186, 395, 406, 410.

5 Julia Kristeva, *Black Sun: Depression and Melancholia*, trans. Leon S. Roudiez (New York, 1989), pp. 3–4. On the underlying consistency of Burton's science, theology and politics see Andrew Gowland, *The Worlds of Renaissance Melancholy: Robert Burton in Context* (Cambridge, 2006). On the day-to-day practice of humoral medicine in the seventeenth century, see Michael MacDonald, *Mystical Bedlam: Madness, Anxiety, and Healing in Seventeenth-century England* (Cambridge, 1981), especially pp. 150–64, on Melancholy and Mopishness. See MacDonald also for contemporary corroboration of the connections Burton sees between melancholy and Satan, and between melancholy and religious 'enthusiasm'; MacDonald pp. 155, 170, 207, 215, 218, 223–4.

6 William Harvey, *Of the Motion of the Heart and Blood in Animals*, trans. Robert Willis (London, 1847), chap. 9.

7 Klibansky, Panofsky and Saxl, *Saturn and Melancholy*, p. 320; Burton, *Anatomy of Melancholy*, vol. I, p. 392.

8 Klibansky, Panofsky and Saxl, *Saturn and Melancholy*, p. 318.

9 See T. S. Eliot, 'Whispers of Immortality', in *Poems, 1920* (New York, 1920); Anna Dostoevsky, *Dostoevsky Reminiscences*, trans. and ed. Beatrice Stillman (New York, 1975), p. 134; Fyodor Dostoevsky, *The Idiot*, trans. David Magarshack (London, 1955), p. 236.

10 See Kristeva, *Black Sun*, pp. 71–94, 106–38.

11 Quotations from Shakespeare are from the current Arden editions. 'Alas, poor Yorick! . . .' *Hamlet*, v.i.182–92; 'I have of late . . .' II.ii.294–309.

12 Burton, *Anatomy of Melancholy*, vol. I, p. 130; Burton cites Ben Jonson on III, pp. 463, 472, 474, 478, 480, 507 and Shakespeare on III, pp. 445, 451; on III, p. 187, he slightly misquotes the last lines of *Romeo and Juliet* without mentioning Shakespeare's name, presumably believing he and everyone else knew them by heart.

13 'Something in his soul . . .' III.i.165–6; 'out of my weakness . . .' II.ii.596; 'my inky cloak . . .' I.ii.75–84. The copperplate engraving to Rowe's edition of 1709 was cut by Elisha Kirkall from a drawing by F. Boitard.

14 To be, or not to be – that is the question . . .
                    To die, to sleep –
    To sleep: perchance to Dream; Ay, there's the rub,
    For in that sleep of death what dreams may come . . .
    Must give us pause . . .
    Who would . . .
            grunt and sweat under a weary life,
    But that the dread of something after death
            . . . makes us rather bear those ills we have
    Than fly to others that we know not of. (III.i.56–82)

15 Burton, *Anatomy of Melancholy*, vol. I, p. 406; the line-references in 'Il Penseroso' are: 'These pleasures . . .' 175–6; 'But hail . . .' 11–21; 'in glimmering Bowres . . .' 27–9; 'Come pensive Nun . . .' 31–3; 'forget . . .' 42; 'flowing . . .' 34; 'sable stole . . .' 35–6; 'most musicall . . .' 62; 'saddest plight . . .' 55; 'Gorgeous Tragedy', 97–9; 'such notes . . .' 106–7; 'the pealing organ . . .' 161–2; 'glowing embers . . .' 79–80. I reproduce Blake's

illustration of the goddess Melancholy in a black gown, and in a companion illustration Blake shows the poet, in the black mortar-board and gown of a Cambridge scholar, gazing in wonder at 'the wandring moon', l. 67.

16 Book and line references to *Paradise Lost* are: 'black tartareous dregs' VII, 238–9; 'bituminous gurge' XII, 41–2 ; sulphurous . . . grain' VI, 512–5; 'black fire . . .' II, 67; 'sad Acheron . . .' II, 578; 'myself am Hell . . .' IV, 75–8.

17 *Hamlet*, III.ii.125–6; Burton, *Anatomy of Melancholy*, vol. III, 392–400; 'extraordinary valour' I, 393; *Paradise Lost*, IV, 75–8.

18 *Paradise Lost*, 'black low mist . . .' IX, 180; 'the other shape . . .' II, 666–72.

SEVEN: Servitude and Négritude

1 This night, *Macbeth*, I.v.50–1; black vengeance, *Othello*, III.vi.31–2; black angel, *Lear*, III.vi.31–2; black gown, *All's Well*, I.iii.92–4; *Love's Labours Lost*, ebony and chimney sweepers, IV.iii.243–62; pitch-balls, III.i.190–92ff. On ebony, in the Arden edition of *Love's Labours Lost* (London, 1998), H. R Woudhuysen notes that Theobald's emendation of 'wood divine' to 'word divine' 'has been widely accepted but is unnecessary': indeed, the emendation seems itself wooden.

2 'For I have sworn', sonnet 147; dun breasts, black wires, 130; raven eyes, 127.

3 *Hamlet*, I.iv.48ff; *Antony and Cleopatra*, 'tawny', I.i.6; Phoebus' pinches, I.v.28–9; strumpet, I.i.13; triple-turned whore, IV.xii.13; hotter hours, III.xiii.123–5; lass unparallelled, v.ii.315; baby at breast, v.ii.308.

4 *Othello*, 'the Moor', I.i.57; thick-lips, I.i.66; ram, I.i.88.

5 *Othello*, chop, IV.i.200; *Antony and Cleopatra*, lingering pickle, II.v.65–6.

6 'Let all . . .' *Merchant*, II.vii.79; 'Zounds', *Titus*, IV.ii.73.

7 For Jonson's text, see C.H.H. Percy and E. Simpson, eds, *Ben Jonson* (Oxford, 1941), vol. VII, pp. 169–80. Because of their obscurity, I do not discuss in my text two poems by Lord Herbert of Cherbury (1583–1648), the elder brother of the poet George Herbert: his 'Sonnet of Black Beauty' and 'Another Sonnet to Black', both published posthumously in 1665. The first quatrain of the former reads:

> Black beauty, which above that common light,
> Whose Power can no colours here renew
> But those which darkness can again subdue,
> Do'st still remain unvary'd to the sight . . .

One might of course say that obscurity suits a 'black' poem. It is possible the poems relate to the occasion of the Masque of Blackness. It is also possible that they were inspired by a beloved whose skin was dark or black, or who had extremely black hair. Lord Herbert was himself swarthy and black-haired, and it is said that the family were known as the 'black Herberts'. Together with the Masque, and the lines from Shakespeare quoted, the poems do reflect a sense, in Jacobean culture, of the intrigue of the colour black. More broadly on the black monarchs and saints of Christian tradition – including also Prester John – see Michel Pastoureau, *Black: The History of a Color* (Princeton, NJ, 2009), pp. 82–7.

8 Numbers 12:1; Petronius, *The Satyricon*, chap. 102. Prejudice is certainly represented, however, since Giton objects, 'We can't make our lips so hideously thick, can we? We can't kink our hair with a curling-iron, can we?'

9 On all the topics in this paragraph, see Winthrop D. Jordan's excellently indexed *White over Black: American Attitudes toward the Negro, 1550–1812* (New York, 1977).

10 On Islamic slavery and the Arab crows see especially Bernard Lewis, 'The Crows of the Arabs', in *'Race', Writing and Difference*, ed. H. L. Gates Jr (Chicago, IL, 1986), pp. 107–16.

11 See Jordan, *White over Black*, p. 6.

12 Sir Thomas Browne, *Pseudodoxia Epidemica* (1646), Book VI, chap. 10, 'Of the Blackness of Negroes'.

13 On Noah, Ham and Canaan, Genesis 9:21–7; Peter Heylyn is quoted in Peter Fryer, *Staying Power: The History of Black People in Britain* (London, 1984), p. 143; for Jeremy Taylor and Sir Edward Coke, see Jordan, *White over Black*, p. 54.

14 On debasement see especially Jordan, *White over Black*, pp. 24–8; Thomas Jefferson, *Notes on the State of Virginia* (London, 1787), Query 14, 'Laws', final paragraph (before table of punishments).

15 *The Interesting Narrative of the Life of Olaudah Equiano; or, Gustavus Vassa the African* (London, 1789), chap. 2. Though densely informed, Equiano's *Narrative* may be in part fictional. Possibly he was born in America and Africanized his origins to assist the success of his book and/or of his active campaigning against the slave trade. See Vincent Carretta, *Equiano, the African: Biography of a Self-Made Man* (Athens, GA, 2005), and also Catherine Obianuju Acholonu, *The Igbo Roots Of Olaudah Equiano: An Anthropological Research* (Owerri, 1989).

16 Adam Smith, *Theory of Moral Sentiments* (Edinburgh, 1759), Part V, chap. 2; James Boswell, *Life of Samuel Johnson, LL.D.* (London, 1980), p. 876.

17 David Hume, footnote added in 1753 to his essay 'Of National Character' (1748), *The Philosophical Works of David Hume* (Bristol, 1996), vol. III, p. 228; Herder's remarks, from his *Briefe zu Beförderung der Humanität* (1797) and his *Philosophieder Geschichte der Menschheit* (1784) are quoted by Robert Palter in 'Eighteenth-century Historiography in *Black Athena*', in *Black Athena Revisited*, ed. M. R. Lefkowitz and G. M. Rogers (Chapel Hill, NC, 1996), p. 373.

18 Johnson, 'An Introduction to the Political State of Great Britain', *The Literary Magazine*, 1 (London, 1758); Cowper, *The Task* (London, 1785), Book IV, ll. 28–30.

19 Charles Darwin, *The Descent of Man* (London, 1871; in facsimile, Princeton, NJ, 1981), Part I, chap. 6, p. 201.

20 C. Lombroso and G. Ferrero, *The Female Offender* (New York, 1895), 'phenomena of atavism', p. 124; 'obsessive obesity of prostitutes', p. 113; 'Hottentot, African', p. 114; 'to kill', p. 171.

21 Benjamin Rush, 'Observations Intended to Favour a Supposition that the Black Color (As It Is Called) of the Negroes is Derived from the Leprosy', *Transactions of the American Philosophical Society*, vol. IV (1789), pp. 289–97.

22 See Sander L. Gilman, 'Black Bodies, White Bodies: Toward an Iconography of Female Sexuality in Late Nineteenth-century Art, Medicine, and Literature', in *'Race', Writing and Difference*, ed. Gates, pp. 223–57.

23 Mungo Park, *The Life and Travels of Mungo Park in Central Africa* (New York, 1858), 'remarkably black', chap. 5, 'black and deep', chap. 9.

24 On the perception and visual illustration of Africa and Africans, see Patrick Brantlinger, 'Victorians and Africans: The Genealogy of the Myth of the Dark Continent', in *'Race', Writing and Difference*, ed. Gates, pp. 185–222.

25 Charles Darwin, *The Descent of Man*, 2nd edn (London, 1874), chap. 7, 'Of the Formation of the Races of Man'.

26 On the changing understanding of 'race', see especially C. Loring Brace, D. P. Tracer, L. A. Yaroch, J. Rob, K. Brandt and A. R. Nelson, 'Clines and Clusters versus 'Race': A Test in Ancient Egypt and the Case of a Death on the Nile', *Yearbook of Physical Anthropology*, 36 (1993), pp. 1–31.

27 Sir Henry M. Stanley, *How I Found Livingstone* [1872], chap. 7, pp. 179–80 (Vercelli, 2006).

28 For 'The Light and the Truth of Slavery, Aaron's History' [1845] and 'The Life, Experience, and Gospel Labours of the Rt. Rev. Richard Allen' [1833] see http://docsouth.unc.edu.

29 For *The Life and Narrative of William J. Anderson* [1857] see http://docsouth.unc.edu.

30 Frantz Fanon, *Black Skin White Masks*, trans. C. L. Markman (London, 1986), especially pp. 3, 5, 116, 86, 95, 106, 108.

31 Ibid., pp. 5, 147, 7.

32 On colour symbolism among the peoples of the lower Congo, see especially Anita Jacobson-Widding, *Red, White and Black as a Mode of Thought* (Stockholm, 1979).

33 On the 'Black Stone' of the White Fathers see for instance *White Fathers White Sister*, 354 (October–November 2000), 21; also Jean-Philippe Chippaux, Ismaila Diédhiou and Roberto Stock, 'Étude de l'action de la pierre noire sur l'envenimation expérimentale' (July–September 2007), available at www.jle.com. In addition to Jacobson-Widding, *Red, White and Black*, see James Faris, *Nuba Personal Art* (London, 1972); Victor Turner, *The Forest of Symbols: Aspects of Ndembu Ritual* (Ithaca, NY, 1967), especially pp. 59ff, 'Colour Classification in Ndembu Ritual: A Problem of Primitive Classification'; Alfonso Ortiz, *The Tawa World* (London, 1969).

34 Frantz Fanon, *The Wretched of the Earth*, trans. C. Farrington (London, 2001), pp. 251–5.

35 Biographical information about Senghor, the French texts and the English translations of them are drawn principally from Sylvia Washington Bâ, *The Concept of Negritude in the Poetry of Léopold Sédar Senghor* (Princeton, NJ, 1973): 'Black Woman', pp. 132, 190; black milk, pp. 88, 250; black blood, p. 251; 'emotion is black', p. 75; '*une negresse blonde*', p. 82; Paris snow, p. 50; '*nuit diamantine*', p. 84; '*mines d'uranium*', p. 50.

EIGHT: Black in the Enlightenment

1 Edward Gibbon, *The History of the Decline and Fall of the Roman Empire* (London, 1781), vol. III, chap. 31, 2nd paragraph; William Cowper, *The Diverting History of John Gilpin* (1782), stanza 6. For the earlier point about Louis XIV and dancing, I am grateful to Professor Peter Burke.

2 Michel Pastoureau, *Black: The History of a Color* (Princeton, NJ, 2009), pp. 148, 156.

3 Isaac Newton, *Opticks: or, a Treatise of the Reflections, Refractions, Inflections and Colours of Light*, 4th corrected edn (London, 1730), Book I, Part IV, Observation 5, p. 326; Book I, Part I, Proposition I, Experiment I, p. 21; Book II, Part III, Proposition VII, 'for the production of black', p. 260.

4 Newton, Book II, Part III, Proposition VII, 'for the production of black'.

5 Robert Boyle, *Experiments and Considerations Touching Colours* (London, 1664), Part the Second, 'Of the Nature of Whiteness and Blackness', chap. 2, section, 2, p. 119.

6 Ibid., pp. 127, 130.

7 The medical details are from a correspondent of Priestley's, Thomas Percival MD, whose letter to Priestley is reprinted as item Number III in the Appendix to *Experiments and Observations on Different Kinds of Air*, 2nd edn (London, 1775).

8 See, in Pepys's diary, the entries for 8, 15 and 17 October 1666.

9 Samuel Richardson, *Pamela or Virtue Rewarded*, letter 24. The blackening of the teeth originated in South Asia, and in twelfth-century Japan was practised by noblemen and samurai; by the eighteenth century, the practice was limited to women.

10 Pepys, diary entry for 12 June 1663.

11 Pepys, diary entry for 18 February 1667.

12 On the history of the London masquerades, see especially Terry Castle, *Masquerade and Civilization* (Stanford, CA, 1986), pp. 1–51.

13 Andrew Marvell, *Miscellaneous Poems* (London, 1681), 'The Gallery', stanza 2.

14 See in William Blake's *Poetical Sketches* (1783), 'Fresh from the dewy hill' ('But that sweet village, / where my black-eyed maid / Closes her eyes in sleep', stanza 5) and 'When early morn walks forth in sobery grey' ('to my black-eyed maid I haste away', line 2), and in Byron's *Don Juan* (1819–24) the Romagnole, Canto IV; 'some female head . . . presumes / To thrust its black eyes through the door', Canto V; 'Mahomet . . . Who only saw the black-eyed girls in green', Canto VIII; 'black-eyed Sal', Canto XI; 'whether black or blue', Canto XIII; 'her black, bright, downcast, yet espiegle eye', Canto XVI.

15 See Fanny Burney, *Cecilia; or, Memoirs of an Heiress* (1782), chap. 3, 'A Masquerade'.

16 Edward Young, *The Complaint; or, Night Thoughts* (1742–5), 'dreadful masquerader . . . devours', Night Fifth, ll. 860–81;

17 Young, *Night Thoughts*, 'sable goddess', Night First, l. 18; 'How populous', Night First, l. 116; Robert Blair, 'The Grave' (1743), ll. 28–40.

NINE: Britain's Black Century

1 George Routledge, *Routledge's Manual of Etiquette* (London, 1860), Etiquette for Gentlemen, chap. 7, 'Dress'; Anthony Trollope, *The Eustace Diamonds* [1872], chap. 28, 'Mr Dove in His Chambers', p. 294 (Harmondsworth, 2004).
2 Anthony Trollope, *The Way We Live Now* [1875], chap. 4, 'Madame Melmotte's Ball', p. 33 (Harmondsworth, 1994); Thomas Hardy, 'The Dorsetshire Labourer', *Longman's Magazine*, 9 (July 1883), p. 258.
3 Benjamin Disraeli, *Tancred; or, The New Crusade* (London, 1847), chap. 1; Catherine Gore (Mrs Gore), *The Banker's Wife; or, Court and City, a Novel* (London, 1843), vol. II, chap. 2, p. 74.
4 Dinah Craik, *John Halifax, Gentleman* (London, 1856), chap. 30; Charlotte Bronte, *Shirley* [1849], chap. 25, p. 417 (Harmondsworth, 2006); Isabella Beeton, *The Book of Household Management* (London, 1861), 'Duties of the Laundry-maid', in chap. 41, 'Domestic Servants', section 2383.
5 Beeton, *The Book of Household Management*, 'In Paying Visits of Condolence' in chap. 1, 'The Mistress', section 30; Sarah Ellis, *The Women of England, Their Social Duties and Domestic Habits* (London, 1839), p. 321.
6 Anthony Trollope, *The Way We Live Now* [1875], chap. 26, pp. 202ff (Harmondsworth, 1994). On black and democracy see p. 243ff later in this chapter.
7 Routledge, *Routledge's Manual of Etiquette*, Etiquette for Ladies, chap. 7, 'Dress'.
8 Charles Eastlake, *Hints on Household Taste* (London, 1869), pp. 116, 166, 191.
9 Beeton, *The Book of Household Management*, 'Duties of the Coach-Man, Groom and Stable-Boy', in chap. 41, 'Domestic Servants', section 2220.
10 See Simon Metcalf and Eric Turner, 'The Conservation of a *c.* 1867 Cast Iron Hat Stand: A Dresser Design and Original Coalbrookdale Paint Scheme Revealed', DAS *The Decorative Arts Society 1850 to the Present*, 26, at www.decorativeartssociety.org.uk.
11 Eastlake, *Hints on Household Taste*, p. 236.
12 John Ruskin, *Elements of Drawing* (London, 1857), p. 232; Letter VIII, 'Of Colour and Composition', Section C, c.
13 The process of mezzotint was invented in the 1640s by the German artist Ludwig von Siegen, as a way of adding tone to a plate without the use of lines. It quickly travelled to England, where Samuel Pepys noted on 5 November 1665, 'Made a visit to Mr Evelyn [John Evelyn, his friend and fellow-diarist], who . . . showed me . . . the whole secret of mezzo-tinto and the manner of it, which is very pretty, and good things done with it.'
14 *The Principles of Harmony and Contrast of Colours and Their Applications to the Arts*, trans. Charles Martel, 2nd edn (London, 1855), uniforms, p. 243; effect on skin colour, p. 251; colours for dark skins, pp. 256ff.
15 *Helmholtz's Treatise on Physiological Optics, translated from the Third German Edition*, ed. James P. C. Southall (Menasha, WI, 1924), vol. II, p. 131; chap. 20, 'The Compound Colours'.
16 Johann Wolfgang von Goethe, *Goethe's Theory of Colours*, trans. Charles

Lock Eastlake (London, 1840, reprinted in facsimile Cambridge, MA,
1970): Newton's castle, pp. xliiff; 'the dark nature of colour', p. 275
(para. 694). Cf. 'Colour itself is a degree of darkness', p. 31 (Para. 69),
'shadow is the proper element of colour', p. 236 (para. 591), 'each colour,
in its lightest state, is a dark', p. 277 (para. 699). Goethe's general view of
blackness is qualified by his translator (who is not the Charles Eastlake
who wrote *Hints on Household Taste*, but his uncle, who was also a painter
and was first Keeper of London's National Gallery). See Eastlake's 'Note
U' (pp. 398–9): 'the cold nature of black and its affinity to blue is assumed
by the author throughout . . . but in many fine pictures, intense black
seems . . . the last effect of heat, and in accompanying crimson and orange
may be said rather to present a difference of degree than a difference of
kind.' Eastlake's 'Notes' remain a valuable corrective to the narrow parts
of Goethe's colour theory – which Eastlake himself still found, on the
subject of colour-harmonies, a more valuable text for artists to read than
the actual *Opticks* of Newton.

17 W. M. Thackeray, 'May Gambols; or, Titmarsh on the Picture Galleries',
in *Ballads and Miscellanies* (London, 1899), XIII, pp. 419–45.

18 Henry Mayhew, *London Labour and the London Poor* (London, 1861),
vol. III, p. 238.

19 John Ruskin, *The Ethics of Dust* (Rockville, MD, 2008), p. 137, Lecture X,
'The Crystal Rest'; Thomas Carlyle, *Latter-day Pamphlets* (Cambridge,
1898, in facsimile 2010), 37 ('The Present Time', 1 February 1850).

20 Benjamin Disraeli, *Sybil, or the Two Nations* (London, 1845):
metal-workers, Book III, chap. 4; miners, Book III, chap. 1. It should
be noted that the Mines and Collieries Act 1842, which followed the
graphic report of the Children's Employment Commission (Mines) in
1842, prohibited the employment of boys under ten and all females in
work underground.

21 Friedrich Engels, *The Condition of the Working Class in England* (*Die
Lage der arbeitenden Klasse in England*) [Leipzig, 1844], trans. Florence
Kelley Wischnedwsky (New York, 1887, London, 1891, reprinted
1943), black spittle, p. 247; black mutinous discontent, p. 117 (Engels
cites *Chartism*, p. 34); the 'Rebecca' disturbances, p. 271; Charlotte
Brontë, *Shirley* [1849], see chap. 8, 'Noah and Moses', pp. 121ff
(Harmondsworth, 2006).

22 Blackened brick, p. 39; Long Millgate, p. 50; Ashton-under-Lyne, p. 44;
Bradford, p. 40; the Medlock, p. 59; the Aire, p. 39; the Irk, pp. 49–50.

23 Mayhew, *London Labour and the London Poor*, vol. III, tall chimneys
vomiting, p. 302; the original hue, p. 338.

24 Black all the way, p. 313; once black, p. 333; a beautiful suit of black,
p. 419; fustian and corduroy, p. 379; squalor and wretchedness, p. 313.

25 William Blake, 'Auguries of Innocence' (from the Pickering Manuscript,
1803?), ll. 123–4.

26 Charles Kingsley, *The Water-Babies, a Fairy Tale for a Land Baby* [1863],
chap. 1, p. 14 (Harmondsworth, 2008).

27 William Cobbett, *Rural Rides* (London, 1830), pp. 494–5 (Northern
Tour, 'Sheffield, 31st January 1830').

28 Charles Dickens, *The Old Curiosity Shop* (London, 1840–41), chaps 44 and 45; Dickens, *Hard Times* [1854], Book the First, chap. 5, p. 27 (Harmondsworth, 2003).

29 Dickens, *The Old Curiosity Shop*, chap. 45, p. 340; Dickens, *Hard Times*, Book the First, chap. 5, p. 27.

30 In *Barnaby Rudge* (London, 1841) the crackling fire, the army of devils and the demon labours are in chap. 55; the legion of devils in chap. 68; the demon heads and savage eyes in chap. 50 and Lucifer among the devils in chap. 65; in Charles Dickens, *A Tale of Two Cities* (London, 1859), see Book the Third, v, 'The Wood-Sawyer'.

31 The quotations from *Bleak House* (London, 1852–3) are all from chap. 63, 'Steel and Iron'; see *Little Dorrit* [1855–7], Book the First, chap. 23, 'Machinery in Motion', p. 285 (Harmondsworth, 2012).

32 Goethe, *Theory of Colours*, p. 329 (para. 843).

33 On the colour changes of the French Revolution, see Aileen Ribeiro, *Fashion in the French Revolution* (London, 1988). See Baudelaire, 'The Salon of 1846', chap. 18, in *Baudelaire: Selected Writings on Art and Artists*, trans. P. E. Charvet (London, 1972), p. 105. Carlyle, *Latter-day Pamphlets*, p. 9 ('The Present Time', 1 February 1850).

34 Eastlake, *Hints on Household Taste* , p. 236; Charles Reade, *Hard Cash* (originally *Very Hard Cash*, London, 1863) (Fairfield, Glos., 2009), chap. 41, p. 400.

35 Bishop Edmund Gibson, 'To the Masters and Mistresses of Families in the English Plantations Abroad', *Two Letters of the Bishop of London* (London, 1727), p. 11.

36 George Berkeley (then Dean of Derry), *A Proposal for the Better Supplying of Churches in Our Foreign Plantations, and for converting the Savage Americans to Christianity by a College to be erected in the Summer islands* (London, 1725), from *The Works of George Berkeley*, ed. A. A. Luce and T. E. Jessop (London, 1948–57), chap. 7, p. 346.

37 See Robert Currie, *Methodism Divided: A Study in the Sociology of Ecumenicalism* (London, 1968), p. 165.

38 Dickens, *Hard Times*, Book the Third, chap. 6, p. 265.

39 Alfred de Musset, *La Confession d'un enfant du Siècle* (Paris, 1880), p. 11; Honoré de Balzac, 'Complaintes satiriques sur les moeurs du présent temps', *La Mode*, February–April 1830; for Eastlake, see *Hints on Household Taste*, p. 236; for Mayhew, see John Morley, *Death, Heaven and the Victorians* (London, 1971), p. 63.

40 W. M. Thackeray, *Vanity Fair* (London, 1847–8), chap. 32, last sentence.

41 The account of Wellington's funeral is drawn chiefly from Joseph Drew, *A Biographical Sketch of the Military and Political Career of the Duke of Wellington, including the most interesting particulars of His Death, Lying in State and Public Funeral* (Weymouth, 1852): 'strength and muscle', p. 24; 'polished mahogany', p. 25; 'fashion of royalty', p. 28; 'black horses', pp. 46–7; 'sentiments sublimer', p. 43.

42 Richard Lovelace, 'To Lucasta, Going to the Wars', from *Lucasta: Epodes, Odes, Sonnets, Songs &c.* (London, 1649), ll. 11–12.

TEN: Our Colour?

1 The Model T moved by stages into monochrome. In early 1909 (the first 2,500 cars) the touring model was red or green, the runabout grey, the town car, landaulet and coupé green. In 1910 all models were brewster green, in 1911–12 dark blue and in 1913–14 increasingly black. See Bruce W. McCalley, *Model T Ford: The Car That Changed the World* (Iola, WI, 1994), pp. 413–21; for Ford's 'black' instruction see Henry Ford, *My Life and Work* (New York, 1922), p. 72. Ford notes that his 'selling people' did not at first agree with him.

2 I quote Le Corbusier and Léger from Mark Wigley, *White Walls, Designer Dresses: The Fashioning of Modern Architecture* (Cambridge, MA, 1995), 'colour . . . the caress', p. 206; 'only one colour, white', p. 115; 'cleans, cleanses', p. 8; Léger, p. 231; 'the delicious brilliance', pp. 253–4.

3 On Premet, Vionnet and Chanel, see Valerie Steele, *The Black Dress* (New York, 2007); also Valerie Mendes, *Dressed in Black* (London, 1999); on practical issues of black-dressmaking see Simon Henry, *The Little Black Dress: How to Make the Perfect One for You* (Lewes, 2008).

4 Yohji Yamamoto is quoted in Brenda Polan and Roger Tredre, *The Great Fashion Designers* (New York, 2009), p. 180; on Versace and Elizabeth Hurley, see Amy Holman Edelman, *The Little Black Dress* (New York, 1997), p. 93; on Balenciaga and Rei Kawakubo see Valerie Steele, *The Black Dress*, n.p.

5 As to the changing dress of witches over the centuries, see especially T. Norris, *The History of Witches and Wizards* (London, 1720), which includes an early woodcut of a witch black in face and dress and with a black beast, though most of Norris's witches do not wear black gowns, and only a minority wear black hats. For further nineteenth-century witches sometimes in black hats and seldom in black gowns see the text and illustrations to William Harrison Ainsworth's novel *The Lancashire Witches* (London, 1849). The Revd Richard Harris Barham's collections of *The Ingoldsby Legends* (London, 1840, 1842, 1847) followed separate publication in *Bentley's Miscellany* and *The New Monthly Magazine*.

6 On Schiaparelli and Balenciaga see Steele, *The Black Dress*; Yohji Yamamoto is again quoted from Polan and Tredre, *The Great Fashion Designers*, p. 180; 'Rolf' is quoted from Armand Limnander at 'Viktor & Rolf Review', 10 March 2001, at www.style.com.

7 See '5 Tips to Creating The Ultimate Bachelor Pad' (3 May 2012), at www.woohome.com; Simona Ganea, 'A Bachelor's Black Dream Home' (10 May 2012), at www.homedit.com; Jordan Davis, 'Decorative Basics for a Bachelor Pad' (17 March 2011), at www.ask.com; and 'Beyond the Bachelor/ette Pad: Living with Black Furniture', at www.apartmenttherapy.com.

8 Newman is quoted from Yve-Alain Bois, 'On Two Paintings by Barnett Newman', *October*, 108 (Spring 2004), pp. 12, 16.

9 Quoted ibid., p. 8.

10 Quoted ibid.

11 Reinhardt is quoted from Barbara Rose, ed., *Art-As-Art: The Selected*

Writings of Ad Reinhardt (Berkeley, CA, 1991), 'black in sunlight', p. 86; 'useless, unmarketable', p. 81; 'timeless, spaceless', p. 83; 'five feet wide', p. 82; see especially 'Black as Symbol and Concept', pp. 86–8.

12 Quoted from Henri Meschonnic, 'Le Rythme et la lumière avec Pierre Soulages', in *Pierre Soulages, noir lumière*, ed. Francoise Jaunin (Lausanne, 2002).

13 Like Reinhardt, Degottex has worked against the dominant lustre of the Western tradition in oils. 'I only find light through mattness', quoted in Par Lydie and Nello Di Meo, eds, *Jean Degottex, 1976–1978* (Paris, 2010), p. 24. Cf. Reinhardt, 'The glossier, texturier, gummy black is a sort of objectionable quality in painting. It's one reason I moved to a sort of dark gray. At any rate it's a matte black', *Art-As-Art*, ed. Rose, p. 87.

14 James Elkins, *Pictures and Tears* (London 2004), 'like traps', pp. 17–18; 'sweep forward', p. 18; 'playing at drowning', p. 10.

15 Rothko is quoted from Selden Rodman, *Conversations with Artists* (New York, 1957), pp. 93–4.

16 Elkins, *Pictures and Tears*, p. 18.

17 See Bridget Riley, 'Colour for the Painter', in *Colour: Art and Science*, ed. Trevor Lamb and Janine Bourriau (Cambridge, 1995), pp. 31–64.

18 Quoted in Veit Gorner and Frank-Thorsten Moll, eds, *Back to Black: Black in Current Painting* (Heidelberg, 2009), p. 123.

19 Especially sinister in Poe is water: there is a presage of death in the 'black and lurid tarn that lay in unruffled lustre' beside the house in 'The Fall of The House of Usher'. In *The Narrative of Arthur Gordon Pym of Nantucket*, the 'dreary water lay intensely black, still, and altogether terrible' (chap. 2), and in 'The Thousand-and-Second Tale of Scheherazade' 'there flowed immense rivers as black as ebony, and swarming with fish that had no eyes'. *Treasure Island* (London, 1883), chaps 1 and 4; also the pirates fly, of course, 'the black flag of piracy' (chap. 19); Blackbeard was 'was the bloodthirstiest buccaneer that sailed' (chap. 6); and the treasure map locates the gold 'ten fathoms south of the black crag' (chap. 6). Black may also be, in Stevenson, the sign of vigour and life: Dr Livesey has 'bright, black eyes' and a 'black poll' under his powdered wig (chap. 1), while Squire Trelawney has eyebrows that are 'very black, and moved readily' (chap. 6). The *Strange Case of Dr Jekkyll and Mr Hyde* (London, 1886), 'Story of the Door', 'Dr Lanyon's Narrative'. There is another 'morning, black as it was' later in the story,when Jekkyll tells us he enters an inn with a black countenance ('Henry Jekkyll's Full Statement of the Case'); Mr Hyde has 'a kind of black, sneering coolness' ('Story of the Door'). Bram Stoker, *Dracula* (London, 1897), chap. 2.

20 Chinua Achebe, 'An Image of Africa: Racism in Conrad's *Heart of Darkness*', *Massachussetts Review*, 18 (1977).

21 Salman Rushdie, *Midnight's Children* (London, 1981), pp. 522, 238.

22 Ted Hughes, *Crow: From the Life and Songs of the Crow*, expanded edn (London, 1974), 'Two Legends', p. 13; 'grinning into the black', 'The Contender', pp. 41–2; 'in the silent room', 'Crow Alights', p. 21; 'Crow-colour', p. 66; 'black is the wet otter's head', 'Two Legends', p. 13; 'Crow's Fall', p. 36; 'Crow Blacker than ever', p. 69; 'Magical Dangers', p. 51.

23 Quoted in Gorner and Moll, eds, *Back to Black*, p. 135.

24 Ibid., p. 107.Fuller thoughts on black can be found in the writings of the British painter Ian McKeever. He is famous especially for the luminosity of his art, but has over the last 25 years produced many black paintings. They were shown together in a retrospective exhibition at the Tønder Museum in Denmark in 2011, 'Black and Black Again . . .'. In the book that accompanied the exhibition he quotes Matisse's remark that black is 'a force' and concludes, 'when we actually do see true black being used as a colour in a painting, it comes as a shock. It takes us by surprise because it is actively black, and carrying with it the force to which Matisse referred.'

25 Ibid., p. 93; Henry James, *The Golden Bowl* [1904] (Harmondsworth, 2009), Book 6, p. 566.

26 Gorner and Moll, eds, *Back to Black*, p. 113.

A Note on Chessboards, Death and Whiteness

1 Charles Dickens, *A Christmas Carol* (London, 1843). The passages quoted come from just before, and just after, the start of Stave IV, 'The Last of the Spirits'. For Albrecht Dürer, see the engravings *Four Horsemen of the Apocalypse* of 1497–8, and *Knight, Death and the Devil*, 1513.

2 D. H. Lawrence, *Women in Love* (London, 1920), chap. 30, 'Snowed Up'. Herman Melville, *Moby-Dick; or, The Whale* (New York, 1851), chap. 42, 'The Whiteness of the Whale'. On Poe see chapter Ten, ref. 17, above. Thomas Mann, *The Magic Mountain* [*Der Zauberberg*, 1924] (London, 1999), p. 293. There was a black element in German military tradition, associated with the regiment known as The Black Brunswickers, founded in the nineteenth century by Friedrich Wilhelm, *Der schwarze Herzog*, the Black Duke of Brunswick, and later renewed in the black uniform of Himmler's fear-police, the ss. Also in *The Magic Mountain*, Hans Castorp is told of an Italian grandfather who wore black 'in mourning for the state of the fatherland': this is the radical use of black, favoured by young libertarian patriots like the *arditti* in Italy, including Gabriele D'Annunzio, and by the Macedonian freedom-fighters in Greece known as the 'black tunics'. Castorp's own German grandfather wore black 'to indicate his oneness with a bygone time and his essential lack of sympathy with the present' – this is the reactionary use of black once prevalent among European ruling classes. For both grandfathers, see *The Magic Mountain*, p. 151.

3 When Mark Twain met Tsar Alexander, he was impressed to find that he wore 'plain white drilling [with no] insignia whatever of rank': *The Innocents Abroad; or, The New Pilgrims' Progress* (Hartford, CT, 1869), chap. 37. In later life Twain (Samuel L. Clemens), who had habitually worn black serge, took to wearing white: he owned fourteen white suits, which he described as his 'snow-white full dress' and also as his 'don't-give-a-damn suit'. See Michael Sheldon, *Mark Twain, Man in White: The Grand Adventure of His Final Years* (New York, 2010).

4 See T. E. Lawrence, *Seven Pillars of Wisdom* (London, 1926), Book 1, chap. 20, paragraph 1.

SELECT BIBLIOGRAPHY

Colour and Sight

Berlin, Brent, and Paul Kay, *Basic Colour Terms: Their Universality and Evolution* (Berkeley, CA, 1969)

Boyle, Robert, *Experiments and Considerations Touching Colours* (London, 1664), Part the Second, 'Of the Nature of Whiteness and Blackness'

Goethe, Johann Wolfgang von, *Goethe's Theory of Colours*, trans. Charles Lock Eastlake (London, 1840; reprinted in facsimile Cambridge, MA, 1970)

Hardin, C. L., and L. Maffi, eds, *Colour Categories in Thought and Language* (Cambridge, 1997)

Helmholtz's Treatise on Physiological Optics, Translated from the Third German Edition, ed. James P. C. Southall (Menasha, WI, 1924)

Lamb, Trevor, and Janine Bourriau, eds, *Colour: Art and Science* (Cambridge, 1995)

Newton, Isaac, *Opticks: or, a Treatise of the Reflections, Refractions, Inflections and Colours of Light*, 4th corrected edn (London, 1730)

Wittgenstein, Ludwig, *Remarks on Colour* (Berkeley, CA, 1978)

Colour and Culture

Bradley, Mark, *Colour and Meaning in Ancient Rome* (Cambridge, 2009)

Bruno, Vincent J., *Form and Colour in Greek Painting* (London, 1977)

Chevreuil, Michel, *The Principles of Harmony and Contrast of Colours and Their Applications to the Arts*, trans. Charles Martel, 2nd edn (London, 1855)

Eco, Umberto, 'How Culture Conditions the Colours We See', in *On Signs*, ed. M. Blonsky (Baltimore, MD, 1985), pp. 157–75

Gage, John, *Colour and Culture: Practice and Meaning from Antiquity to Abstraction* (London, 1993)

Ling, Roger, *Roman Painting* (Cambridge, 1991)

Pastoureau, Michel, *Blue: The History of a Colour* (Princeton, NJ, 2001)

Turner, Victor, *The Forest of Symbols: Aspects of Ndembu Ritual* (Ithaca, NY, 1967)

Culture and the Colour Black

Carr, Gillian, 'Woad, Tattooing and Identity in Later Iron Age and Early
    Roman Britain', *Oxford Journal of Archaeology*, XXIV/3 (2005), pp. 273–92
Jacobson-Widding, Anita, *Red, White and Black as a Mode of Thought*
    (Stockholm, 1979)
Metcalf, Simon, and Eric Turner, 'The Conservation of a *c.* 1867 Cast Iron
    Hat Stand: A Dresser Design and Original Coalbrookdale Paint Scheme
    Revealed', DAS: *The Decorative Arts Society 1850 to the Present*, 26, at
    www.decorativeartssociety.org.uk
Mollard-Desfour, Annie, *Le Noir: Dictionnaire des mots et expressions de
    couleur, XXe–XXIe siècle* (Paris, 2005)
Pastoureau, Michel, *Black: The History of a Color* (Princeton, NJ, 2009)
Wright, W. D., 'The Nature of Blackness in Art and Visual Perception',
    Leonardo, XIV (1981), pp. 236–7

Black Clothes

Harvey, John, *Men in Black* (London, 1995)
Hollander, Anne, *Seeing through Clothes* (Berkeley, CA, 1993)
Holman Edelman, Amy, *The Little Black Dress* (New York, 1997)
Mayo, Janet, *A History of Ecclesiastical Dress* (London, 1984)
Mendes, Valerie, *Dressed in Black* (London, 1999)
Norris, Herbert, *Church Vestments: Their Origin and Development* [1949]
    (Mineola, NY, 2002)
Ribeiro, Aileen, *Dress and Morality* (London, 1986)
Routledge, George, *Routledge's Manual of Etiquette* [1860] (Fairford,
    Gloucestershire, 2007)
Shkolnik, Amiram, C. Richard Taylor, Virginia Finch and Arieh Borut,
    'Why Do Bedouins Wear Black Robes in Hot Deserts?', *Nature*, 283
    (24 January 1980), pp. 373–5
Steele, Valerie, *The Black Dress* (New York, 2007)

Black in the Arts

Bois, Yve-Alain, 'On Two Paintings by Barnett Newman', *October*, 108
    (Spring 2004)
Elkins, James, *Pictures and Tears* (London, 2001)
Gorner, Veit, and Frank-Thorsten Moll, eds, *Back to Black: Black in Current
    Painting* (Heidelberg, 2009)
Graham-Dixon, Andrew, *Caravaggio: A Life Sacred and Profane* (London,
    2010)
Jaunin, Francoise, ed., *Pierre Soulages: noir lumière* (Lausanne, 2002)
Langdon, Helen, *Caravaggio: A Life* (London, 1998)
Lydie, Par, and Nello Di Meo, eds, *Jean Degottex, 1976–1978* (Paris, 2010)
Rodman, Selden, *Conversations with Artists* (New York, 1957)
Rose, Barbara, ed., *Art-As-Art: The Selected Writings of Ad Reinhardt*
    (Berkeley, CA, 1991)

Schama, Simon, *Rembrandt's Eyes* (London, 1999)
Wigley, Mark, *White Walls, Designer Dresses: The Fashioning of Modern Architecture* (Cambridge, MA, 1995)

Black and Melancholy

Burton, Robert, *The Anatomy of Melancholy*, ed. Holbrook Jackson [1922] (facsimile edn New York, 2001)
Gowland, Andrew, *The Worlds of Renaissance Melancholy: Robert Burton in Context* (Cambridge, 2006)
Klibansky, Raymond, Erwin Panofsky and Fritz Saxl, *Saturn and Melancholy: Studies in the History of Natural Philosophy, Religion and Art* (London, 1964)
Kristeva, Julia, *Black Sun: Depression and Melancholia*, trans. Leon S. Roudiez (New York, 1989)
MacDonald, Michael, *Mystical Bedlam: Madness, Anxiety, and Healing in Seventeenth-century England* (Cambridge, 1981)

Race

Bâ, Sylvia Washington, *The Concept of Negritude in the Poetry of Léopold Sédar Senghor* (Princeton, NJ, 1973)
Bindman, David, and Henry Louis Gates, Jr, *The Image of Black in Western Art*, 4 vols (Cambridge, MA, 2010–12)
Brace, C. Loring, D. P. Tracer, L. A. Yaroch, J. Rob, K. Brandt and A. R. Nelson, 'Clines and Clusters versus "Race": A Test in Ancient Egypt and the Case of a Death on the Nile', *Yearbook of Physical Anthropology*, 36 (1993), pp. 1–31
Browne, Sir Thomas, *Pseudodoxia Epidemica* (London, 1646), Book VI, chap. 10, 'Of the Blackness of Negroes'
Burnel, Martin, *Black Athena: The Afroasiatic Roots of Classical Civilization*, 2 vols (New Brunswick, NJ, 1987–91)
Equiano, Olaudah, *The Interesting Life of Olaudah Equiano; or, Gustavus Vassa the African* (London, 1789)
Fanon, Frantz, *Black Skin White Masks*, trans. C. L. Markman (London, 1986)
Gates Jr, H. L., ed., *'Race', Writing and Difference* (Chicago, IL, 1986)
Jordan, Winthrop D., *White over Black: American Attitudes Toward the Negro, 1550–1812* (Durham, NC, 1977)
Lefkowitz, Mary R., and Guy MacLean Rogers, *Black Athena Revisited* (Durham, NC, 1996)

ACKNOWLEDGEMENTS

MY BLACK STUDIES began with a lecture on black in the nineteenth century given in Bristol in 1981, which in time became a history of the colour black in men's dress (*Men in Black*, Reaktion, 1995). Following what now seems a clear obsession, I here attempt a fuller history. In the process I have sometimes travelled far from my academic home in the study of the relations between the novel and visual art, and I am sincerely grateful for the guidance kindly given by experts in fields where my need was great. I am especially grateful to Professor Tarif Khalidi of the American University in Beirut, who has given invaluable advice on Arab and Islamic culture. Also to Professor Mark Bradley of the University of Nottingham, who has advised most helpfully on the colours, and the blacks, of ancient classical civilization; and to Professor Patrick Chabal of King's College London for his keen advice on African and African-Gallic questions. I am grateful to Anita Desai and Eric Auzoux for advice on the gods and goddesses of India. On contemporary art I have been particularly grateful for steers and comments from Barry Phipps, Fellow and Curator of Works of Art at Churchill College, Cambridge, who also arranged for me to meet the 'black' painter Peter Peri.

I am grateful above all to my wife, Julietta Papadopoulou Harvey, for insights, ideas, many patient comments, and for putting the bright colour in my life, though she is also smart in black. I want also to thank warmly my colleagues at Emmanuel College, Cambridge. One advantage – or perhaps a danger – of working in a college is that, while one seldom sees one's colleagues in one's own teaching area, one is surrounded by experts in other fields, who are like hospitable hosts in their willingness to feed the most wayward curiosity. I am particularly grateful to Robert Henderson, Julian Hibbard, John MacLennan, Nigel Spivey and James Wade for their guidance on physiological, botanical, geological, classical and medieval questions, and to David Tolhurst for his patience in explaining the mechanisms of sight. For advice on many points, including the neat footwork of Louis XIV, I am grateful to Professor Peter Burke. But I would also like to give a more general thanks for decades now of friendly exchange. That is why this book, imperfect as it may be, is dedicated to that generous-minded community. More materially, I gladly thank the College for the grant from the Research Expenses Committee, which helped buy scans and rights for the illustrations.

PHOTO ACKNOWLEDGEMENTS

The author and publishers wish to express their thanks to the following sources of illustrative material and/or permission to reproduce it. Some locations are also supplied here, not given in the captions for reasons of brevity.

Photo © 2012 The Ansel Adams Publishing Rights Trust: 101; from William Harrison Ainsworth, *Mervyn Clitheroe* (London, 1858): 75; from William Harrison Ainsworth, *The Tower of London* (London, 1840): 74; photo akg-images: 91; photo akg-images/Album/M.G.M.: 94; photo akg-images/Album/Oronoz: 58; photo akg-images/Album/RKO: 92; photo akg-images/British Library, London: 84; photo akg-images/Erich Lessing: 34, 66, 68; photo akg-images/Rabatti-Dominigie: 12; photo akg-images/Schütze/Rodemann: 57; photo akg-images/VIEW Pictures Ltd: 95, 96; Gnadenkapelle, Altötting, Bavaria: 18; Antalya Museum, Turkey: 17; reproduced courtesy of the artist (Peter Peri): 104; from *L'Association mensuelle* (18 January 1834): 77; photo Philipp Bier: 96; British Library, London (Add. Ms. 42130): 30; British Museum, London (photos © The Trustees of the British Museum): 4, 6, 7, 11, 16, 28; photos © The Trustees of the British Museum: 8, 20, 22, 51, 76, 88; photo courtesy Dr Angelandrea Casale: 14; photo De Agostini Picture Library/Bridgeman Art Library: 3; © Dedalus Foundation, Inc./DACS, London/VAGA, New York 2013: 99; from the *First Report of the Commissioners for Inquiring into the Employment and Condition of Children in Mines and Manufactories* (London, 1842) [Parliamentary Papers, London, 1842 – B.S.Ref.18 (vol. 17, 65)]: 84; The Frick Collection, New York: 21; Galleria degli Uffizi, Florence: 13, 39; Galleria Nazionale d'Arte Antica, Rome: 49; Gemälde-gallerie, Berlin: 45; photos © Georgia O'Keeffe Museum/DACS, 2013: 79, 100; The J. Paul Getty Museum, Malibu, California: 65; photo by Hickey-Robertson, Rothko Chapel, Houston, Texas: 100; © 1998 Kate Rothko Prizel & Christopher Rothko ARS, NY and DACS, London: 100; Kelvingrove Art Gallery and Museum, Glasgow: 24; Kunsthistorisches Museum, Vienna: 37; Kunstmuseum, Basel: 23; from Mårten Lange, *Anomalies* (Göteborg, 2009 – reproduced courtesy of the artist [Mårten Lange]): 102; photos Library of Congress, Washington, DC (Prints and Photographs Division): 27, 59 (Frank and Frances Carpenter Collection), 64 (Civil War Photograph Collection), 90; from Cesare Lombroso and Guillaume Ferrero, *La Donna deliquente: La Prostituta e la donna normale* (Turin, 1893): 60; © Victor Man, courtesy the artist (Victor Man), Gladstone Gallery, New York and Brussels, and Blum & Poe, Los Angeles: 105; Marienkirche, Halle an der

Saale, Saxony-Anhalt, Germany: 57; Mauritshuis, the Hague: 44; Metropolitan Museum of Art, New York: 14, 32, 43, 68, 80; photo R. & S. Michaud/akg-images: 9, 26; from *Milton's 'Paradise Lost' illustrated by Gustave Doré* (London, 1882): 56; Musée du Louvre, Paris: 36, 42, 66, 85; Museo e Gallerie Nazionale di Capodimonte, Naples: 40; Museo Gregoriano Etrusco, Rome: 10; Museo del Prado, Madrid: 31, 38; The Museum of London: 70; National Gallery, London: 48, 52, 86; National Gallery of Art, Washington, DC (Widener Collection): 83; Offentliche Kunstsammlung, Basel 53; photo Timothy O'Sullivan: 59; Palazzo Pitti, Florence: 12; Palazzo Vecchio, Florence: 33; Pierpoint Morgan Library, New York: 55; private collections: 1, 3, 34, 67; courtesy of Raster Gallery, Warsaw: 106; photo Reinraum: 18; Royal Collection: 35, 73, 89 (photo courtesy Victoria and Albert Museum, London); Royal Geographical Society, London (photo RGS Library): 61; Royal Holloway College Picture Collection (University of London): 87; photo Bibi Saint-Pol: 19; Sant'Agostino, Rome (Cavaletti Chapel): 41; Staatliche Antikensammlungen, Munich: 19; Städelsches Kunstinstitut, Frankfurt: 46; State Hermitage Museum, St Petersburg: 50; Stedelijk Museum, Amsterdam: 97; photo © Succession H. Matisse/DACS 2013: 98; Tate, London: 81; photo courtesy Topfoto: 93; Topkapı Palace Museum, Istanbul: 25; photo Hugh Tuffen: 2; from *Vathmethon*: Photographies (Thessaloniki, 2011): 103; from a set of prints, the *Vita et Miracula Sanctissimi Patris Benedicti* (1658): 20; from Herbert Ward, *Five Years with the Congo Cannibals* (London, 1890): 62; from *The Works of Mr William Shakespear in Six Volumes* (London, 1709): 54; from *The Yellow Book* (15 April 1894): 78.

INDEX

332

09/09/2014